THE FALSE TRAITOR:
LOUIS RIEL IN CANADIAN CULTURE

The nineteenth-century Métis politician and mystic Louis Riel has emerged as one of the most popular – and elusive – figures in Canadian culture. Since his hanging for treason in 1885, the self-declared David of the New World has been depicted variously as a traitor to Confederation; a French-Canadian and Catholic martyr; a bloodthirsty rebel; a pan-American liberator; a pawn of shadowy white forces; a Prairie political maverick; a First Nations hero; an alienated intellectual; a victim of Western industrial progress; and even a Father of Confederation.

Albert Braz synthesizes the available material by and about Riel, including film, sculpture, and cartoons, as well as literature in French and English, and analyses how a historical figure could be portrayed in such contradictory ways. In light of the fact that most aesthetic representations of Riel bear little resemblance not only to one another but also to their purported model, Braz suggests that they reveal less about Riel than they do about their authors and the society to which they belong. The most comprehensive treatment of the representations of Louis Riel, *The False Traitor* will be a seminal work in the study of this popular Canadian figure.

ALBERT BRAZ is an assistant professor of comparative literature at the University of Alberta.

Date Due
JUL 2 3 2009

The False Traitor

Louis Riel in Canadian Culture

ALBERT BRAZ

UNIVERSITY OF TORONTO PRESS
Toronto Buffalo London

© University of Toronto Press Incorporated 2003
Toronto Buffalo London
Printed in Canada

ISBN 0-8020-4760-2 (cloth)
ISBN 0-8020-8314-5 (paper)

Printed on acid-free paper

National Library of Canada Cataloguing in Publication

Braz, Albert Raimundo, 1957–
    The false traitor : Louis Riel in Canadian culture / Albert Braz.

    Includes bibliographical references and index.
    ISDN 0-8020-4760-2 (bound)   ISBN 0-8020-8314-5 (pbk.)

    1. Riel, Louis, 1844–1885 – In literature.   2. Canadian literature –
    History and criticism.   3. Riel, Louis, 1844–1885 – Art.   I. Title.

    PS8101.R5B72 2003   C810.9′351   C2002-905039-1
    PR9185.7.R5B72 2003

University of Toronto Press acknowledges the financial assistance
to its publishing program of the Canada Council for the Arts and the
Ontario Arts Council.

This book has been published with the help of a grant from the Humanities
and Social Sciences Federation of Canada, using funds provided by the
Social Sciences and Humanities Research Council of Canada.

University of Toronto Press acknowledges the financial support for
its publishing activities of the Government of Canada through the
Book Publishing Industry Development Program (BPIDP).

To Jonathan and Alison – and to Carolyn,
without whom much would not have been possible,
most especially Jonathan and Alison

Contents

viii   Contents

Illustrations follow page 116

Preface

This is a study of Louis Riel's image in Canadian culture, particularly as it is articulated in novels, poems, plays, cartoons, films, paintings, statues, and one opera. As we will see in the following pages, there are such glaring discrepancies among the aesthetic representations of the Métis leader that one cannot help but wonder if they refer to the same individual. Of course, no attempt has been made either to mask the contradictions in different portraits of Riel or to minimize the idiosyncracies in a given work, even if unpalatable. Still, being cognizant of the way in which language may not only reflect but constitute reality, I feel that I should describe my terminology in order to give a better indication of the reasons for my own choices.

It has been said that every war has at least two names. This is certainly true of the two military clashes between the Métis and Canada with which Riel is so indelibly identified. The conflicts at Red River in 1869–70 and at Batoche in 1885 have been known by a series of monikers, usually incorporating the highly judgmental words 'insurrection,' 'rebellion,' or 'uprising.' Starting with the historian W.L. Morton in the mid-1950s, there has been a growing consensus that the first conflict was really a defensive one, since Canada did not yet have a legal claim to the territory. Consequently, following Morton's lead, I describe it as the Red River Resistance. Perhaps it could also be argued, as some writers have, that the Saskatchewan troubles too were a defensive action. But considering that Canada had by then acquired stewardship of the territory, the second Riel conflict will be characterized as the North-West Rebellion.

The terms 'Métis' and 'North-West' themselves need some clarification. In the second half of the nineteenth century, the North-West comprised not only most of what is now northern Canada and the Canadian Prairies but also much of Ontario and Quebec. For Riel, however, it meant essentially the provinces of Manitoba, Saskatchewan, and Alberta, especially the first two. The word 'North-West' will be hyphenated throughout this study both in order to reflect the most common (although not universal) usage at the time and to differentiate it from the present-day Northwest Territories. The meaning of the term 'Métis,' French for the offspring of different races, also has undergone considerable change over the years. There were actually two groups of mixed Aboriginal and European ancestry in the North-West, the predominantly Protestant, English-speaking Halfbreeds and the mainly Catholic, French-speaking *métis*. Since 'Métis' is now generally applied to both communities, I will use that term here – except when it is necessary to specify that someone belonged to either of the two subgroups.

This study covers the representations of Riel from the early 1860s, beginning with his first letters home from the Collège de Montréal, to about 2000, with the television series *Canada: A People's History*. Needless to say, such a comprehensive undertaking is not possible without the assistance of many individuals. Thus, I would like to take this opportunity to thank Ted Chamberlin, who first green-lighted the project and who remained unflagging in his support, even when our interpretations did not necessarily coincide. Equally critical, and appreciated, was the encouragement given to me by Roseann Runte, who, in spite of her busy schedule as (then) President of Victoria University, somehow always managed to find time to discuss Riel and to suggest a way out when nothing seemed to make much sense. Thanks are also in order to the many colleagues and friends who either read my manuscript at various stages of its development or who provided me with information about (usually) obscure works on Riel: John Baird, Peter Baxter, Jennifer Chambers, Stan Dragland, William Harvey, Armando Jannetta, Neil Semple, Ricardo Sternberg, Rosemary Sullivan, and Tracy Ware. In addition, I would like to thank the two anonymous readers from University of Toronto Press, especially the first one, who not only gave me two extremely attentive readings of my work but who did so while granting it its starting point. Last but definitely not least, I would like to express my deep gratitude to my wife, Carolyn Kapron, and to our children, Jonathan and Alison, the trio that makes everything both possible and worthwhile.

Parts of the manuscript have appeared in 'The Vengeful Prophet: Revenge in Louis Riel's Writings,' *Dalhousie French Studies* 35 (1996): 19–32; 'The Absent Protagonist: Louis Riel in Nineteenth-Century Canadian Literature,' *Canadian Literature* 167 (2000): 45–61; and 'Promised Land / Cursed Land: The Peculiar Canada of Mathias Carvalho,' *Interfaces Brasil/Canadá* 1.1 (2001): 119–28.

Excerpts from Steven Michael Berzensky (Mick Burrs), *The Names Leave the Stones* (Regina: Coteau Books, 2001), reprinted by permission of Coteau Books. Excerpts from Frank Davey, 'Riel' (*The Louis Riel Organ and Piano Company*, 1985), reprinted by permission of the author. Excerpts from Don Gutteridge, *Riel: A Poem for Voices* (1968), reprinted by permission of the author. Excerpts from Erin Mouré, 'Riel: In the Season of His Birth,' reprinted by permission of the author. Excerpts from Kevin Roberts, 'Riel,' reprinted by permission of the author. Excerpts from Tom Wayman, 'Canadian Culture: Another Riel Poem' are from *In a Small House on the Outskirts of Heaven* (Madeira Park, BC: Harbour Publishing, 1989). Reprinted by permission of the author.

THE FALSE TRAITOR:
LOUIS RIEL IN CANADIAN CULTURE

Introduction

Louis Riel: A Central Voice from the Margins

> ... The nice thing about Louis [Riel]
> was my mother always called him 'real'
> *Frank Davey (1985)*

Louis Riel is simultaneously one of the most popular and most elusive figures in Canadian literature, and culture in general. Since his hanging for treason on November 16, 1885, he has been depicted variously as a traitor to Confederation, a French-Canadian and Catholic martyr, a bloodthirsty rebel, a New World liberator, a pawn of shadowy white forces, a Prairie political maverick, an Aboriginal hero, a deluded mystic, an alienated intellectual, a victim of Western industrial progress, and even a Father of Confederation. This tremendous fluidity in the aesthetic representations of the Métis leader calls into question the necessary connection between an individual and the manner in which he or she is portrayed by novelists, poets, playwrights, and other artists. Yet the fact Riel was a historical figure, someone who ostensibly lived in a particular place and time, gives him a certain concreteness or realness, to echo Frank Davey's play on his surname ('Riel' 49). The primary objective of this study is to document and analyse the many faces of Riel in Canadian literature. While the focus is on the contrasting ways he has been conceived by Canadian creative writers in both English and French, aesthetic representations in other media and from other countries are also examined. My thesis is that the reason Riel changes so markedly over time, and across space, is that most of the purported representations of the politician-mystic are less about him than about their authors and their specific social reality. I am not quite convinced that, as Michel Foucault proposes, 'power ... produces reality; it produces domains of objects and rituals of truth' (*Discipline* 194). Nevertheless, it seems incontestable that there is a direct link between the fact the discourse on Riel is dominated by Euro-Canadians and the fact he is usually situated not in a Métis context but in a Canadian one.

In his book on the poet (and Ministry of Indian Affairs bureaucrat) Duncan Campbell Scott, Stan Dragland states that, in research, 'we find what we look for' (104). Although I have tremendous admiration for Dragland's scholarship and intellectual acuity, I must say that my experience does not support his contention. On the contrary, my conclusions about Riel's place in Canadian culture are shaped heavily by my not finding what I was looking for. Like most other people today, I would presume, I was introduced to Riel, not through his writings, but through other people's representations of him, especially recent ones. These works tend to be highly positive, accentuating both the Métis leader's magnanimity and his pan-Canadianism. As his biographer Maggie Siggins writes, Riel is 'truly a humanitarian,' who gives up 'prestige and wealth to fight for the underdog.' He is the most successful mediator between Natives and Newcomers in Canada, striving to establish 'a sympathetic and equitable relationship between the two. That Canadians may someday achieve this vision remains Louis Riel's legacy' (448). Or, as another commentator affirms, Riel is 'the first reform member of parliament from the prairies' and 'does not need to be pardoned' but 'historically exonerated' (Arnold 76, 83). Judging by most literary works on him since at least the end of the Second World War, Riel would seem to be basically a Canadian visionary who advocated nothing less than the social welfare and multicultural policies that the nation would embrace a century later. He is very much a precursor of Joy Kogawa's Emily Kato, a fervent patriot denied full citizenship because of white racism. But when I finally read Riel's own writings, I was struck by his lack of identification with Confederation. Instead of someone who sees himself deeply enmeshed in the country's fate, 'for better or worse,' like Kato (Kogawa 40), I encountered an individual who seems remarkably sceptical about the whole Canadian project, even claiming that Canada is the worst enemy of the Métis people, whom it yearns to 'détruire' (Riel, 4: 118).[1]

Needless to say, there were numerous reasons why Riel should have entertained deep reservations about Canada, from the fact he was born a Métis, in a distinct jurisdiction, to his people's subsequent ignoble treatment in Confederation. That, though, would be the topic for another book. What I wish to explore in this study is why Euro-Canadian writers have been so intent on claiming as their own an individual who appears to have such apprehensions about their country and their ancestors. 'Appeals to the past,' it has been remarked, 'are among the commonest of strategies in interpretations of the present' (Said, *Culture* 3), which suggests that representations such as those of Riel are likely excursions into the author's own time as much as the subject's. Thus, one must inquire why contemporary Euro-Canadian writers have become so adamant about depicting Riel as some sort of quintessential Canadian, particularly the 'archetypal' outsider. Or, conversely, why they are so reluctant to deal with Riel's often-declared Métis nationalism, to contemplate the possibility that he belongs to a different, and adversarial, polity.

In *Orientalism*, Edward Said asserts that the European representations of the Middle East were so ubiquitous that 'the Orient was almost a European invention' (1). Considering the sheer volume of works on Riel by Euro-Canadians, perhaps one could also argue that he is almost a white invention. However, as in Said, the key word here is *almost*, for Riel is seldom absent from the discourse about himself. While best-known as a political and religious figure, he produced a substantial body of writing, poetry and prose in which he often challenges the representations of him by his enemies as well as his supporters. Indeed, Riel's writings provide a perfect illustration of Said's thesis, in his later book *Culture and Imperialism*, that the arrival of the white man in the non-European world inevitably precipitated 'some sort of resistance' (xii).

The manner in which Riel's writings can contest the dominant narratives about the Métis leader is never more evident than when it comes to what one might call the national question, his place in Canada. Joan Scott has said that one should avoid creating 'an illusory sameness' by referring to an entity, such as a nation, 'as if it never changed, as if not the category, but only its historical circumstances varied over time' (285). The point is especially germane in terms of Riel's relations with Canada or, perhaps more correctly, the Canadas. As we will see in the next chapter, Riel was predominantly of French-Canadian/Québécois extraction and always had strong affinities with the Franco-Canadian community not only in Quebec but also in the United States. Because of his Aboriginal roots, his identification with his eastern and southern cousins is sometimes complicated by race, yet one cannot help but notice his sense of oneness with *le Canada*. As he writes in a poem like 'Le peuple Métis-Canadien-français' (1883),

Métis et Canadiens ensemble
Français, si nos trois éléments
S'amalgament bien, il me semble
Que nous serons un jour plus grands. (4: 324)

That solidarity, though, rarely extends to Confederation. Quite the opposite – Riel usually sees the Canada that emerges in 1867 as inimical to his people. Thus, rather than wishing that the Métis become part of the new country, he stresses their collective 'droit' not to join it (1: 106).

Riel's discordant views on Canada suggest that, for him, there is more than one Canada, and that one should always be aware of the specific Canada to which he refers. They also underscore the paradox of how someone who is so wary of a country could gradually be transformed into its very personification, a development that raises many questions about the political implications of the lionization of Riel by contemporary Canadian writers and other artists. One fact about the Métis leader that one must bear in mind is that he is a member of a vanquished group who is memorialized mainly by members of the group that defeated him and his people. As the Anishnabe writer and painter Sherry Farrell Racette notes, he has become 'Canada's Riel' (46). The embrace of Riel by the descendants of his enemies might be easily interpreted as an act of appropriation, a manifestation of what Dennis Duffy terms 'the Walter Scott syndrome, whereby the conquering, modernizing culture dons the kilts of whatever group it has exterminated[2] and goes on to celebrate the charming fossil in story and song' (*Gardens* 56). But perhaps one should not discount the possibility that Riel's Canadianization may also reflect the profound ambiguity about the nature of citizenship that still prevails in Canada.

One of the most flagrant examples of the Canadian bewilderment about nationality is Hugh Hood's assertion that 'un-Canadianism is almost the very definition of *Canadianism*' (32). In the context of Riel, the untenability of the statement becomes obvious the moment one considers his antagonists. If Riel becomes a Canadian patriot by opposing the federal government, what is the national status of the volunteers who battled him on behalf of that government – traitors? Indeed, it is probably not an accident that the 1885 volunteers have vanished from the consciousness of Canadians. Following the fall of Batoche, the young soldiers who responded to the call to fight Riel and the Métis became the toast of the nation. Poem after poem was devoted to the selfless patriots who preserved the North-West for, as one Quebec writer phrases it, '"la loi" et la Reine' (DeGuise 16). However, as the one-time renegade began to be metamorphosed into a hero, the volunteers disappeared. They were not vilified but simply ignored, unacknowledged, as if their presence would call into question the new discursive order of things. What soon also becomes apparent about Hood's comment is the assumption that the nineteenth-century Métis are just another ethnic group fighting for their rightful place in the land. Hood acknowledges as much when he describes 'the displacement of the Acadians' and Riel's story as two instances of 'the mistreatment of minorities [in the country] and therefore typically Canadian' (32).

A similar confusion about the national status of the Métis is revealed by Pierre Trudeau. While unveiling a statue of Riel in front of the Saskatchewan Legislature in 1968, the then prime minister delivered a most eloquent meditation on the place of protest in a democracy, in the past as much as in the present. As he addressed a crowd gathered by Regina's picturesque Wascana Lake,

> ... this very setting, this very tranquility, this sense of orderliness and propriety makes me think how difficult it is for any of us to understand Louis Riel. What forces motivated this man? What social conditions led him to believe that nothing short of rebellion would serve the cause to which he had pledged himself? How many other Riels exist in Canada, beyond the fringe of accepted conduct, driven to believe that this country offers no answer to their needs and no solutions to their problems? (109)

The moral that Trudeau drew from the story of the man who suffered more 'reversals of fortune during his life' than anyone else in the nation's history was the urgent need for Canadians to respect minority rights, since 'a democracy is judged by the way the majority treats the minority' and 'Louis Riel's battle is not yet won' (109–10). Yet, in the same speech, Trudeau then proceeded to imply that the North-West conflicts were not really about minority rights but about national determination. As he added, 'We can agree that Riel's dream of a vast, autonomous Metis nation-state in the middle of North America could never have been realized. The economic and political momentum of the two young countries which share this continent was too great to justify or to permit further fragmentation' (110). In other words, for Trudeau, Riel and his people were not a Canadian minority but a distinct polity whose territorial ambitions the new Dominion simply could not – or would not – accommodate.

Riel's sense of national separateness, which is arguably the central motif in his writings – such as when God presumably reveals to him the divine desire to efface 'la ligne' between Canada and the United States (3: 312) – of course complicates considerably his relationship with post-Confederation Canada. But not all the challenges that Riel poses to the students of his representations pertain exclusively to him. Some of those obstacles are inherent in historical figures in general, notably the fact that our knowledge of those individuals is usually mediated by a third party, or parties. The Cree painter Gerald McMaster has captured the phenomenon brilliantly. In his 1985 drawing *Riel Remembered* (pl. 1), he shows a partly obscured man holding a photograph of Riel for the viewer. McMaster seems to be underlining the difficulty of interpreting historical figures or events, since his own impression is already influenced by previous responses to the subject. It is as if he wishes to remind the spectator that his is not the only interpretation of Riel but one 'among many' (Mattes, 'Rielisms' 20). The complexity increases even further if one happens to know that the photograph in McMaster's drawing was taken soon after Riel surrendered at Batoche and that the photographer was an officer with the Canadian forces, Captain James Peters. As Kim Morrissey writes in a poem about Peters and his famous photograph, it is not enough to take a picture of someone, 'you must learn to aim / to establish the shot,' which is particularly challenging if the individual in question, like Riel, keeps 'shifting' (*Batoche* 51).

Another difficulty in understanding historical figures resides in the medium in which they are commonly portrayed, historical fiction. A hybrid, half of whose name qualifies if not nullifies the other half, historical fiction is a problematic if not 'impossible' genre. Because it is torn between the need to be anchored in the real and the suspicion that true art is possible only by escaping the real, it tends to be found wanting in relation to both of the entities that constitute it (Manzoni 72). Historical fiction clearly does not possess history's claim to veracity, even if history's own factualness is being increasingly contested by writers and scholars who contend that 'history is a kind of fiction' and that 'as verbal artifacts histories and novels are indistinguishable from one another' (Doctorow 25; H. White 122). No less significant from a literary perspective, it also lacks the textual autonomy of more purely aesthetic genres in which the writer is supposedly 'judged [only] by the integrity or consistency of his verbal structure' (Frye, *Fables* 53). After all, even the creators of such realistic personages as Emma Bovary or

Duddy Kravitz do not have their characters measured against their specific empirical models. But that is invariably what happens in the analysis of historical novels, poems, and plays, which derive much of their power from the conviction that they are not invented but reflect some tangible, paratextual reality.

In *The Distinction of Fiction*, one of the most spirited critiques of postmodern relativism, especially its tendency to conflate the factual and the fictive, Dorrit Cohn concludes that historical fiction is 'unmistakably and distinctively fictional.' As she approvingly quotes the German novelist Alfred Döblin, 'The historical novel is, in the first place, a novel; in the second, it isn't history' (121, 153). Yet historical fiction remains distinct from purely non-referential discourse. It may well be the case that it is usually not presented as 'history,' as Cohn asserts (121), but paratextual truth claims seem endemic to the genre. James Reaney, for instance, evokes a non-aesthetic aspect of historical fiction when he confesses that he has 'anxious' fears about the possible discovery of documents critical of the Donnellys. Such documents presumably could undermine his own plays about the controversial nineteenth-century Ontario family (Reaney, 'Scapegoats').[3] Similarly, Margaret Atwood has stated that what 'terrified' her while writing her historical novel *Alias Grace* 'was that I would get a letter from somebody saying "I was up in the attic and I found this old biscuit box full of letters from Grace Marks and you were very wrong about everything." That hasn't happened, but you never know, it might' (quoted in Martin R4). Michael Ondaatje is more nonchalant about the implications of using real-life individuals in his work, asserting that the subject of one of his historical fictions was 'important to me only as I knew him' at the time of the writing (quoted in Pearce 132). Yet, judging by the controversy over *The English Patient*, even Ondaatje cannot escape the congenital hybridization, or incompleteness, of historical fiction. Cohn herself claims that her 'initial admiration' for Ondaatje's novel 'dropped down a few notches' after she 'learned some biographical facts' about its protagonist, the desert explorer László Almásy (159), a response that incidentally qualifies her contention that 'fiction never refers to the real world outside the text.' For if it were true that literary characters were purely 'imaginary beings' (Cohn 14, 16), then one's feelings about a personage would not likely be affected by a biography of him or her.

If nothing else, what the current debate on the nature of textual reality underscores is the need to recognize the unique relationship between historical fiction and the world, notably when writers attempt to reconstruct the lives of people who actually lived. In particular, one must acknowledge the ontological difference between fictional and factographic representations, to borrow Uri Margolin's term for those literary narratives with a referential component (269). Even when produced by people who either participate in or witness empirical events, factographic representations are not necessarily more faithful than fictional ones. This is evident in Riel's self-figuration not only as the 'David' of the New World but also the Christian 'Daniel,' 'Jerimiah,' and 'Elijah' (2: 75; 3: 322–3). Yet the reason factographic and fictional representations should not be collapsed is that, along with the fact they are shaped by different narrative techniques (Cohn 109–31), they are subject to dissimilar 'truth conditions' (Doležel 792). As Lubomír Doležel states, 'fictional gaps are created' by the writer in the process of constructing his or her fictional world, and are thus 'ontological and irrecoverable.' Factographic or historical gaps, in contrast, 'are due to the lack of evidence or the historian's selectivity' and, therefore, are 'epistemological' (795–6). In other words, a fictional world cannot be altered, since it is complete. But a factographic world can, if either new archival evidence is unearthed or a new way of seeing materializes.

In the case of a study of the representations of Riel, that 'shapeshifter' who has become a symbol not only of 'both Canadian unity and Canadian disunity' but also of 'the dividing line between fact and fiction' (Francis, *National Dreams* 127; Moore, 'Haunted' 413), one must begin with the primary texts by the Métis leader himself and his contemporaries. It is only from those works, whether produced by friend or foe, that one can sketch an empirically informed portrait of the subject. Considering that Riel exhibited different selves at different stages of his life, it is possible that two or more seemingly contradictory characterizations of him could be historically accurate, depending on their time frame. Still, it does not follow that every play, novel, or poem about the 'crucifix waving dude' who has become the most prominent figure in Canadian culture is equally sound (Suknaski 3; Moore, 'Haunted' 411). The rationale for privileging Riel's archival record is precisely that it enables one to differentiate between the aspects of a representation that are shaped by collective memory and those that are the wilful invention of its author. It is because of this foundational yardstick that one can establish the relation – if any – between the man who was convicted of being a 'traitor' to the Canadian Crown (*Queen* 3, 371) and his portraits as 'Canada's Joan of Arc' (Lusty 5); a modern-day Guy Fawkes, who by hanging 'got exactly what he deserved' (C. Woodcock); 'the Métis founder of Manitoba' (Wiebe, 'Night' 237); a 'self-seeking adventurer' (Pocock 97); an 'egotist' and 'coward' (E. Young 467); a 'wise m[a]n from the West' (Klassen 275); 'the mad [Métis] messiah' (Nicol, *Dickens* 242); Canada's own 'Che Guevera [*sic*]' (Morrissey, *Batoche* 69); 'the David Koresh of his day' (Bercuson and Cooper); the 'Marat of the Grasslands' (Ferguson 102); 'a saint and martyr' (Zinovich 178); the precursor and 'modest Canadian counterpart' of the Ayatollah Khomeini (D. Morton, 'Reflections' 59); or 'a true Father of Confederation' (Doyle 183).

Needless to say, there are limitations to such a historical approach. Except in passing, it does not allow one to evaluate a given text's literary value. It also does not permit one to investigate whether a historical fiction can succeed as literature even though it is historically inaccurate. But as I stated at the outset, while this study deals mainly with literary texts, its focus is less strictly literary than cultural. Its aim is not to identify the great masterpieces on Riel, which it has been convincingly argued tend to be not literary but historical (Duffy, 'Wiebe' 209), but to trace the tremendous permutations his reputation has undergone in Canadian literature. More specifically, I will attempt to ascertain the political motivation for such disparate views of the same historical individual and, at the same time, to show how a society must come to terms with competing narratives when it transforms into a national hero someone it had hanged as a traitor.

History, as the totality of the recorded or articulated past, is necessarily a mere fraction of what transpires in space and time. It is also inherently biased. History favours privileged individuals and groups in society, the famous and the notorious, as well as those either powerful enough to commission their own life stories or eloquent enough to produce them themselves. Traditionally, it has been peopled chiefly by so-called world historical men, the cultural and political leaders who, among other characteristics, share the privilege of having their lives widely documented. Oppressed figures seldom enter the hallowed domain of history. Moreover, when they do, their stories tend to be framed, not from their perspective, but from that of the very people who have subjugated them. For example, the earliest accounts of the Ghost Dance movement that emerged in the U.S. Great Plains in the 1870s emanated, not from its 'messiah,' the Paiute prophet Wovoka, but from antagonistic white journalists (Mooney 7). The dominant narrative about Antônio Conselheiro's role in the Canudos War of 1896–7 was also not written by the millenarian preacher or one of his followers but by a representative of the 'cosmopolitan' Brazilian coastal society that obliterated them (Cunha 474–8).[4] Lastly, the pivotal text about Jandamarra's rebellion against white settlement in the Kimberleys of Western Australia was not authored by the Bunuba 'rebel' or some other Aborigine but by a white writer (Idriess).

Riel, however, is an exception to this general invisibility of marginalized political figures. In her elegiac poem 'Riel: In the Season of His Birth' (1979), Erin Mouré decries the fact that following the Métis leader's death all that were left were 'accusations – / words of the priests / spoken against you' (66). This is not quite the case. It may be true that Riel was hanged because he lived in a colonial backwater, too 'far away' from merry Windsor Castle, as charges the Byron of Oregon, Joaquin Miller (113). But if the words of any of the participants in the North West troubles have endured, it is not those of the priests (or soldiers) who clashed with Riel but his own. As Mouré herself implies at the end of her poem,

> you are falling   Riel
> but your voice dangles
> wild & liquid   focussed
> as grass reborn
>   to breathe in the white spring
>   of prairie rivers (68)

So fecund has Riel's voice become that he is the single most important generating-source of his own mythology. Despite the 1885 Regina verdict, he has emerged not so much as a martyr, to say nothing of a traitor, as a 'posthumous victor' (Fetherling 30). His interpretation of his quarrels with Ottawa is so widely accepted that it has virtually silenced all his opponents. As the historian Desmond Morton complains, the idea of presenting the people who fought Riel as patriots, even if it would do no 'offence to the known facts,' is simply too outlandish ('Reflections' 51).

Riel's triumph has never been more pronounced than when the Canada Council (now the Social Sciences and Humanities Research Council of Canada) and several universities marked the centenary of his hanging by contributing generously to the publication of all his known papers, a five-volume bilingual edition entitled *The Collected Writings of Louis Riel / Les écrits complets de Louis Riel*. The singularity of the event becomes even more striking when one realizes that no such honour has been bestowed on any other major Canadian cultural, military, or political figure, including the country's first prime minister – and Riel's nemesis – Sir John A. Macdonald (Owram, 'Riel' 207, 215; Bumsted, 'Mahdi'). Furthermore, this is not an isolated incident. Most of Canada's current political establishment, like the cultural one, seems to have come to accept Riel as a patriot. Governor General Adrienne Clarkson, for instance, describes the Métis leader as a champion of 'western rights and the rights of his people, [who] helped to lay the framework for minority rights – and as a result for cultural cooperation – in this country' (1). Former Prime Minister Joe Clark, too, feels that Canada should show 'respect' to today's Métis by officially 'recognizing "the unique and historic role of Louis Riel as a founder of Manitoba and his contribution in the development of Confederation"' (80–1). Parliament itself appears ready not only to declare 'Louis Riel a Canadian hero' but even to name May 12 'Louis Riel Day' (D.B. Smith, 'Right' F6). In the words of Liberal MP Denis Coderre, the head of the all-party campaign to 'innocenter' Riel, he is 'un grand Canadien' (quoted in Gratton).

The consensus among both writers and politicians about Riel's status is worth noting. Like other artists, writers tend to perceive themselves as oppositional figures, iconoclasts battling the entrenched powers-that-be. But at least when it comes to the Métis leader, there is no significant difference between their stance and that of the overwhelming majority of politicians. Rather than challenging the 'official' view of Riel, writers simply echo it. Equally significant, despite the wholehearted embrace of the 1885 rebel by the political and cultural elites, it is not easily discernible how the citizenry feels about him. The one plebiscite on Riel suggests that the general populace is highly divided. When the government of Saskatchewan decided to rename Highway 11 the 'Louis Riel Trail,' there was a storm of protest. According to a report, at least '75 percent' of respondents to one survey were opposed to changing the designation of the north-south artery connecting Regina and Prince Albert (Racette 46). In the time-honoured Canadian tradition, the government went ahead and did it anyway ('Highway 11').

In any case, the transformation of the architect of two armed conflicts against Canada into the epitome of Canadianness, the very gauge of Canadian authenticity, could not occur without creating some ironies, if not outright contradictions. Peter Goldring, for one, sees the 'unhanging' of Riel as another example of 'political correctness.' The Canadian Alliance MP for Edmonton claims with some justification, but little support from his federal colleagues, that 'Riel didn't "Father" Confederation; he "fought" those who did' ('Louis Riel'; 'Riel').[5] For somewhat different reasons, George Bowering also has raised a series of objections to the Métis leader's ubiquity in Canadian culture. As the West Coast poet and novelist protests, 'You do not have to shovel snow or Louis Riel into your book to write a Canadian text' ('Great' 12). Bowering is the author of one of the most racialized treatments of mixed-race life in Canada, the historical novel *Shoot!*, in which people like his protagonists, the McLean brothers, are supposedly feared by nineteenth-century British Columbia society because they give evidence of 'the sexual union of native women and hairy-faced men from the outside world' (141). Yet Bowering is not convinced that contemporary examinations of Riel's life will 'tell us how we are living today' (12). He is also doubtful that any individual can be so representative of a nation, particularly when the person in question 'wasnt [sic] even a citizen' (*Short* 184). Of course, the matter of Riel's citizenship or national identity is precisely the detail that most recent Canadian writers tend to ignore, a curious omission given his unswerving identification with the Métis, as his writings attest.

One of the reasons that I am reluctant to accept Foucault's equation of power and truth is that I do not believe this is quite the case in non-absolutist societies. In totalitarian countries, it is probably accurate that those in power are able not just to rewrite history but to 'remake the actual past,' such as when Stalin had his adversaries removed from photographs (Doležel 799). That is, through their brute power, totalitarian rulers can produce truth. However, it is not self-evident that in democracies 'power and knowledge directly imply one another' (Foucault, *Discipline* 27). Foucault's theory of power is a complex one, notably his suggestion that power has a multiplicity of sources and is 'never localised here or there, never in anybody's hands, never appropriated as a commodity or piece of wealth' (*Power* 98). Still, even though Foucault concedes that 'where there is power, there is resistance' (*History* 95), one cannot help but sense that he seriously underestimates the extent to which power is contested. It is certainly difficult to dispute Said's contention that Foucault has 'a singular lack of interest in the force of effective resistance' and that one must ask why such a formidable mind 'went as far as he did in imagining power to be irresistible and unopposable' (*Reflections* 241).

The limits of power are apparent everywhere, including in such enterprises as literary or cultural criticism, in which one's claims are open to verification by others. The aforementioned publication of Riel's *Collected Writings* is a case in point. In his 'General Editor's Remarks' introducing the last volume, George F.G. Stanley writes that the Alberta-based endeavour was bound to be a source of 'pride' to Canadians, especially Western Canadians (2). By collecting and making accessible the totality of Riel's poetry and prose, Stanley and his associates seem to have believed that they would be helping cement the reputation of a great Canadian 'folk hero' (1). But something peculiar transpired: Riel resisted the embrace. The very words that were so painstakingly compiled undercut the intentions of both the editors and their financial backers by suggesting that the subject of this nation-building project is a problematic Canadian. Whatever else they may achieve, Riel's writings clearly demonstrate that his discursive victory since the end of the Second World War must be qualified, for it may be a pyrrhic one. The fact is that something fundamental occurs to the Prophet of the New World in his journey from pariah to hero: he is Canadianized. Riel may still be considered the quintessential 'marginal ex-centric,' but he is a Canadian symbol of peripheralness; he is 'the Canadian' (Hutcheon 4–5). However, his own words intimate that this transformation has been achieved at a price – by depriving him of his Otherness, his national specificity as a Métis.

Since the violence that the denationalization – and dehistoricization – of Riel does to his story is most apparent in his writings, my study opens with a close reading of them. Chapter 1, 'The Red River Patriot: Riel in His Biographical and Social Context,' attempts to situate him in relation to the mixed-race milieu that produced him. It focuses especially on the Métis leader's construction of himself and the New Nation, proposing that neither entity is constant. Throughout Riel's writings, his idea of the Métis nation evolves from being a branch of the greater French-Canadian family in North America, to a pan-Métis confederation (French-speaking as well as English, Catholic and Protestant), and finally to a unitary Franco-Catholic Métis society. Not surprisingly, as his collective identity evolves over time, so does his personal one. In fact, it may not be amiss to contend that his work is basically a quest for a feasible and stable body with which he can identify, and that the failure of his political dream is directly connected to his inability to poetically imagine or construct such a reality.

Entitled 'The Traitor: Riel As an Enemy of Confederation,' chapter 2 traces the image of Riel as a nation-wrecker. These representations are most popular at the end of the nineteenth century and beginning of the twentieth and are predominantly, but not exclusively, in English. One of the more fascinating works on the theme is actually Robert de Roquebrune's *D'un océan à l'autre*, a 1924 novel whose avowed intention is to prove to the outside world that Canadians are of pure French and English stock and that 'il n'y a pas de métis chez nous' (10). In addition to their proclivity to minimize Riel's political significance, to the point of asserting that Riel was only the nominal leader of the two North-West conflicts, the most common characteristic of these texts is how their authors depict as an arch-traitor someone they do not usually perceive as a fellow citizen.

Chapter 3, 'The Martyr (I): Riel As an Ethnic and Religious Victim of Confederation,' concentrates on English Canada's alleged bigotry toward the Métis leader. In contrast to the representations in the previous chapter, these emanate mainly from French-speaking, Catholic Quebec. Like the former, they are most prominent at the end of the nineteenth century. They also tend not to focus on their reputed protagonist, giving credence to Gilles Martel's thesis that both French- and English-speaking Canada are unable to transcend their 'querelles ethnocentriques' and accept that the Métis leader's story is not their own but 'le drame d'une *autre* collectivité' ('Louis Riel' 155).

As its title suggests, 'The Go-between: Riel As a Cultural Mediator,' chapter 4 centres on those texts that portray Riel as an intermediary among the various ethnocultural, religious, and regional groups in Canada. Largely a post–Second World War phenomenon, the topic reflects the gradual 'collapse, for North American eyes, of the meta-narrative that once went by the name Europe. Europa' (Kroetsch, *Lovely* 23). Following the catastrophic events across the Atlantic, many Euro-Canadian writers embark on a journey of self-indigenization. As Margaret Laurence writes, 'Canadians who, like myself, are the descendants of various settlers ... must hear native peoples' voices and ultimately become part of them' or 'perish' ('Man' 235). But instead of trying to bond directly with the country's indigenous inhabitants, those authors regularly opt to use Riel as a bridge between themselves and Aboriginal people.

Chapter 5, 'The Martyr (II): Riel As a Sociopolitical Victim of Confederation,' is in many ways a continuation of chapter 3. The key difference is that Riel is no longer perceived as a victim of English-Canadian ethnic or religious chauvinism but rather of Canada's transcontinental dream, if not of Western civilization itself. Riel, like the Métis people as a whole, is just another casualty of the all-consuming ideology of progress. He is the symbol of the pastoral world that seems destined to give way to the new industrial universe. Increasingly, at least for English-speaking writers, the Métis leader also emerges as the quintessential ancestor. He is the representative of a truly American culture that, instead of perceiving the land as an enemy, is at one with it. Of course, such a genealogical embrace is not without its consequences. In order to claim Riel as their own, those writers 'en mal d'identité' (Morisset, 'Louis Riel' 60) are often forced either to demonize their own biocultural ancestors as some sort of psychological freaks or, what is more common, to pretend they never existed.

The subject of the representations examined in chapter 6, 'The Mystic/Madman: Riel As a Para-rational Individual,' constitutes unquestionably the most controversial aspect of the Métis leader's life, his mental state. For some writers, Riel is an enlightened but misunderstood mystic, and thus sane. Other writers, however, are no less certain that he is a megalomaniac with visions of grandeur who would stop at nothing to achieve his goals. Ironically, at least at the end of the nineteenth century, it is Riel's supporters who strive most passionately to prove he is insane, while his enemies, particularly the federal government, systematically attempt to show he is mentally responsible.

Finally, extrapolating from the enormous diversity of representations of Riel in the last 150 years, the study explores why the 'footnote to minor colonial history' who has made 'it into the company of William Tell, Robin Hood and El Cid' (Moore, 'Haunted' 411) is likely to remain central to the Canadian imagination for some time to come. As well, it ponders the ambiguity of the charges levelled against the Métis leader in 1885 as a 'false traitor' to Canada (*Queen* 3), an accusation that gives this work its title and that simultaneously connotes an evil person and a non-traitor. It then concludes with the contention that the appropriation of Riel as an ancestor in Canadian literature since the middle of the twentieth century reflects a major cultural shift, a change in consciousness that has culminated in non-Aboriginal people increasingly seeing themselves as Americans. That is, the transformation of Riel into the archetypal Canadian probably says less about the Métis leader than it does about the evolving collective identity of the descendants or at least 'héritiers spirituels' of the people who hanged him (Morisset, 'Louis Riel' 50).

1

The Red River Patriot
Riel in His Biographical and Social Context

Je suis le Prophète, le Pontife Infaillible, le Prêtre Roi ...

Louis Riel (1876)

In his testimony during his 1885 trial for treason, Riel made three central points: he was not, as his own lawyers urged him to claim, insane; he was divinely inspired, both politically and poetically; and he was a child of the North-West. The matters of his sanity and divine inspiration, which will be examined in greater detail in the last chapter, are perhaps ultimately insoluble. At this juncture, suffice it to say that Riel was well aware that his self-perception was not universally shared. As he acknowledged, instead of accepting him as God's 'Infaillible témoin,' the world considered him 'fou' and 'se rit de moi' (2: 86; 4: 140). The question of his collective identity, however, is far more tangible, and more problematic. Contrary to the impression created by the later Riel, his ethno-national affiliation was not constant throughout his life. While he almost always described himself as Métis, he envisaged the group with a radically different composition across time, ranging from a branch of the greater French-Canadian family in North America, through a bilingual and bi-religious society, to a unitary Franco-Catholic people. As Glen Campbell notes, for Riel 'the lexeme "Métis" is not monosemic'; 'the signifier ... does not always refer to the same signified' ('Dithyramb' 33, 31).

Riel was not the most typical Métis, a people of mixed European and Aboriginal ancestry whose principal occupation was hunting buffalo and trading furs. The oldest of eleven children, he was born to a devout Catholic, French-speaking family in Saint Boniface, Red River Settlement – present-day Winnipeg – on either October 22 or 23, 1844 (Flanagan, *Louis 'David' Riel* 4; G. Martel, *Messianisme* 389–90). Riel's mother was Julie Lagimodière, the Western-born daughter of a couple from Lower Canada (Quebec) – her own mother was the legendary Marie-Anne Gaboury, the first white woman to become a permanent resident of what are now the Canadian Prairies. His father, also named Louis Riel, was the son of a voyageur originally from Quebec and a Métis woman of Québécois and Chipewyan descent (Champagne 151). In short, the future Métis leader, who later would base his people's 'titre' to the North-West almost exclusively on their 'sang indien,' was only one-eighth Aboriginal. Or, as he himself boasts, 'presque tout mon sang vient de la France' (3: 279; 2: 72).[1]

Riel's father, too, was not a buffalo hunter or freighter, but a farmer and mill owner. That is, he was part of the small, Quebec-centred Métis bourgeoisie, although bourgeoisie may be a misnomer for a community that had as yet 'given no priest to the church, no lawyer to the courts of Assiniboia, no doctor to practise among his people' (W.L. Morton 16). Raised and educated in Quebec – he entered the Oblate novitiate but soon realized that he did not have the calling and left the seminary – the senior Riel had played a critical role in the historic 'affaire Sayer' of 1849. This was an embryonic rebellion, provoked by the arrest and imprisonment of Guillaume Sayer and three other Métis hunters, which virtually ended the Hudson's Bay Company's monopoly in fur trading in the North-West (Stanley, *Louis Riel* 3, 14). The incident would also become for the Métis people 'un prototype héroïque d'une lutte nationale' and for Riel's oldest son and namesake, 'un catalyseur d'espérance' (G. Martel, *Messianisme* 93). But despite the family's enviable standing in the community, its economic circumstances were chronically precarious, being 'always deeply in debt' to 'the Great White Company' (Flanagan, *Louis 'David' Riel* 5; Colmer vi). Thus, when the thirteen-year-old Riel was sent to study for the priesthood in Quebec in June 1858 – along with two other *métis* boys, the unlikely surnamed Daniel McDougall and Louis Schmidt – he was not supported financially by his parents but by Bishop Alexandre Taché and, through the Catholic prelate of Saint Boniface, the influential Masson family of Terrebonne, Quebec (Siggins 46).

The Red River seminarian appears to have been acutely aware of his dependency on others from the moment he arrived at the Sulpician-run Collège de Montréal, as is evident in the earliest of his extant texts. In two end-of-year letters to his 'Vénérée Bienfaitrice' Sophie Masson, one in 1861 and the other in 1862, Riel expresses his discomfort at being 'l'objet d'une bienveillance dont je suis si indigne' and regrets that he will probably never be able to repay the seigneuresse of Terrebonne for 'les monuments de bienfaisance dont vous me dotez tous les jours' (1: 1–2). Even considering the formal tone of the letters, which suggests that they may have been dictated by the priest-teachers, it is difficult not to notice his sensitivity concerning his position. The reason for Riel's self-consciousness about his indigence is that it is not just personal and familial – he notes that the Massons had already done 'la même faveur ... à mon cher papa' (1: 9; Stanley, *Louis Riel* 17) – but also ethno-national. Throughout his writings, Riel actually draws a parallel between his marginality and that of the Métis. As he is individually dependent on the patronage of Bishop Taché and the Masson family for his education, so must the Métis people collectively rely on the spiritual and political protection of Quebec against all external foes.

Especially for the young Riel, his sense of collective insecurity leads him to regard Quebec not just as his people's protector but also as its progenitor. For him, after divine Providence, only the French-speaking Catholic society on the Saint Lawrence River can shield the Métis from the rapacious designs of their mortal enemy, Ontario. As he writes in the poem 'O Québec' (1870),

> Des ennemis fort à craindre
> Menaçant le berceau de tes enfants chéris.
>   Mais ils ne pourront atteindre,
> O Québec! Malgré toi, jamais notre pays!
>   Que la sainte Providence
> Inspire à notre égard tes hommes d'ottawa
>   Souviens-toi combien la France
> Te fit mal! O Québec! Lorsqu'Elle t'oublia! (4: 95–6)

Riel contrasts favourably Quebec's 'gloire,' its 'religion,' to Ontario's crass material 'politique' (4: 96). However, his appeal is less spiritual than historical or cultural. Quebec ought to support the Métis, he argues, not because it is a Catholic society, but because it is its 'Mère Colonie!'[2] Therefore, like any loving parent, it must not abandon its offspring and spare itself 'la douleur / de voir écraser tes braves / Tes fiers enfants du Nord, héritiers de ton Coeur!' (4: 95–6).

The degree to which Riel perceives the Métis as an extension of Quebec is particularly discernible in his Collège de Montréal poems, none of which deals directly with what he would later call 'la nation métisse' (4: 90). For instance, the fable 'Le chat et les souris' (1864–5) is an allegorical exploration of the brutal consequences of political oppression; or, more specifically, English oppression of foreign subjects. In the poem, an aristocratic and pitiless English cat lives exclusively from hunting mice. As the cat holds one of his sumptuous feasts, in which the 'plat plus délectable' is always 'la chair de souris,' the mice decide to meet in 'assemblée' and their worst fears are confirmed. When they count themselves, they discover that their numbers have dwindled precipitously because of the cat's activities. Still the mice, who are described as a 'nation' and a 'peuple,' do not despair about their fate (4: 26). Convinced that every oppressive act engenders its own retribution, they form an army and advance toward the cat's palatial residence, determined to attack their enemy 'en masse. / De le dévorer vif, l'écorcher, le manger, / De s'en venger' (4: 28). After much waiting, the battalion at last spots the cause of its misery and, as one, attacks him. The incensed cat somehow manages to escape, yet, in the end, he is unable to deprive his subjects of the 'joies de la vengeance.' He subsequently dies 'enragé,' and the battered but proud mice emerge victorious, as was their destiny. In the poem's final words, 'Le bon droit est ainsi toujours vengé' (4: 28).

'Le chat et les souris,' which is one of Riel's most critically respected works, is important for two distinct reasons. First, it typifies what has been called the author's 'moralle ... vengeresse' or 'conception némésiaque de la vie humaine' (Runte 21; G. Martel, *Messianisme* 115), his conviction that the oppressed can never be defeated since God will intervene in temporal affairs and punish whoever has abused them (Braz, 'Vengeful Prophet' 22). Second, and more important in terms of his collective identity, the poem illustrates the extent to which Riel considers Quebec not just his people's ancestral homeland, but their actual homeland. Whereas the cat is unambiguously described as 'Anglais' or 'Saxon' – the poem was the object of stylistic and political 'corrections,' which resulted in the word 'Anglais' being replaced by 'Noble' and 'Saxon' by 'héros' (Runte 19) – it is not easily discernible who the mice are supposed to be, either the *métis* (Runte 27; Siggins 55) or all French-speaking Canadians (Campbell, 'Notes' 128; Flanagan, *Louis 'David' Riel* 11).

Although Riel's 'national' identification with Quebec never ceases completely, it becomes far less pronounced after the mid-1860s. This is an ideological shift likely precipitated by the tumultuous events in his private life, notably the death of his father in 1864. The then nineteen-year-old had always idealized, if not idolized, his begetter. Posterity has tended to judge the senior Riel as a somewhat ineffectual farmer and businessman, 'the famous "Miller of the Seine" who never milled nothing,' to cite a partisan account (Wiebe, *Scorched-Wood* 12). But for his oldest son, he was a symbol of Métis national pride and moral rectitude. He was the dauntless hero who, through his courage and faith, had 'renversé un colosse d'iniquités' and whose name was destined to grow 'd'âge en âge dans tout le Nord Ouest' (Riel, 3: 267). Thus it is not surprising that the young man would be deeply affected by the news that his father had died suddenly after an undetermined but 'painful illness.' So traumatized was Riel by the loss that, before long, he would discard his plans to become the first Métis priest in the North-West and leave not just the Collège de Montréal but Montreal itself (Siggins 58).

There was probably one other factor that led Riel to reassess his relationship with Quebec, the social rejection he purportedly experienced there. Soon after abandoning his sacerdotal studies (Siggins 62), or being forced to abandon them (Flanagan, *Louis 'David' Riel* 20), Riel became secretly betrothed to a young Montreal woman named Marie-Julie Guernon. Guernon's parents, however, did not approve of her romance with the impecunious Métis divinity student and demanded that she cancel the wedding, a decision generally interpreted as being racially motivated (Stanley, *Louis Riel* 33). The rejection by his fiancée's family appears to have crystallized Riel's growing estrangement from Quebec society, his 'conscience d'être un étranger parmi ses semblables' (G. Martel, *Messianisme* 114), and convinced him that it was time to return home. Consequently, after eight years in Montreal, he left the city and embarked on a fateful journey that would lead him to two years of wandering through various communities of the Quebec diaspora in the eastern half of the United States, from New England to Minnesota; the command of two Métis armed confrontations with Canada; a series of mental breakdowns; a religious epiphany in which he supposedly was declared the Prophet of the New World; and, finally, his hanging for high treason at Regina in 1885.

Whether triggered by his father's death, the rebuff by Marie-Julie Guernon's family, or a combination of the two, after Riel arrived back in Saint Boniface in July 1868, he for the first time began to articulate an explicit Métis nationalism. There is certainly no equivalent in his Montreal works of the unambiguous celebration of his mixed-race roots expressed in the poem 'La métisse' (1870):

Je suis métisse et je suis orgueilleuse
D'appartenir à cette nation
Je sais que Dieu de sa main généreuse
Fait chaque peuple avec attention
Les métis sont un petit peuple encore
Mais vous pouvez voir déjà leurs destins
Etre haïs comme ils sont les honore.
Ils ont déjà rempli de grands desseins. (4: 88)

Or, as the heroine adds, if she ever falls in love, she will choose as 'mon fidèle amant / Un des soldats de la petite armée,' the valiant soldiers who are making it possible for the Métis to have 'notre Province' (4: 88–9).

The same Métis national pride is also evident in Riel's emotional reaction to the incendiary comments made by the poet Charles Mair about the people of Red River, especially its women. The author of Confederation's 'first significant collection of verse' in English, and an avid promoter of Canadian expansion, Mair had arrived recently from Ontario as the paymaster of the crew sent by Ottawa to build a road between the Lake of the Woods and the Settlement (Shrive vi, 55). In a letter to his brother Holmes, published in several eastern newspapers, Mair waxes poetic about the North-West, a land 'boundless and rich beyond all description or comparison' and blessed with a 'delightful' climate. The soil is so fertile, he stresses, that the 'half-breeds are the only people here who are starving. Five thousand of them have to be fed this winter, and it is their own fault, they won't farm' (Letter 396, 398). Even less tactfully, Mair also remarks on the social relations in the community. After stating that 'I received hospitalities to my heart's content,' he alleges that there are 'jealousies and heart-burnings' between the local mixed-race and white women. Many prosperous white men, Mair writes, 'are married to half-breed women, who, having no coat of arms but a "totem" to look back to, make up for the deficiency by biting at the backs of their "white" sisters.' The latter, in turn, 'fall back upon their whiteness, whilst the husbands meet each other with desperate courtesies and hospitalities, with a view to filthy lucre in the background' (Letter 396).

While Mair's appraisal of social life at Red River is believed to contain at least 'a germ of truth' (Van Kirk 239), it is obviously graceless, and the response to it by his injured hosts was both swift and unequivocal. Annie Bannatyne, a Halfbreed woman married to one of the richest white merchants in the community, cornered Mair in the post office and publicly horsewhipped him, reportedly telling the author that 'c'est ainsi que les femmes de la Rivière-Rouge traitent ceux qui les insultent' (Dumas 27–8; Shrive 73). Alexander Begg, the business partner of Bannatyne's husband and a future historian, sought his revenge by savagely lampooning 'the celebrated!! poet' as a braggart with a weakness for 'the Red River belles' (*Red River* 156; 'Dot It Down' 281; Shrive 74–7). Riel's riposte was also literary, but no less personal. In a long letter to the Montreal newspaper *Le nouveau monde*, he ridicules Mair's claim to know the North-West. Riel particularly resents the Ontarian's insinuation that the Métis have become dependent on 'la charité,' and sarcastically suggests that Mair should restrict himself to verse, 'car par là au moins ses écrits auraient le mérite de la rime puisqu'ils n'ont pas toujours celui du bon sens.' Tellingly, to establish his authority to speak on behalf of the people of Red River, he states simply, 'je suis métis moi' (1: 14).

Considering that several conflicting nationalisms coexist in Riel, the enunciation of any of them can never be systematic or uncomplicated. This becomes quite apparent when one realizes that 'La métisse' and the reply to Mair's letter were written about the same time as 'O Québec,' a poem that speaks of the Métis, not as a separate people, but as Quebec's children, 'tes Métis-Canadiens' (4: 95). Nevertheless, there is little doubt that upon leaving Montreal, Riel became far more conscious of his Métis identity, of belonging to 'la nation naissante des Métis' (4: 165). If anything, this awareness becomes even more pervasive after his religious epiphany in 1875, a development for which again there may be biographical explanations.

When Riel returned to Red River in 1868, he arrived just in time to assume the leadership of the amorphous forces beginning to resist the planned sale of the North-West by the Hudson's Bay Company to the newly formed Canadian Confederation. The transaction, which was finally scheduled to occur on December 1, 1869, was opposed by most of the residents of the Settlement for a variety of reasons, not the least of which was the fact they had not been consulted on what amounted to 'la vente et l'achat' of a people (Groulx, *Louis Riel* 4). Resistance was especially pronounced amongst Red River's two mixed-race groups, the French-speaking *métis* and the English-speaking Halfbreeds. Riel thus proceeded to rally the 'deux sections de la Population' to work together to repel the Eastern invaders by appealing both to their sense of solidarity and to that great cement of collectivities, their 'grievances' (Riel, 1: 24; Lipking 205, 213).

Riel managed to convince the inhabitants of Red River that, if they wished their foes to deal with them on a 'noble pied d'égalité,' they had to form a government and army of their own. Then he and his almost exclusively francophone followers, led by his adjutant-general Ambroise Lépine, captured Fort Garry (Riel, 1: 91; Schmidt, 'Mémoires' 8 Feb. 1912, 4). The chief aim of their 'bloodless coup' was to prevent the Canadians from taking possession of the Hudson's Bay Company headquarters. However, their behaviour was severely criticized by the Halfbreeds, who judged it 'inconstitutionnel,' and by the local Canadian minority (Siggins 109; Riel, 1: 25). The Red River Canadians, who instead of feeling threatened by Canada's imminent acquisition of the Settlement actively promoted it, were strident in their protestations. Under the general leadership of John Christian Schultz, a medical doctor originally from Ontario and with close links to the expansionist Canada First Party, they began to plot to recapture Fort Garry. But Riel learned of their plans and promptly had all those involved arrested (Stanley, *Birth* 48–52, 115–17). As the Métis leader would later inform the colony's inhabitants, his government would not tolerate any breach of the 'sûreté publique,' and anyone who caused any public disturbances would be treated 'avec toute les sévérités de la loi' (1: 81).

Several of the prisoners soon escaped, though, a political embarrassment that caused Riel much grief and may have precipitated his first major mental breakdown (Siggins 158). Among the escapees were the aforementioned Mair and Schultz, as well as Tom Scott, an Irish-born Orangeman who had recently migrated from Ontario. Scott was subsequently arrested again and, upon being tried in a 'conseil de guerre' presided over by Lépine, was executed by firing squad (Riel, 1: 404). The treatment of Scott by Riel and his government remains controversial to this day not only because they killed the Ontarian for rather obscure reasons but also because they never returned the body – while there are many theories, the most common belief is that the corpse was dropped through the ice of the Red River.[3] Curiously, despite the fact Scott was the only person killed by his government, Riel is extremely reticent on the subject. He usually dismisses it as a case of political expediency, telling two observers that the Orangeman had to be executed because 'we must make Canada respect us' and 'I must make an example to impress others and lead them to respect my government' (quoted in D.A. Smith 40; Young 135). The historian J.M. Bumsted, about the only contemporary scholar who gives Scott the benefit of the doubt, suggests that the reason Riel had the Ontarian executed was because of the latter's marginality. Bumsted writes that, contrary to his image as an influential Protestant, Scott was 'a transient Canadian newcomer' who 'was not regarded as being very important by anybody' and thus Riel must have felt that he could sacrifice him, since he was 'one of life's expendables' ('Why' 209).

Looking back at the episode some years later, Riel would seem to support Bumsted when he states that, in the context of the 'troubles du nord'ouest ... l'exécution de Th. Scott n'est qu'un détail' (1: 362). However, rather than being a non-issue, Scott's killing would become 'le grand événement' or 'central and defining event of the Red River Resistance,' basically ending it (Frémont, *Sur le ranch* 113; Bumsted, 'Crisis' 26; 'Thomas Scott' 146). As even Riel concedes, it was his great 'political mistake' (Riel, 3: 583; Bumsted, 'Thomas Scott's Body' 10). The twentieth-century poet and playwright James Reaney has written that 'anyone who can think up a name like Manitoba deserves to live, no matter how many Tom Scotts he himself has hanged' ('Local Grains' 27). But the response was rather different at the time. The affair provoked such indignation in Ontario that the government of Prime Minister Macdonald felt compelled to organize a military expedition to ensure its possession of what would soon be named the province of Manitoba. The Métis realized that they had little chance against the better-armed Canadians and began to disperse, having 'abandoned any idea of resistance' by the time troops arrived at Fort Garry in August 1870 under the British colonel Garnet Wolseley (Stanley, *Louis Riel* 140). Riel himself at first hid in the woods around Saint Boniface, waiting to see if he would be treated with the civility he thought his position as head of the provisional government and 'le droit des gens' merited. But he soon concluded that Wolseley's 'Expédition de paix' had entered the Settlement 'comme un ennemi' (1: 236). Believing Canadian 'assassins' were plotting to murder him – his suspicions were partly confirmed the following year when the Ontario Liberal leader, Edward Blake, offered a $5,000 reward for his capture – Riel fled to the United States and to a new life as an international fugitive (1: 101–2; Stanley, *Birth* 167).

Ironically, Riel's status as an outlaw would not prevent him from initiating one of the most unlikely careers in Canadian federal politics. While living on the run from what Don Harron's Charlie Farquharson calls 'yer just sassiety' (99), he won the Conservative party's nomination for the new Manitoba riding of Provencher. Then, when Sir George-Étienne Cartier was unexpectedly defeated in his Quebec riding – the Eastern election took place weeks before the Western – he was approached through Bishop Taché to resign his candidacy in favour of the prime minister's French-speaking lieutenant (3: 260). After demanding that the Métis be allowed 'the exercise' of their traditional land rights, Riel assented to be replaced by the 1837–rebel-turned-statesman, someone he had once eulogized as 'l'honneur des Canadiens français' (1: 224; 4: 71), but would later describe both as his 'vrai' political ancestor and as a deceitful practitioner of the 'politique anglaise' (3: 572; 4: 127). To render the situation even more implausible, Cartier died soon afterwards and Riel would again contest, and win, the riding. He then travelled surreptitiously to Ottawa and, with the assistance of a former schoolmate and Quebec member of Parliament, slipped into the House of Commons long enough to take the oath of allegiance and sign 'the register as member for Provencher' (Riel, 2: 419; Stanley, *Louis Riel* 202).

Parliament, which was already humiliated by Riel's election, responded to its newest member's audacious appearance in Ottawa by expelling him (Stanley, *Louis* 203). The Métis leader somehow had managed to embarrass both parties in the Commons, which reacted in contrasting ways. Whereas the Liberals were calling for Riel's head, the Tories were doing all they possibly could to keep the 'rebel' out of the country. The country's first prime minister is actually alleged to have been channelling money through Bishop Taché to bribe Riel not to return to Canada until the crisis was over (*Queen* 363, 369). This was a masterful game of double-speak, to which no one has paid better homage than J.W. Bengough, the founder and editor of the influential nineteenth-century satirical magazine *Grip*. In one cartoon, the Liberal Bengough depicts MP Riel escaping from Ottawa while 'warden' Macdonald conveniently looks the other way. The Liberal leader, Alexander Mackenzie, is seen in the background exclaiming that he would like to arrest the two supposed adversaries (pl. 2). In another cartoon, after the fall of Batoche, Bengough responds to the suggestion that a memorial to Riel be erected at Toronto's Queen's Park by sketching a 'combination' statue of Riel and Macdonald. The prime minister's half shows the moccasin-clad Macdonald holding a note about a $1,500 payment to Riel. On the base of the monument is inscribed, '1872, Would to God I could catch him!' and '1886, Would to God I had not caught him!' (pl. 3).

The awkward political situation created by Riel's election finally seemed to be resolved in 1875, when Parliament granted the Métis leader amnesty for his role at Red River, presumably including the execution of Tom Scott, 'conditional on five years' banishment from Her Majesty's Dominions' (quoted in Stanley, *Birth* 174). But Riel's exile from Canada would neither silence him nor sever his political and emotional ties to his cause. On the contrary, his Métis nationalism grew ever stronger after he was forced to move away from his people and land. As he writes to his mother from Worcester, Massachusetts, 'Pendant les cinq années que je passerai dans l'exil, je n'ai que cela à faire, et à dire aux Métis: rester Métis, devenir plus Métis que jamais!' (1: 167). This is particularly true after December 8 of that year, when he experienced what would be unquestionably the pivotal event in his life. Riel was attending mass at Saint Patrick's Catholic Church in Washington, DC:

> Au moment même où le prêtre, ayant terminé son sermon, disait le *Credo*, et pendant que le peuple était debout et moi avec lui, je sentis soudain dans mon coeur une joie si maîtresse de moi, que pour cacher à mes voisins le rire de mon visage, je fus contraint d'étendre mon mouchoir à sa grandeur et de le tenir ainsi avec ma main sur ma bouche et sur mes joues ...
>
> Après que ces consolations m'eussent réjoui environ deux minutes, je fus immédiatement saisi par une immense douleur d'âme. Et si ce n'eut été des grands efforts que j'ai faits pour contenir mes sanglots, mes cris et mes larmes eussent éclaté terriblement dans l'enceinte de l'église. C'est par discrétion que j'ai fait taire la douleur presque insupportable que j'éprouvais dans mon âme. Or cette grande peine qui avait été égale à ma joie, passa en aussi peu de temps qu'elle. Et mon esprit resta plein de cette pensée: 'Les joies et les douleurs de l'homme ici-bas sont courtes.'
>
> Pas longtemps après, à la suite seulement de quelques jours, on commença à me traiter de fou. (2: 163–64)

It was that wondrous winter in the capital of the United States, Riel would assert later – writing of himself in the third person – that 'God anointed him ... prophet of the new world' (3: 261).

Needless to say, Riel's Washington revelation raises serious questions. As he notes, it is often perceived as a sign of his faltering mental health. In a case fraught with political overtones, his 'bons et ... nombreux amis' would soon afterwards spirit the exile to Quebec and have him institutionalized in psychiatric hospitals for the next two years, in order to protect him not only from his Orange 'enemies' but also from himself (Mousseau 90; H. Howard 644). Even more critical from a textual perspective, Riel assumes the authenticity of whatever occurred in Saint Patrick's Church, based not on what God purportedly imparted to him but rather on a previous letter by Montreal's ultramontane Bishop Ignace Bourget. Dated July 14, 1875, Bourget's text would become for Riel 'le livre de ma guidance' and the irrefutable proof of his messianic destiny. Yet all the letter states is that 'Dieu qui vous a toujours dirigé et assisté ... vous a donné une mission qu'il vous faudra accomplir en tous points' (Riel, 2: 35; Bourget 437). Moreover, Bourget himself would later inform his protégé that Riel had 'mal interpreté' his words and that no heavenly significance should be attached to them (Riel, 2: 315–20).

In any case, Riel's vision completely transformed his image of himself. After December 8, 1875, he is no longer a failed political leader driven into exile by a rapacious foreign power. Instead, he is 'le Prophète, le Pontife Infaillible, le Prêtre Roi,' the David of the New World – starting in May 1876, he would usually sign his name 'Louis "David" Riel' (2: 73, 75; Flanagan, 'Louis Riel's Name "David"'). Claiming to be 'plus grand que Samson,' Riel is not just the pope but the Catholic Church itself: 'Je me reconnais, ô mon Dieu, je suis votre épouse, la sainte église des Elus' (4: 143; 3: 374). In his words, 'Quand je vous parle, c'est la voix de Dieu qui sonne / Et tout ce que je dis vous est essentiel. / Je suis le joyeux téléphone' (4: 146). Or, as Orland French asserts in 'Pope Louie I' (1985), 'Riel had a grand impression of his version of the Holy Trinity: He, Himself and God, in that order' (104).

Furthermore, it is not just Riel's self-image that undergoes a metamorphosis as a result of his Washington epiphany. With the Prophet of the New World also rises a new people, the Métis. In a prescient letter written to Bourget on the eve of the revelation, in which Riel seems to anticipate the blissful event by declaring that 'j'accepte avec le plus grand bonheur la mission que vous m'annoncez,' he expresses the desire that the pope be informed 'un nouveau peuple catholique surgit dans le monde en ce temps-ci: le peuple Métis' (1: 474–5). One of the reasons he wishes the pontiff be made aware of the development is that the pope is the 'Protecteur naturel du Peuple Métis.' Riel evidently comes to embrace the idea that the Métis are a chosen people, favoured not only by the 'Christ visible de l'Eglise militante,' 'le Roi des Rois,' but also by the transcendent Christ of the Church Triumphant (1: 475–6; 2: 83).

Riel's belief in the providential role of the Métis has a strong genealogical and religious foundation, his conviction that he and his people are the new Israelites, since 'les sauvages de l'Amérique du Nord sont Juifs et du plus pur sang d'Abraham, à l'exception des esquimaux qui viennent du Maroc' (2: 39). But this belief, which was not uncommon in the nineteenth century and has some currency even today (Chamberlin 14), is not devoid of political implications. At least from the time of the Guernon affair, Riel begins to perceive the Métis people as a separate ethnic and political entity. The challenge for him, then, is not so much to prove that his nation exists as to demonstrate that it has a legitimate claim to the North-West, a 'droit' he initially concludes it possesses through its 'sang sauvage' (1: 292). In his revelations, by contrast, he takes quite a dissimilar approach, deriving his national rights not from his Aboriginal ancestral inheritance but from natural law. As he writes, 'Dieu est le Père des nations et des tribus. Il ne peut les créer sans les localiser' (3: 274). In short, by virtue of its existence alone, a people has a divine right to a territory of its own, a homeland. This is a concept that becomes central to Riel's vision and that he develops more fully in his later writings and in his testimony at his treason trial.

In 1878, two years after being taken secretly to Quebec for psychiatric treatment, Riel was again smuggled across the border. This time he travelled in the opposite direction, back into the United States, as his hosts apparently feared the political repercussions of having sheltered him 'illegally' for such a long period (Siggins 271). Riel would do some farming in a French-speaking area in northeastern New York, while travelling occasionally across the state and throughout New England, but before long he started to entertain the idea of returning to the West. At first he expressed the intention of acquiring a homestead in Nebraska, presumably attracted by its 'tempéré' and 'doux' climate (2: 174, 184). However, late in 1879 he decided to relocate not to Nebraska but to Montana, a choice that seems to have been less motivated by the weather than by the fact the territory had a sizable Métis population.

Riel's Montana life, at least on the surface, appears to have been uneventful. He married a local Métis woman named Marguerite Monet *dit* Bellehumeur, with whom he would have two children, and settled down as a schoolteacher in a Jesuit Métis mission. Especially after taking United States citizenship, a 'delight[ful]' occurrence that he felt had 'effacé la ligne entre le N.O. et les Etats-Unis' (quoted in Botkin 19; Riel, 3: 307), Riel became actively involved in Montana politics on behalf of the Métis. In an attempt to better support his family, he even began writing verse in English, offering to use his pen to sell anything from mineral resources to political parties and tourism:

I can sing in my poetry
Right and wealth. I can advertize
Your trade. I can sing the country
And every great enterprise.

My poems can show the big trains
Run by Northern Pacific
Over Hills and through rowling plains:
I can celebrate their trafic.

My pen can invite emigrants
To come and buy along the line
Acres of those beautiful grants
Where a land is worth a rich mine.

I can sing our gentle ladies
Innocent girls and good young boys
And that pure love which remedies
To sorrows and makes us rejoice. (4: 279)

Unfortunately for Riel, neither his political nor his poetic endeavours met with much success. So he again began to doubt himself, asking in 1884, 'Que suis-je? Que suis-je pour essayer à mener les événements? Un néant, c'est moi' (2: 355).

Riel's political fortunes would soon change dramatically, though, with the arrival of the fabled buffalo hunter Gabriel Dumont and three other Saskatchewan Valley Métis. Sent by both the white and mixed-race residents of the region, which was beset by a series of economic and political problems, the visitors had travelled over a thousand kilometres on horseback to entreat the hero of Red River to help them prepare a list of grievances to present to the Canadian government (Stanley, *Louis Riel* 265–8). Riel immediately grasped the potential significance of 'gabriel / the messenger' journeying to Montana to bring back 'david / the prophet' (Morrissey, *Batoche* 23), noting that 'your coming to me has the proportions of a remarkable fact. I record it as one of the gratifications of my life' (Riel, 3: 4). He pondered the invitation for some time, but there was never much doubt what would be his response. Thus, within a few days, on June 10, 1884, Riel headed north toward the Métis village of Batoche, a historic trek that would culminate in 'the final brave and desperate attempt to assert a kind of native sovereignty in Canada' (Chamberlin 200) and his own hanging.

As just mentioned, the stated objective of the Dumont delegation was to request Riel's 'advice on various difficulties which have rendered the British North West as yet unhappy under the Ottawa Government' (Riel, 3: 4). But even the prospect of such a relatively inconsequential role before long began to transform his sense of self, making him wonder if it did not augur more grandiose events ahead. As he writes to members of his family back in Manitoba,

Il n'y a pas longtemps, j'étais humble maître d'école sur les bords éloignés du Missouri. Et me voici aujourd'hui au rang des hommes publics les plus populaires de la Saskatchewan. L'an dernier personne ne voulait de moi dans les cercles politiques influents du Manitoba, cette année le peuple s'émeut à ma parole dans le coeur du Nord Ouest. Les banquiers m'invitent à leur table. Et leur bienveillance leur fait battre des mains, en signe d'approbation. Ils m'applaudissent avec la foule. Et le mauvais riche qui me regardait l'an passé avec un air de pitié, s'inquiète à présent. Il ouvre les yeux dans son étonnement; il est alarmé; il se fâche. Qui est-ce qui fait arriver tout cela? (3: 12)

He answers his own question by saying that 'c'est Dieu' and then adds, underlining his words for effect, 'Le Seigneur a fait pour moi de grandes choses' (3: 12).

Riel became convinced that his call to Batoche was part of God's larger providential plan for him. He was not just to counsel the local populace on federal-territorial relations but was a divine emissary sent by God 'to establish a new code of laws in the North West' (quoted in Ross 26). More specifically, he was the 'second David' chosen to redress all the wrongs done to his suffering nation and to 'lead my people, Israel, out of tyranny' (quoted in Schultz 382; Banks 256). However, Ottawa's unresponsiveness to his petitions led Riel to conclude that 'Justice commands [us] to take arms' and that 'a war of extermination' should be waged 'upon all those who have shown themselves hostile to our rights' (3: 54, 56). Yet his struggle was as much religious as political, since the people of the North-West had to fight Canada as well as 'Rome.' After the majority of white settlers and Halfbreeds refused to heed his call to battle the Canadian government, he persuaded his largely French-speaking followers to form a new council called the 'Exovedate,' meaning that everyone is 'equal' like the members of a flock (Riel, 3: 70–1; *Queen* 322). The council soon started to arrest those individuals who did not support its policies, including Riel's cousin, Charles Nolin, a prominent figure at both Red River and Batoche, whose ambiguous activities have given rise to the suspicion he was a Métis Judas (H. Adams, *Tortured People* 91–7; Payment 110). But while his community began to turn on itself, Riel appeared less concerned with military or political matters than with spiritual ones. Instead of devising a strategy to win over his local opponents or to forestall the coming Canadian forces, he contemplated the transfer of a revitalized Catholic Church to the New World. Believing that fashionable secular ideas were threatening to turn Rome into a·'ville d'ateliers et de boutiques,' he felt that the only way the Church could save itself was by relocating to the Americas, with the new Holy See in his hometown of Saint Boniface. The new pope, too, would hail from the New World. He would be none other than Riel's mentor, Archbishop Taché,[4] replacing the now deceased Bishop Bourget, who was originally scheduled to be the first New World pontiff (3: 144–7).

Since Riel was increasingly immersed in religious matters, he entrusted the defence of Batoche to his 'parent' Dumont, a man he claimed had 'le génie des opérations militaires' and 'connaît le Nord ouest comme le creux de sa main' (3: 119). Under Dumont's command, the Métis began propitiously, inflicting serious losses on the shocked Canadian forces at nearby Duck Lake. The buffalo hunter, though, attributed his success, not to his own proficiency as a marksman, but to the 'prières de Riel, qui pendant tout le temps de l'engagement, priait les bras en croix et faisait prier les femmes et les enfants' (G. Dumont, 134–5). In response to the news of the Métis victory, the Plains Cree chief Poundmaker and his men marched to Battleford, some distance northwest of Batoche. The anxious residents promptly sought refuge in the local Mounted Police barracks, and that night 'a few of the Indians raided several of the abandoned farms and houses.' More ominously, farther west at Frog Lake, Big Bear's mixed band of Plains and Woods Cree took advantage of their chief's absence from the community and shot in 'cold blood' the village's 'Indian Agent, the Farm Instructor, two priests and five others including a French half-breed' (Stanley, *Birth* 335, 339). Members of the two groups then proceeded toward Fort Pitt and 'peremptorily demanded' that Inspector Francis Dickens and the Mounted Police surrender to them (Stanley, *Birth* 341). The English novelist's son, or 'Dickens the Lesser,' as the satirist Eric Nicol calls him (*Dickens* 53), at first resisted. But he ultimately capitulated and, after taking several civilians hostage, 'the Indians' plundered the fort and 'set fire to it' (Stanley, *Birth* 343).

With the so-called Frog Lake Massacre and the attacks at Battleford and Fort Pitt, the last of which 'finally destroyed any lingering doubts as to the invincibility of the white men' (Stanley, *Birth* 343), Riel's hopes of a Métis–First Nations alliance against Canada seemed about to be realized. However, no other First Nations would elect to clash directly with the Canadian forces and help the Métis and their leader end 'our difficulties … in an American 4th July,' a failure arising from a variety of both personal and cultural factors (Riel, 3: 76; Dempsey, *Crowfoot* 119–20; *Big Bear* 92–4). While Riel was expecting Poundmaker to join the Métis at Batoche, Poundmaker was counting on Riel to support him at Battleford, 'as we are unable to take the fort without help' (quoted in Stanley, *Birth* 365). Similarly, the main reason Big Bear chose not to support Riel was that he mistrusted not just the Métis leader but his people. Even though the Métis tended to be largely the product of Cree and Caucasian relationships, often being described as 'the Cree mixed-bloods,' Big Bear apparently considered them 'interlopers' who were 'living off Cree buffalo' (Dempsey, *Crowfoot* 55, 124; *Big Bear* 53). He was also deeply resentful of Métis chauvinism, the fact that, instead of adopting the time-honoured ways of their Aboriginal ancestors, the Métis demanded that the Cree follow their customs. This was especially true of the buffalo hunt, which the Métis conducted 'in their own fashion, travelling in large companies and using a militaristic type of organization that went beyond the Cree idea of co-operative hunting.' Indeed, an incident at a buffalo hunt under Dumont's command allegedly provoked much of Big Bear's antagonism toward the Métis. When Big Bear refused to hunt according to Métis rules, Dumont publicly humiliated the Plains Cree chief, a 'bitter experience for Big Bear' which 'created a rift that never healed' (Dempsey, *Big Bear* 53–5).

Riel was even less successful with Crowfoot and Red Crow. The Blackfoot and Blood chiefs, both members of the Blackfoot Confederacy that controlled the strategic area along what is now the Alberta-Montana border, were partial to any group that vowed to take 'possession of the North-West' and return it to its first occupants. Yet, despite extensive pressure from their younger warriors, neither Crowfoot nor Red Crow deemed it wise to show solidarity with Riel. This was a turn of events that is explained not only by their scepticism about the 'self-appointed savior' but also by the fact the two chiefs tended to perceive the Métis as an extension of their 'age-old' enemy, the Cree[5] (Dempsey, *Crowfoot* 120–1, 170; *Big Bear* 11). Without general support from the First Nations, the Métis were no match for the more numerous and better-armed Canadian police-militia contingent, which had been reinforced by the enigmatic Lieutenant Arthur Howard of the U.S. Army and his state-of-the-art Gatling gun, the '"patent murdering machine"' which produced 'that "music by Handle"'/ That lulled Riel's "breeds" to rest' (Mulvaney, *History* 245; Anonymous 2). Thus, by May 1885, a mere two months after it had started, the North-West Rebellion was over. Dumont, the consummate guerrilla fighter, would escape to the United States. The more introspective Riel, by contrast, would neither flee nor be captured, but strategically surrender to the victors (G. Woodcock, *Gabriel Dumont* 11; Riel, 2: 93; Middleton 56).

Excluding his sanctioning of the execution of Tom Scott, which would forever give him a certain 'baggage' (Dowbiggin 167), Riel's actions during what he termed 'our bold but just [Saskatchewan] uprising' constitute the most controversial aspect of his life (3: 59). According to the usually laudatory Dumont, Riel was responsible for the military defeat at Batoche by forbidding his lieutenant to 'aller devant les troupes et de les harceler pendant la nuit,' a guerrilla tactic Riel considered 'trop sauvage' (127). Likewise, the anarchist thinker and Dumont biographer George Woodcock argues that Riel 'developed desperate policies that could succeed only by means of violence, and yet he shrank from violence when it came' (*Gabriel Dumont* 13). The Métis historian Howard Adams goes further, claiming that the reason the Métis lost both of their 'wars of national liberation' was that 'our supposed hero' did not act as 'a revolutionary' but as 'a pacificist and a negotiator.' As Adams explains, 'If Riel had not been at Batoche, the Metis and the Indians may have had a much better chance of winning their liberation battle, and may have maintained control of their territory and established a nation' (*Tortured People* 119). Even the more sympathetic Margaret Laurence, a writer who as early as 1948 stated that the 'fiery' Métis leader is one of the 'few Canadian historical characters ... who gather into themselves the salient features of their times' ('In the Air' 205–6), is critical of Riel. Laurence maintains that the Métis 'could not have held out indefinitely' against the mightier Canadians. At the same time, she feels that there are 'degrees of failure' and that, under a strategy other than Riel's, the Métis might at least 'have achieved ... bargaining power' ('Man' 229).

Riel attempted to justify his behaviour at his trial, but he did so in a way that was quite revealing of his state of mind. He contended that the Métis did not initiate the 'agitation' in the Saskatchewan Valley but simply responded to attacks by Canada. He also asserted that the North-West Rebellion was really a 'continuation' of the Red River Resistance of 1869–70. To Riel this was made evident by the fact of the earlier conflict being called 'the troubles of the North-West, and the troubles of 1885 being still [known as] the troubles of the North-West' (*Queen* 317, 352). He suggested that the Saskatchewan clash was rendered inevitable by Ottawa's refusal to accept what one might call the 'natural' sovereignty of nations. In his famous words to the court, which have made an indelible impression on several Canadian poets (Colombo, 'Last Words'; Souster, 'Found Poem'; Morrissey, *Batoche* 55),

Do you own the lands? ... Who starts the nations? The very one who creates them, God. God is the master of the universe, our planet is his land, and the nation and the tribes are members of His family, and as a good father, he gives a portion of the lands to that nation, to that tribe, to everyone, that is his heritage, that is his share of the inheritance, of the people, or nation or tribe. (*Queen* 358)

That is, even when a nation outgrows its land-base, it never has the right to displace any other nation by dispossessing it of its divinely granted territory. As Riel concluded, 'you cannot exist without having that spot of land. This is the principle[:] God cannot create a tribe without locating it. We are not birds' (*Queen* 358).

During his trial, Riel also insisted vehemently that 'I believe that I have a mission' and that 'I am naturally inclined to think of God at the beginning of my actions' (*Queen* 314, 311). While he did not specify the precise nature of his calling, except to say that it would bring about 'the triumph of religion in the world,' it is evident that he was convinced he was favoured by 'a spirit who guides and assists me and consoles me' (*Queen* 315, 320). However, since he sensed that people would only believe he had been 'blessed by God' if they were convinced he was sane, he almost welcomed the prospect of being condemned to death by the court. Such a verdict would prove to the world that his mind was not unbalanced and, he stated, 'I cannot fulfil my mission as long as I am looked upon as an insane being' (*Queen* 315, 351). In light of Riel's religious beliefs, it is not difficult to understand why he would not concern himself unduly with military matters during the Saskatchewan campaign. No matter how militarily inferior the

Métis might have been, they were bound to emerge victorious, for God would assure his chosen people's final triumph.

Another significant point Riel made at his trial was that he decided to travel to Batoche in 1884 because the 'North-West is ... my mother, it is my mother country' (*Queen* 312). This is clearly not the case in his early writings, and it is not always so even in his later work. Riel's identification with Quebec evolved considerably over the years, from his envisaging the Eastern society as his motherland in the Collège de Montréal period, through the 'Mère Colonie' of 'O Québec,' to a 'sister colony' at his trial (3: 95; *Queen* 359). As late as July 1885, while incarcerated in Regina, he could still refer to France as 'ma mère,' suggesting that he had at least another collective mother, a caring European parent who 's'intéresse à mon sort / En protégeant ma vie auprès de l'Angleterre' (4: 429). In fact, Riel considered himself to be not just a child of France but also a royal pretender to its throne, since 'par sa mère Julie de la Gimodière [il] est un des princes descendants de Louis xi' (3: 209; Flanagan, 'Louis Riel: Icon' 224).

The question of Riel's national affiliation actually remained unresolved to the day he died, which was perhaps inevitable given his profound ambivalence toward his Aboriginal ancestors. As we have seen, Riel derives the Métis' title to the North-West from their 'droit d'indien' (1: 290). Yet, especially in his early writings, he tends to treat the First Nations as an amorphous mass, describing them generically in the dominant discourse of the day as the 'nations sauvages' or just 'les sauvages' (1: 65; 3: 65). It is true that, after Riel migrated to Montana, he did become more aware of the particularity of the First Nations, referring to them as Blackfoot, Cree, Teton, or Sioux (2: 212–18). Still, even toward the end of his life, he is not above boasting about the numerous defeats that the Métis have inflicted on the First Nations. As he writes in 'Le peuple Métis-Canadien-français' (1883),

J'aime sans mesure et j'admire
Les Métis-canadiens-français:
Ce peuple nouveau qui se mire
Déjà dans de brillants succès.

Il a fait connaître sa gloire
Aux indiens du Minnesota.
Il a toujours gagné victoire
Sur les tribus du Dakota. (4: 319)

Or, as he states elsewhere, 'Avant la Confédération les Métis, par leur supériorité sur les tribus indiennes les dominaient'; and, 'Les métis sont les hommes qui domptèrent ces nations sauvages par leurs armes' (3: 281, 284).

Riel's dissonant views of the First Nations are linked to his concept of *métissage*, an idea crucial to an understanding of his thought and identity and which exposes his general pessimism about the future prospects of Aboriginal people. For example, he develops a master plan to divide the North-West into several parts in order to create a new Bavaria, Belgium, Denmark, Ireland, Italy, Norway, Poland, and Sweden. He even expresses the desire to build a New Judea for those Jews who 'acknowledge Jesus Christ as the son of God and the only Saviour of human kind' (*Queen* 355–6; 3: 312–13, 148). Tellingly, Riel does not allocate any section of those lands either to a specific First Nation or to all First Nations, since he believes they are destined to disappear into the Aboriginal-European melting pot or 'métissage global' that would characterize the northern half of the continent (G. Martel, 'Indiens' 130). In his words, 'toute la race sauvage de l'Amérique du Nord ferait place à une race nouvelle[,] la race métisse' (2: 409).

Jan Vansina has written that 'culture can be defined as what is common in the minds of a given group' and that 'every culture has its imagery, collectively held and understood by all' (124, 137). If this is the case, which seems unlikely given that even the most homogeneous of nations are deemed to have a multiplicity of 'lieux' or 'nœuds de mémoire' (Nora xii), then the only culture or nation to which Riel could ever have belonged was the French-speaking, Catholic Red River Métis, what he calls the 'nation manitobaine / Des Métis-canadiens-français.'⁶ The Red River *métis*, that 'branche de l'arbre Canadien français,' are certainly the only 'national' group with which he consistently identified throughout his life (4: 325; 1: 368). Yet, at least following his return from Montreal in 1868, Riel also developed close affinities with the Settlement's other mixed-race community, the Anglo-Protestant Halfbreeds. Indeed, in his writings, he never questions the latter's title to the North-West, and his main concern during the Red River Troubles is to avert a 'horrible civil war' between the two hybrid groups that he envisages will form the core of 'une puissante nationalité dans le Manitoba et le Nord Ouest' (1: 54; 2: 120).

Riel's pan-Métisism, as might have been surmised, is not without complications. After all, it is articulated by someone who at different times claims that the French language is a 'moyen d'union morale très forte' (1: 390) and that Catholicism is not only 'la seule foi vraie une' but also that 'Jésus Christ Notre Dieu défend à tout catholique d'épouser aucune personne protestante' (3: 258; 2: 152). Still, Riel's need to accommodate his larger community's linguistic and religious duality leads him to endorse a form of Christian ecumenism for all 'dénominations religieuses du Nouveau Monde,' which he feels 'ont besoin d'être reliées ensemble, d'une manière étroite' (2: 231). Moreover, this universalism is religious and cultural as well as racial, since the Métis are destined to become a trans-racial nationality. Like Símon Bolívar's 'middle species' [especie media] in Latin America (48), Riel's people will supersede both their European and Aboriginal forerunners. As he explains, 'Le nom métis serait agréable à tout le monde, parce qu'il n'est pas exclusif' and has 'l'avantage de mentionner d'une manière convenable, le contingent pour lequel chaque nation contribuerait à fonder le peuple nouveau' (2: 120).

Nevertheless, even with the two traditional mixed-race groups fused into one, Riel realizes that the Métis remain vulnerable. Thus, he contemplates forging a series of alliances with other societies, from Quebec and the Québécois diaspora in the United States, through France and several other European countries, to the United States itself. For Riel, the republic to the south is a friend and protector of the Métis as well as their mentor, the nation from which all the future mixed-race societies of the North-West will learn 'l'art de gouverner.' He is especially grateful to the U.S. Republican party, which supposedly 'saved Manitoba in 69' (2: 410, 307). Yet Riel's relationship with the United States is not unproblematic. For example, he contends that 'la race Anglo-Saxone des Etats-Unis' should support the mass emigration of its non-British citizens to Canada because such a development would enable it to remain 'd'autant plus homogène' and to preserve 'les qualités de son caractère d'autant plus intactes' (3: 312–13; Bumsted, 'Louis Riel'). He also claims that the United States discriminates against its French-Canadian citizens, who 'n'ont pas dans les emplois publics la quottepart qu'ils ont droit d'avoir' (3: 380). Just before Dumont and his companions arrive in Montana in 1884, Riel even prays to God, 'Délivrez-moi des Etats,' a country he calls 'un enfer pour l'honnête homme' (2: 357; 3: 404). But after the fall of Batoche, as an 'american citizen,' he asks the U.S. president Grover Cleveland not just to come to the assistance of the Métis but to annex 'the Northwest to the great american republic' and to 'blot out' the 'international line between the United States and the Northwest ... from lake Superior to the Pacific ocean' (3: 187).

Paradoxically, in light of his emergence as the most popular figure in Canadian history and a 'Canadian true' (Hope vii), the one country with which Riel never seems to consider forging an alliance is Canada. The Métis leader is clearly a Red River patriot, often expressing his love for his homeland:

> O cher Manitoba! Province que j'adore
> Puisse-tu prospérer! Puisse Dieu te bénir.
> Dieu! bénis mon pays! Tu charmas son aurore
> Fais-luis des jours sereins, sereins dans l'avenir. (4: 94)

Riel's Manitoba, however, does not have to be part of Canada. As his political career attests, he is not overly enthusiastic about forging links between his 'patrie / Chérie' and 'la Puissance' (4; 221; 1: 173). Indeed, for Riel, Canada is not merely 'a foreign power and ... a foreign jurisdiction' but 'notre injuste agresseur' (1: 111, 416), and Confederation 'une fraude immense, une tyrannie colossale' (3: 299). So, rather than desiring to become part of the Canadian experiment, he strives to shelter his people from the evil predator who 'usurped the title of the aboriginal Half breeds to the soil' (3: 60). The extent to which Riel does not associate his individual and collective dreams with Canada is conspicuously evident at his trial. During the proceedings, he frequently draws attention to his U.S. citizenship, which he says makes him 'simply a guest of this country – a guest of the half-breeds of the Saskatchewan' (*Queen* 324). Even more significant, Riel refers to his cross-examiners, not as Canadians, but as 'British,' a sentiment fully reciprocated by one of his own lawyers, who describes the Métis leader as 'an alien in race and an alien in religion' (*Queen* 315, 310). Needless to say, as we shall see in the following chapters, Riel's lack of identification with Canada has not deterred contemporary Canadian writers from celebrating him as a national hero, as it did not hinder earlier ones from condemning him as a traitor.

2

The Traitor
Riel As an Enemy of Confederation

> We'll hang Riel up the Red River,
> And he'll roast in hell forever,
> We'll hang him up the River
> With a yah-yah-yah.
>
> *E.J. Pratt (1952)*

Riel's impact on the Canadian consciousness was almost instantane-
ous. The first literary work on the Métis leader, depicting him as an
enemy of Confederation, appeared the very winter he entered the political scene. In February 1870, a retired Hudson's Bay Company officer
named Alexander Hunter Murray responded to the Métis seizure of
Fort Garry by writing a martial ballad threatening to recapture Red
River's economic and administrative centre. In the two-verse 'The Marching Song,' Murray leaves little doubt regarding his feelings about the
mixed-blood upstart:

> Riel sits in his chamber o' state
> Wi' his stolen silver forks an' his stolen silver plate,
> An' a' his braw things spread out in style so great;
> He'll not breakfast alone this morning.

> O Hey, Riel, are ye waking yet,
> Or are yer drums a-beating yet?
> If y're nae waking we'll nae wait,
> For we'll take the fort this morning. (50)

Later that year, the Scottish-born author would add several verses to
his work and rename it 'Capture of Fort Garry, or Riel's Retreat,' and

further lambaste the Métis and their 'President elate' for being not just rebels but also cowards. As Murray writes, the moment Riel and his supporters sensed the Canadian soldiers were approaching the Settlement, they sank 'intae the groun', or vanished i' the air / Like Macbeth's weird sisters' (58–9).

The two versions of Murray's ballad occupy a privileged place in the literature on Riel not only because of their primacy but also because they are so representative of the cultural amnesia that marks so much of the work on the Métis leader. 'The Marching Song' and 'Capture of Fort Garry' are based on 'Johnnie Cope,' an air by the Scottish poet Adam Skirving. Marking the 1745 Jacobite rout of General John Cope's royalist forces at Prestonpans, Scotland, Skirving's poem ridicules the overconfident and cowardly Hanoverian commander for running away 'like a frighted bird' when he ran into the Highlanders (Skirving 412).[1] But perhaps because of the ambiguous role played by Scots as both victims of English expansionism and critical instruments of Anglo-British imperialism, by the time the tale crosses the Atlantic it has been transformed into a pro-British narrative. Indeed, 'The Marching Song' and 'Capture of Fort Garry' exemplify Ernest Renan's axiom that forgetting is as 'essential to the creation of a nation' as is remembering (19). Writers on the Métis leader are seldom as blatant as the good folk of W.O. Mitchell's fictional Crocus, Saskatchewan, who express their pan-Anglo solidarity through the 'Looie Riel Chapter IODE' (266). Nevertheless, the contemporary celebrations of Riel clearly show that, like all other collectivities, Canadians have been forced to forget 'a great deal' (Renan 21).

Also in 1870, J.C. Major published a longer poem on the subject entitled *The Red River Expedition* (1870). A mixture of Anglo-Canadian nationalism and British imperialism, Major's work is a eulogy for those heroic 'Sons of Canada's rich frought land' and 'Albion's distant sons' who defied the Canadian Shield in order to 'avenge a murder'd martyr's fall' (3–4, 14). Its focus, though, is not on the volunteers' clash with Riel and the Métis but on their epic confrontation with nature, especially the 'tiresome and heavy work' of carrying 'Cartridge and arm chests, boats and tents,' over an endless chain of portages (17). So captivated is Major by the obstacles faced by the soldiers that he does not even name the fiend whose opposition to Confederation proves that 'God's blessing [is] on our nation's arms, and on our noble / Queen' and that those who fight 'beneath the Crimson flag' belong to 'God's avenging side' (28).

In contrast, the Métis leader is very much present in a poem written not long after, 'The Ballad of Monsieur Riel' (1873), as is evident from its opening stanzas:

There once was a Frenchman called RIEL,
Who troubled the land a good deal,
   For he rallied his boys,
   And kicked up a great noise,
And trampled the law under heel.

In the midst of the riot so hot,
Rose a patriot by name THOMAS SCOTT;
   Who, refusing to kneel
   To Le President RIEL,
Was tied to a pillar, and shot. (Anonymous 1, n.pag.)

Although composed anonymously, 'The Ballad of Monsieur Riel' was first published in *Grip*, and its gentle anti-Tory satire suggests that it is likely the work of the humour magazine's editor. The poem certainly ends on a characteristic Bengough note. After Riel escapes to the United States, we are told, 'the land thirsted still for his gore,' and Macdonald and his cabinet promise the populace to do their utmost to capture the fugitive. But when the politicians finally locate 'the bold and red-handed outlaw,' instead of having him arrested, they decide that he should join the government's ranks in 'the Commons at brave Ottawa!' That is, for the poet, Scott is a patriot, whose gruesome murder is greeted by the country with 'a great howl' of indignation. Riel, by contrast, is not just a rebel but a foreigner of sorts, a Frenchman. He is clearly not a full-fledged member of the Canadian family (Anonymous 1, n.pag.).

None of the above poems, however, appears to have left a lasting imprint on other writers or the public. Thus, one must trace the beginning of the literature on the treacherous Riel, not to them, but to J. Edmund Collins's *The Story of Louis Riel the Rebel Chief* (1885).[2] An instant-novel written anonymously while the Saskatchewan campaign raged, Collins's work possesses little aesthetic merit. The author himself subsequently declared that the reason he did not attach his name to the text was that he was 'unwilling to take responsibility for the literary slovenliness' (*Annette* 143). Still, despite its numerous shortcomings, the novel is pivotal in the evolution of Riel's image in Canadian culture.

Born and raised in Newfoundland (which would not join Confederation until 1949), Collins became a fervent Canadian nationalist soon after immigrating to Canada in 1874, at the age of nineteen. While working on newspapers first in New Brunswick and then in Ontario, he embraced the national optimism that reigned in much of the country's nascent literary community, even writing 'the first significant study of the Macdonald era' (J. Adams 5–7, 9; Collins, *Life*). He became particularly close to the 'Confederation' poets Archibald Lampman and Charles G.D. Roberts, the former considering him 'almost the literary father' of a new generation of writers, while the latter would continue to communicate with him even after the Newfoundlander's death – through a Ouija board (Lampman 40; Pomeroy 85). But the most notable virtue of Collins's novel is that it is believed to reflect so well the cultural milieu in which the author circulated that it is an excellent barometer of 'the mentality of Ontario,' if not of much of English-speaking Canada, during the later Riel years (Lamb 343).

The Story of Louis Riel is a rather confused work, both politically and psychologically. For instance, early on Collins depicts the young Riel as being motivated mainly by the prejudice he experiences in Montreal. It is in reaction to his schoolmates' frequent taunting references to the Métis as 'savages' that the would-be priest determines 'to follow in the footsteps of my father' instead and become a political leader. This way, Riel reasons, he will be able to avenge all the slights and humiliations he and his people have suffered at the hands of more powerful groups. As he confides to 'God[,] who made all men, the white man and the savage, I will, if the propitious day ever come, strike in vengeance, and my blow will be with an iron hand, whose one smiting shall wipe out all the injustice and dishonor' (10–11). Yet, at the same time that Collins implicitly condemns Quebec's chauvinism, he draws a blatantly racist picture of Riel. He states that the Métis leader is 'only one-eighth Indian,' a genetic technicality that supposedly makes him not so much a 'half-breed' as an 'Octoroon' (6). The author also suggests that it is Riel's 'small measure of Indian blood,' which can 'assert itself in many ways,' that is responsible for his violent and vindictive personality, for his becoming the 'apostle of insurrection and unrest' (46, 5).

The focal point of Collins's novel is the Riel-Scott relationship, a whimsical portrait that was accepted as historically factual until as recently as the 1970s (Swainson, 'It's the Real Thing' 14; Collins, *Annette* 142–3). Like their historical models, the Red River Métis and the Ontario Orangeman remain implacable enemies. The crucial difference is that the source of their conflict is not religious or political but romantic; both men fall in love with the same woman, a beautiful young Métisse who loves Tennyson, talks to birds, and inadvertently precipitates the troubles of 1869–70. Riel is smitten by the dark-haired Marie before he ever sees her. He is out hunting with a friend, soon after returning from Montreal, when he hears the eighteen-year-old singing in the middle of the prairie. Since Riel, 'like Mohammed, El Mahdi, and other great patrons of race and religion,' has a strong will but is 'weaker than a shorn Samson' when facing an attractive woman, he immediately succumbs to the singer's charms. He becomes especially infatuated when he overhears Marie confide to 'a lonely thrush' whose mate has flown south that she too is lonely and 'nobody loves me[,] woos me, cares for me, or sings about me' (49–50). So overwhelmed is Riel by the 'ravishing beauty of the girl' that, as they walk toward Marie's home, he forces himself on her and attempts to 'kiss her.' But to his shock, 'the soft-eyed fawn of the desert' not only rebuffs his graceless advances but categorically rejects the possibility of any future romantic dalliance between the two, since 'your very sight is already hateful' (51–2).

Notwithstanding Marie's confession to the thrush about not having a lover, at least part of the reason for her antipathy toward Riel is that there is another man in her life, someone she loves deeply and to whom she owes her life. During the previous flood season, the intrepid young woman went canoeing on the Red River just above a waterfall. When she reached a series of eddies, she started circling them playfully, but then she lost her paddle and began drifting toward 'the rending fans' of a nearby mill. A group of Métis men watched her from the riverbank but, cognizant of the risks involved, chose not to intervene. Then a 'young white man,' paddle in hand, appeared out of nowhere and, 'without a word, leaped into the mad waters.' After swimming to Marie and handing her the paddle, he selflessly guided her and her canoe over the fall (58–9).

The 'young white man' turns out to be Tom Scott, and, not surprisingly, both Marie and her family are very grateful to 'the heroic stranger' they consider 'the benefactor of [us] all' (59, 55). For his part, Riel develops an instant animosity toward the 'manly, sunny-hearted lad' from Ontario. At first, he attempts to minimize Scott's courage, asserting that it is not much of a feat for a swimmer to go over a waterfall. In an effort to dissociate himself from the Métis men who elected not to help Marie, he even denies his own ethno-national affiliation, declaring: 'I am not a half-breed' (56, 59). When that fails to convince Marie and her family that Scott is unworthy of their trust, Riel starts to insinuate that the Ontarian is 'a paid spy' for the Canadian government. Not only that, acting like the national leader he prematurely considers himself to be, he forbids the entire family to have any further contact with the Orangeman, since Red River is the Métis homeland 'and any man who opposes its welfare is a traitor and a common enemy' (65, 64). But Marie is anything but intimidated by the threats and, in front of Riel, asks her father to tell the 'coward' and 'snake' to 'never enter our doors again' (65).

Marie's rejection of Riel, and implied preference for Scott, signals the beginning of the open warfare between the two men, a conflict that ends with Riel and his associates framing the Ontarian for murder. When he learns through a Métis friend that Riel is plotting to kidnap Marie and her father, under the pretext that they are 'both in league with Canadian spies, and enemies of Red River,' Scott persuades the pair to let him take them to a safe haven on the U.S. side of the border (76). Later, a vengeful Riel instructs his commander Ambroise Lépine to have his guards goad Scott 'to commit an assault' and arrest him for insubordination (108). The Métis leader then offers to 'spare' the prisoner on the condition that he reveal the whereabouts of Marie and her father, but the steadfast Orangeman will not betray his beloved or her begetter even at the prospect of saving his own life (116). So, after being subjected to a court martial under Lépine, he is summarily executed in such a 'revoltingly cruel' fashion that the author confesses 'it is with pain one is obliged to write about it' (120). However, before being killed, Scott entrusts a sealed letter to his minister to deliver to Marie in case the execution is carried out. The clergyman duly honours his parishioner's last wish and personally conveys the missive to the young woman at her secret dwelling. A few days later, Scott's 'letter in her hand and his ring upon her finger,' a heartbroken Marie too dies (122).

What is most striking about *The Story of Louis Riel the Rebel Chief* is how untypical it is of the literature on Riel and Scott. The novel does not merely clash with the dominant views of the Métis leader and the Orangeman at the beginning of the twenty-first century but completely reverses them, transforming the modern hero into a sex-crazed buffoon and the quintessential 'bigot' (Snell 54) into a martyr. Collins's Riel is obviously not the 'great humanitarian' and 'pacifist' that the latter's biographer Maggie Siggins judges him to be (quoted in Poitras 3), but a bloodthirsty traitor. He is an unscrupulous libertine who, even though he 'rejoices in the possession of three wives,' leads his people into a rebellion they cannot win simply because a woman has the temerity to choose another man over him (131). Riel is simultaneously a despot, who 'lord[s] ... over' his community while he knows his army stands behind him, and a coward, who flees the moment 'he sees the bayonets from Canada' (73). Above all, he is a hypocrite, someone who orchestrates his arch-enemy's show-trial but then absents himself from the court in order not to be held accountable by either justice or history for the 'sorry proceedings' (116).

In contrast, the Scott depicted by Collins is a genuine hero. The same individual who has inspired only one fifty-page monograph and a handful of essays in the last 130 years (Robertson; Bumsted, 'Thomas Scott,' 'Thomas Scott's Body,' and 'Why Shoot Thomas Scott?') and whose overriding image is that of an 'agitateur orangiste' so obnoxious that even his confederates seem relieved when he is killed (Lemay, 'Épisodes' 163; Sanderson 128–32)[3] is presented as nothing short of a knight in shining armour. He is the Ontario gallant who risks life and limb to rescue a total stranger from the treacherous waters of the Red River, a Métisse whom he will affectionately (albeit ungrammatically) come to address in her native tongue as 'ma amie' (97). More important, Scott is a freedom-loving patriot ready to sacrifice all for country and empire. Certain that his ideas are just and will one day emerge victorious, he is a loyalist willing to die in an attempt to clear 'the plains ... of the mutinous blind, unreasoning hordes' that the villainous Riel has incited into open rebellion. As one of Scott's friends comforts him before his execution, the cause of Canadian patriotism will forever be associated with the Orangeman's name and the 'tyrant who prevails over you, will not triumph for long' (Collins, *Story* 85, 117).

An identical perspective on Riel and Scott informs Collins's next novel, *Annette, the Metis Spy: A Heroine of the N.W. Rebellion* (1886), which was published right after the fall of Batoche. Since the second work is uncannily similar to the first – whole sections being simply lifted from the earlier text – it would be redundant to relate the plot. There are, however, some differences worth noting. While the characters remain basically the same, Collins transfers them to a higher social stratum. With the exception of Riel, he also changes their names, fictionalizing Scott's. Thus the father of the eponymous protagonist is no longer a buffalo hunter but a colonel and 'ex-officer of the Hudson's Bay Company,' and the Scott figure is now a captain with the North West Mounted Police named Philip Edmund Stevens. As the title suggests, the heroine is not named Marie but Annette, although Stevens betrays a too understandable confusion about his beloved's identity and at least once refers to her as 'ma Marie' (86). Collins's motivation for fictionalizing Scott's name becomes apparent toward the end of the novel. The strategy enables him to allow his hero not only to eclipse Riel but also to survive him and marry Annette once the rebellion is over, a momentous occasion that transforms the 'Duck Lake Mata Hari' into the 'most popular woman in the North-West Territories' (McCourt, *Canadian* 15; Collins, *Annette* 141).

Like *The Story of Louis Riel, Annette* is not a significant contribution to Canadian letters. Actually, the most interesting element in Collins's second Riel novel is the short epilogue he appends to it. Only two pages long, 'Notes' is 'one of the gems' of nineteenth-century Canadian literature, as well as one of the truly curious documents in the theory of historical fiction. In it, Collins explains that he incorporates into the second work 'a few passages, with little change,' from his earlier one because the 'most notable authors have done this sort of thing; and chief amongst them I may mention Thackeray' (McCourt, *Canadian* 15; Collins, *Annette* 142). In a statement that wreaks havoc with Alessandro Manzoni's dictum that, in a historical novel, one must 'be able to distinguish fact from invention' (64), Collins also declares that 'I present some fiction in my story, and a large array of fact. I do not feel bound, however, to state which is the fact, and which is the fiction' (*Annette* 142). He writes:

> The preceding story lays no claim to value or accuracy in its descriptions of the North-West Territories. I have never seen that portion of our country; and to endeavour to describe faithfully a region of which I have only a hearsay knowledge would be foolish.
>
> I have, therefore, arranged the geography of the Territories to suit my own conveniences. I speak of places that no one will be able to find upon maps of the present or of the future. Wherever I want a valley or a swamp, I put the same; and I have taken the same liberty with respect to hills or waterfalls. The birds, and in some instances the plants and flowers of the prairies, I have also made to order. (142)

Concerning *The Story of Louis Riel*, Collins adds that his first novel 'has been quoted as history; but it is largely fiction.' He also admits that there is 'no historic truth' in his characterization of Riel and Scott as romantic rivals and thus in the claim that the Métis leader had the Orangeman killed because the woman they both love 'gave her heart to that young man. I have seen that story printed again and again as truth; but there is in it not a word of truth' (142–3).

Regardless of Collins's cavalier attitude toward geography and the historical past, as well as his undeniable ethno-cultural chauvinism, the fact remains that he is captivated by Riel. It is true that he never perceives the Métis chief as a fellow human being, let alone as a co-citizen (but, then, Riel probably would not consider Collins a co-citizen either). Still, Riel is central to both of his novels. While the protagonist may be described in a single paragraph as an 'Arch Rebel,' an 'arch disturber,' an 'autocrat,' and 'a heartless Rebel ruffian' (*Story* 96), he is an individual whom one can underestimate only at one's peril, for Collins's Riel has power. In an allusion to the recent assassination of U.S. president James Garfield by another self-declared mystic, Riel is the 'thrice-dangerous [Charles] Guiteau [of] the plains' who has the support not only of most of his people but also of the hierarchy of the Catholic Church and of Quebec's political establishment (*Story* 47; Rosenberg 5). He is the 'miscreant-fiend' who, even after sanctioning the 'cold-blooded murder' of a young Canadian and indefensibly refusing to allow his body to be given a proper burial, is somehow able to escape 'the vengeance of the law' (*Story* 119, 125). In short, for Collins, Riel is a satanic force that has infiltrated his world and that the author is unable to evade.

Riel, however, does not enjoy the prominence he has in Collins's novels in many other early works dealing with the events of 1869–70 or 1885 (Owram, 'Myth' 317). He does not even figure as a character in two contemporaneous plays about the latter conflict, George Broughall's *The 90th on Active Service; or, Campaigning in the North West* (1885) and L. Dixon's *Halifax to the Saskatchewan: 'Our Boys' in the Riel Rebellion* (1886). Written by soldiers, the burlesques focus almost exclusively on military concerns, especially the alleged mistreatment of the volunteers. The grievances of the troops in both texts are not so much against Riel and his 'breeds' as against their own inconsiderate officers and the haughty media. In the words of one foreign-born soldier, 'Sometimes, mine friend, and this is true, / One meal a day was all we get' (Dixon 20–1). Or, as another soldier complains fatalistically about the press, 'No matter what sacrifice a poor volunteer may make ..., there will always be in this world, a certain class who never contribute anything to the cause, but who live only to criticize and condemn' (Broughall 40).

The Métis leader also plays a somewhat marginal role in the numerous '"poetic" effusions' (Mulvaney, *History* 246) elicited by the North-

West Rebellion. There are exceptions, such as Cleomati's 'To One of the Absent' (1885). Perhaps as befits a work that first appeared in the memoirs of two white women who survived the killings at Frog Lake, Theresa Gowanlock and Theresa Delaney, the poem is uncompromising in its celebration of the Canadian volunteers and settlers and in its condemnation of Riel. As Cleomati writes of her 'darling' fighting 'poor Scott's heartless murderer' (63),

Let justice be done now unfailing
   Nought but *death* can atone for his sin;
Let the fate he has meted to others;
   By our dauntless be meted to him,
Don't return until quiet contentment;
   Fills the homes now deserted out west,
And the true ring of peace finds an echo,
   In each sturdy settler's breast. (64)

Most other works on the subject, though, hardly acknowledge the Métis leader. Instead, they focus on his enemies, especially the 'noble' Canadian soldiers (F. Scott 174). For the majority of writers, the 'brave' and 'loyal volunteers' (Stefansson 174; Bengough 70) ought to be celebrated not only because 'Grim Privation and Peril followed them hand in hand' as they marched to battle but also because, in Riel and his allies, they encountered 'crueller enemies still; – treacherous, scarcely human' (Wetherald 538). Indeed, the reason Canada should shed its collective tears for the soldiers was that it was those 'vaillants enfants, grandis dans les alarmes,' who obliterated all its 'anxious fears' (Desaulniers 13; Imrie 24).[4]

By the mid-1970s, in *The Diviners*, Margaret Laurence has one of her Métis characters state that the 'young *Anglais* from Ontario' who confront Riel in Saskatchewan 'don't know what they're fighting for' (282). Similarly, in her acclaimed song 'Maria's Place / Batoche,' Connie Kaldor writes that in 1885 'the red coats lay hiding / With only the Queen on their side' (178). However, that is not the impression one gets from the writings produced at the time. Particularly after Riel's surrender, there was such a consensus about the heroism of the soldiers, and the perfidy of their opponents, that even a poet of Isabella Valancy Crawford's stature is not able to escape the prevailing jingoism. As Crawford declares in 'The Rose of a Nation's Thanks' (1885),

A welcome? Why, what do you mean by that, when the very stones
  must sing
As our men march over them home again; the walls of the city ring
With the thunder of throats and the tramp and tread of feet that rush
  and run? –
I think in my heart that the very trees must shout for the bold work done!
Why, what would ye have? There is not a lad that treads in the gallant
  ranks
Who does not already bear on his breast the Rose of a Nation's Thanks!
  (45–6)

Or, as she comments in 'Songs for the Soldiers' (1885), 'It was a joyous
day for us' when the volunteers 'made that bold burst at Batoche, /
And with their dead flesh built a wall about / Our riving land' (70–1).

So sweeping was the demonization of Riel at the end of the nineteenth century that even the rare writers who are sympathetic to the
First Nations tend not to mention him. It is as if they believe that, had it
not been for the politician-mystic leading his people astray, the Métis
somehow would have found a modus operandi with Canada and no
blood would have been shed. For example, in 'A Cry from an Indian
Wife' (1885), the poem that launched her career as a recitalist, Pauline
Johnson subtly undermines the moral superiority that permeates the
Euro-Canadian works, by addressing 'the most important ... question'
in the relations between Natives and Newcomers in the New World,
land ownership (Chamberlin 4, 118; Keller 57–8). For the part-Mohawk
poet, the 'white-faced warriors' are not the heroic defenders of the
motherland but intruders into foreign territory, invaders who are 'marching west to quell / Our fallen tribe that rises to rebel.' Thus, rather than
bidding them welcome, she curses 'the fate that brought them from the
east / To be our chiefs – to make our nation least' (457). Significantly,
Johnson does not say a word about Riel. Likewise, in poems such as
'Metis, 1885' and 'A Cry from the Saskatchewan, March 1885,' John
Logan asks, 'How many buffets must the bondsman bear, / Till in just
anger he return the blow / With a swift stroke that lays the tyrant low?'
('Metis' 95). He also bewails the wrongs that Canada's 'favoured race'
has inflicted on the country's Aboriginal inhabitants, who have not
done it 'a single wrong' ('Cry' 119, 123).Yet, like Johnson, he never
alludes to Riel, underscoring the ignominy into which the Métis leader's name had fallen in the immediate post-Batoche period.

Riel is again largely absent from Ernest Henham's *Menotah: A Tale of the Riel Rebellion* (1897), but for more 'subversive,' not to say nefarious, reasons (Osachoff, 'Louis Riel' 63). Macdonald may have considered the Métis leader 'the moving spirit' behind the two North-West conflicts, even suggesting that he be recruited 'as an officer' for Canada's future national police force (Letters 408). For Henham, however, Riel could never have been anything other than a nonentity. By virtue of his mixed racial heritage, he was simply born not to lead but to be led – by one of his 'purer' European cousins. As Henham writes in his preface, Riel is not portrayed as 'an active character' in the novel because he was 'dull-witted, heavy-featured and obtuse – in fact, a French half-breed of the ordinary stamp.' The architect of that 'hopeless [Saskatchewan] enterprise' was 'so colourless, so commonplace, that a true picture must have been uninteresting, while a fictitious drawing would have been unsatisfactory and out of place' (ix).

Written by someone about whom little is known, except that he composed other romances about the Canadian West, *Menotah* is a relatively long and ambitious work. Among its aims are a condemnation of First Nations–Caucasian sexual relations and a vindication of Archbishop Taché's heroic role in 1885. According to Henham, 'one of the principal reasons' for the North-West Rebellion was 'the unscrupulous treatment of the Indian women by the white invaders' (ix). He is especially critical of the Hudson's Bay Company, asserting that its conduct 'well paved the way for this laxity in matters of morality.' Henham also draws attention to the extent to which the events at Batoche were influenced by the 'truly unselfish prelate' of Saint Boniface, a cleric who, 'almost unaided, crushed the rising spirit of independence in half-breeds and Indians, and brought the insurrection to a close' (x). Still, at the centre of *Menotah* is neither interracial marriages nor Taché, to say nothing of Riel, but the elusive (and imaginary) Hugh Lamont, a Euro-Canadian sharpshooter who becomes known as the White Chief.

Lamont's shadowy involvement with the Saskatchewan uprising unravels, gradually but inexorably, through the undaunting persistence of an old hunter named Billy Sinclair. A Métis who claims to 'know Riel' (11), Sinclair discovers that there is a sinister third party behind the 'nickle[sic]-plate god' and his alleged plan to incite the First Nations 'to stamp the whole crowd of whites clean out of the land,' an unknown individual 'who's stirring him up, who's supplying the brains to run this rebellion, and all the rest of it' (12, 13). As Sinclair relates the situation,

Riel was *not*, never had been, the prime factor of the revolution. Himself a dull man of irregular habits, yet one whose mind might easily be moulded, in unscrupulous hands, he was powerless to act as a sole leader; he could not forecast future chances without assistance. Left to himself, he would never have struck the blow for right and liberty. But, when sitting outside his shanty one summer evening, a young man came to him. His sudden arrival was in itself mysterious, and from the first he cast a powerful glamour over the great half-breed ... Riel talked with the young Canadian, who was, on his own confession, the finest rifle shot in the Dominion, perhaps in the world at the time ... The heavy-featured man became delighted with the skill and flattery of the fascinating white, who soon began to pour into his ears a vividly painted word picture where his own name recurred frequently; in conjunction with such expressions as power and wealth unbounded. He was aware of Riel's intentions – his desire to reclaim the land from the oppressor. To be brief, he had come to aid him. (270)

Riel, Sinclair underlines, is only the 'nominal leader' of the insurrection. Its real head is Lamont, a white man who disguises himself 'as a blood Indian, with the paint, feathers, buckskin and bead work of the native warrior.' While the newcomer fails to deceive Aboriginal people about his true identity – it is they who name him 'the "White Chief," or "Father's Friend"' – he wreaks havoc with the Canadian forces. With his 'unerring rifle,' he slaughters many of the enemy, leading the troops 'to dread the report of the Indian marksman's weapon.' But when Lamont realizes that his new allies cannot possibly avoid defeat at the hands of the police and militia, he secretly defects to the soon-to-be-victorious side (270–1).

Sinclair is informed about Lamont's activities by 'an Indian traitor' to the Riel cause – evidently 'there were many of them.' The Métis hunter then proceeds to search for the white Canadian, whom he knew before under a different name, and confronts the latter with the accusation of treason. Lamont is unmoved and, when Sinclair threatens 'to capture and hand him over to the Government,' the adventurer snatches a revolver and fires at the old hunter (271). Sinclair somehow manages to avoid the bullet and disappears into the nearby woods. Yet the two men's destinies remain interlinked. Knowing that he is the only person who knows of the White Chief's real identity, Sinclair becomes obsessed with Lamont. He tracks the younger man to Winnipeg, where, after abandoning his Cree lover, the Menotah of the title, Lamont has started a new life with a white wife named Marie Larivière. Like the tragic Menotah, who becomes estranged from her people because of her liaison with Lamont, Larivière is oblivious to both her husband's romantic and political past. With the help of the two betrayed women, Sinclair corners the impostor but is unable to capture him. The last one hears of Lamont, he has just landed in Rio de Janeiro. A rebellion has broken out in Brazil – likely Conselheiro's Canudos War of 1896–7, considering the novel's date of publication – and Lamont is ready for further action. In his words, 'A new rifle, and then for the strongest side. Besides, there are fine women among the Creoles' (316).

The most remarkable aspect about the characterization of Riel in *Menotah* is that he is depicted not so much as a traitor as a nobody. Confederation's nemesis turns out to be one of the great frauds of all time. As Henham's narrator describes Lamont's motivation for joining forces with Riel,

> He [Lamont] had previously gone over all ground, had reckoned every chance, as he thought, to finally arrive at the conclusion that an insurrection of Indians and half-breeds must be successful. He was but an ordinary adventurer, yet of more than average intellect. He would sway the mind of Riel, the invaders would be conquered and driven out, the half-breed leader would be chief of the entire country – nominally only. The reins of power would actually rest in his own hands. To depose the dull-witted half-breed and obtain entire leadership would then be a comparatively simple matter. (272)

That is, for Henham, Riel is such a simpleton that there is little justification for including him in representations of the two watershed events in Canadian history usually associated with his name.

Notwithstanding its title, John Mackie's *The Rising of the Red Man: A Romance of the Louis Riel Rebellion* (1902) is also only indirectly, and negatively, about Riel. The prologue is basically an exposé of the 'fanatic and rebellion-maker' who exploits his formal education to deceive his 'ignorant' followers (9, 10). It is early in 1885, and Riel assembles a massive group of Aboriginal people and Métis on a bank of the South Saskatchewan River in order to persuade them that it is a propitious time not only to organize 'a rising' but also 'to start a church of his own!' Since the 'red-bearded, self-constituted prophet of the *metis*' has learned from an almanac that there is going to be an eclipse of the sun that day,[5] he informs the gathering that the celestial phenomenon augurs the dawn of a new age of 'unlimited food, tobacco and firewater' for all members of the First Nations who 'would do as he told them' (9–10). Predictably, and to the utter terror of Riel's audience, the moon begins to block out the sun and darkness descends upon everyone. But before long the sun reappears and the crowd shouts in jubilation, convinced the eclipse is a sign of the approval of Riel's prophecy by 'the Manitou, the Great Spirit.' As the prologue concludes, 'Never perhaps in the history of impostors from Mahomet to the Mahdi had an almanac proved so useful' (11, 13).

After such a impassioned introduction, though, Mackie seems to lose interest in Riel. The author does not completely ignore the Métis chief, since Riel's activities have such a devastating impact on the Saskatchewan countryside that they affect even the lives of the work's main characters: a widowed settler named Henry Douglas, his eighteen-year-old daughter, Dorothy, and a Sergeant Pasmore of the Mounted Police. It is only when the Métis capture Dorothy, as she attempts to seek refuge at Fort Battleford, that one discovers how truly depraved Riel has become in his determination to have white people 'utterly exterminated, so that the elect might possess the land undisturbed' (61). In the chapel he has converted into his political and military headquarters, the 'self-constituted dictator' tries to gather information about the young woman's companions with a combination of 'bombast, threats and flattery.' But she refuses to cooperate, and Riel, feeling 'his absurd self-esteem ruffled,' orders that she be jailed indefinitely, 'until we decide what fate shall be hers' (61–2). Yet, once Dorothy is imprisoned, Riel practically disappears from the scene and, perhaps as befits the work of an ex-Mountie who became the most prolific author of 'adventure fiction of the nineteenth-century prairie West,' *The Rise of the Red Man* turns into another paean to 'the red-coated soldiers of the Great Queen' (D. Harrison, *Unnamed Country* 54; Mackie 34). Still, despite his glaring absence from much of the text, there is never much doubt regarding the ultimate fate of the renegade 'who hearkens to a false Manitou' (166). As a disaffected Métis prophetically tells Riel, by the end of his mission their people will be 'scattered and homeless' and 'the red-coats will catch you, for there is no trail too long or too broken for the Riders of the Plains to follow' (149).

The Métis leader occupies a similarly peripheral place in several novels that proclaim to be about events intimately bound to his life and career. For example, Douglas Reville's *A Rebellion: A Story of the Red River Uprising* (1912) opens with a forceful prologue in which the author states that 'Riel ... was mistakenly allowed to escape punishment for the brutal killing of Scott' and that he was 'very properly hanged' for his actions during the second North-West conflict, 'as he should have been in the first place' (n.pag.).Yet Reville, a southern Ontario newspaper editor best known for his role in the publication of the first poem by his long-time friend Pauline Johnson (Keller 43), then goes on to write a saccharine romance about Scottish Canadians to which Riel and the Métis serve merely as an exotic but faint backdrop. The author does explore what he considers Riel's barbarous treatment of Scott, including the macabre disposal of the Orangeman's body 'through a hole in the ice' of the Red River (108), but only cursorily. The inescapable impression one gets from reading the novel is that Reville is not interested enough in Riel, or does not think enough of him, to portray him fully even as a traitor.

Ralph Connor's *The Patrol of the Sun Dance Trail* (1914), too, is not so much about Riel as it is about the North West Mounted Police, the valiant third party that supposedly persuades Crowfoot and the Blackfoot not to join forces with Riel at Batoche. Written by that most popular of Canadian historical romance writers, *The Patrol* does acknowledge the Métis, those 'remote, ignorant, insignificant, half-tamed pioneers of civilization' and their 'hair[sic]-brained four-flusher' of a leader (10, 24). But, as one might deduce after such a description, Connor is not exactly enamoured of either Riel or his people. On the contrary, the author appears to wish to celebrate the heroic role played by the Mounted Police in thwarting the purported Métis plan to establish 'an empire of the North, from which the white race shall be excluded' (25). As Connor has one of his characters state toward the end of the narrative, the reason Riel 'failed utterly in his schemes and that Crowfoot remained loyal I believe is due to the splendid work of the officers and members of our Force' (362).

A somewhat more complex portrait of Riel, or at least more contradictory, emerges in Robert de Roquebrune's *D'un océan à l'autre* (1924). First published in Paris, Roquebrune's novel is a panegyrical celebration of the building of the Canadian Pacific Railway, particularly the role played by Father Albert Lacombe in making possible the monumental engineering project that would finally unite Canada 'd'un océan à l'autre' (253).[6] The protagonists are a Quebec City ethnologist named Augustin Ménard and his teenaged nephew Jacques, an orphan of whom he has custody. It is 1869 and the renowned '*sauvagiste*,' who has devoted his life to studying Quebec's indigenous peoples, travels to the

North-West with his ward in search of First Nations that have not yet been Christianized and thus have 'conservé les mœurs cruelles des races indiennes' (19, 38). By the time the two men arrive at Fort Garry, the disturbances have broken out and the senior Ménard becomes directly involved in the conflict, even warning Riel that Tom Scott has assembled 'une troupe de gens et qu'il a l'intention de vous attaquer' (126). The focus of the novel, however, never shifts to Riel or the Métis. Instead, it remains very much on Augustin Ménard's ethnological involvement with the militant Cree chief L'Ours and the adventures of his nephew, who, partly as a result of having met a young Red River white woman named Aline Guilbault, decides to settle in the West once the troubles are over. Quite symbolically, the work concludes with 'les deux jeunes Canadiens' being married, not in a church or chapel, but 'dans un wagon du Pacifique, entre Winnipeg et Calgary' (253). The priest who blesses the nuptials is none other than Father Lacombe, the Oblate missionary frequently credited with persuading Crowfoot, Red Crow, and other leaders of the Blackfoot Confederacy to remain loyal to Canada in 1885 and inducing them to permit the Canadian Pacific Railway to cross their lands – the latter an achievement for which he was made 'président honoraire' of the railway company (Roquebrune, 'Défense' 31; K. Hughes 277, 298–307).

There are several intriguing elements in *D'un océan à l'autre*, not the least of which is its peculiar treatment of the historical past. Roquebrune was for many years the director of the Canadian Archives in Paris. Yet this 'archiviste-historien,' as one of his critics describes him (Chadbourne 44), has the Orangeman Scott operating, not out of the Protestant strongholds on the west bank of the Red River, but in the heart of Franco-Catholic Saint Boniface (126). As well, when the Canadian troops capture Fort Garry, the then bachelor Riel does not begin the long period that would lead to his mental breakdowns and wanderings through eastern North America, but migrates directly to the western United States 'avec ma femme et mes enfants [pour] m'établir sur une terre dans le Montana' (141). Finally, in the work's most poignant scene, Archbishop Taché's refusal to bless Riel's Saskatchewan campaign, the Métis leader makes a pilgrimage to Saint Boniface to receive 'le geste sacré' (184). Similarly, at the beginning of the North-West Rebellion, Riel does not resurface in Batoche but in Winnipeg, creating the impression that the two communities are, if not contiguous, at least relatively close to each other (167).

The most striking aspects of Roquebrune's novel, though, are its unadulterated Canadian nationalism and its ambivalence toward the Métis, in general, and Riel, in particular. For the author, as he writes elsewhere, the Confederation of 1867 is not merely the amalgamation of a group of provinces but 'l'union de deux peuples en une seule nation'; it is a seemingly mystical political act by which the country's French- and English-speaking inhabitants 'ont cessé d'être étrangers, les uns pour les autres,' and collectively transformed themselves into 'Canadiens' (*Canadiens* 186–7). Roquebrune's pan-Canadianism is conspicuously evident in the ubiquitous image of the transcontinental railroad, signifying the realization of the nation's long-awaited linkage from the Atlantic Ocean to the Pacific. But it is also manifest in his novel's national determinism, the belief not just in the desirability but the inevitability of the expansion of the Western frontier, since 'c'est une loi humaine que les invasions se dirigent vers l'Ouest' and the region is 'destinée à être envahie par l'Est' (142). As the Hudson's Bay Company chief representative Donald Smith tells Aline's parents, 'La civilisation est plus forte que tout ... [L]e Nord-Ouest appartient au Canada et les Canadiens vont venir le coloniser, le peupler et l'habiter' (48). Or, as the narrator summarizes Father Lacombe's reaction to the imminent marriage of Aline and Jacques, 'Une promesse de fécondité lui sembla venir de cette terre puissante et neuve et ce couple lui parut symboliser la jeune race [canadienne, blanche] qui la posséderait' (252).

Needless to say, such a transcontinental vision of Canada would be seriously threatened by the establishment of a Métis homeland in the middle of the country. Still, Roquebrune is not always dismissive of the 'métis révoltés contre la Confédération canadienne' (109). At the beginning of *D'un océan à l'autre*, Augustin Ménard is not so much antagonistic toward Riel and his people as indifferent to them. The erudite student of pre-contact First Nations is simply not interested in the 'sang-mêlé [*sic*], des gens qui ont pour pères des agents de la Compagnie de la Baie d'Hudson et pour mères des Indiennes christianisées et qui portent des chapeaux ridicules et des cotonnades achetées à Fort-Garry' (18). Later, after he reaches Red River and actually meets some Métis, he becomes openly sympathetic to their struggle and declares that it would be 'tellement curieux cet Etat indépendant auquel rêve Riel.' But by the end of the novel, even Ménard accepts that 'Riel sera vaincu' in his 'guerre contre les hommes de l'Est' (118, 218). Someone like Father Lacombe is even less equivocal in his evaluation of the Métis leader. The part-Saulteaux missionary, whom the Métis revere 'comme ... Dieu' (Roquebrune, 'Défense' 33), contends that Riel is deeply religious. But his 'mysticisme,' the priest adds, 'est d'une nature parfois inquiétante,' for 'en lui le mélange de la race indienne avec le sang français semble avoir produit un déséquilibre.' Moreover, Lacombe agrees with Smith's assessment that the Métis leader 'déteste les Canadiens,' whom he 'considère comme des étrangers' (*D'un océan* 62). Indeed, there are few indications in the text any of the main personages questions that Riel and his people are destined to be displaced by the white settlers, the collectivity embodied in the conjugal union between Jacques Ménard and Aline Guilbault, 'la fille de la Prairie, la représentante de la nouvelle race qui s'était emparée de l'Ouest' (164). The extent to which the white characters do not identify with the Métis is illustrated by the jubilant manner in which Aline greets the announcement that the Canadian forces have captured Batoche: 'Le Père Lacombe ... a de bonnes nouvelles à porter là-bas. Riel est vaincu. Il a été arrêté ...' (249).

Roquebrune's conclusion that Riel and the Métis people ultimately will not be able to withstand modern civilization's westward advance is perhaps inevitable considering his equating miscegenation with degeneration and his cognate desire to prove to Europeans, particularly the French, that Canada is a pure white country. In a candid preface to *D'un océan à l'autre*, which curiously was excised from the work's second edition (1958), he writes that one of the most exasperating circumstances facing 'l'homme du Canada à l'étranger' is the general assumption that all Canadians are, if not 'sauvages,' at least of mixed race. The Canadian promptly tells those misinformed foreigners that his people are neither Aboriginal nor Métis – since 'les derniers Indiens achèvent de mourir dans leurs *réserves* où ils sont conservés comme des bibelots rares' (9) – but he senses that he will not be able to eradicate what he considers prejudiced stereotypes about his nation. Unlike his hypothetical fellow citizen, Roquebrune does not capitulate as easily in his quest to enlighten the outside world about the real Canada. As he states, after admitting that there is a 'petite population métisse' in the Canadian West, his novel's central aim is nothing less than to 'faire comprendre aux étrangers que les Canadiens ne sont ni des sauvages ni des métis' (10). In other words, the resistance by Riel and the Métis to the Canadian intrusion into their territory cannot be but 'un échec' (Viau 54), since they themselves barely exist.

Although Roquebrune's Riel may be the inconsequential leader of a doomed people, he is incontestably the Métis chief. That is not the case in Cecil B. DeMille's film *North West Mounted Police* (1940), a work in which – as in Henham's *Menotah* – Riel is presented, not as the architect of the two North-West conflicts, but as a creation of (fictitious) third parties who manipulate him at will. DeMille's film opens with Riel being visited at the Montana school where he teaches by two Canadian Métis, Jacques Corbeau and the Dumont-like Dan Duroc, who have come to ask him to lead their people in Saskatchewan and 'wipe the whites out of Western Canada.'[7] But it soon becomes apparent that the northern visitors intend to have the Red River hero merely as the titular leader of the new First Nations / Métis nation. The mastermind of the insurgence is not to be Riel but Corbeau, a heavily armed whisky trader and murderer who dreams of controlling the liquor business in the North-West. Riel protests when he first learns of Corbeau's plans, but before long he accepts them, since the half-Cree Corbeau is supposedly the only individual who can persuade strategic First Nations to join their people in a common front against the Canadian government.

In any case, not long after Riel re-enters Canada he disappears from the screen to be hardly seen again until near the end, as he is about to be transported to Regina under arrest. Obviously not driven by matters of historical fidelity, *North West Mounted Police* is less concerned with Riel's plight or that of his people than with the adventures of a Mountie and a Texas Ranger. Portrayed by Gary Cooper, the Ranger travels to Canada with a warrant for the arrest of Corbeau for crimes committed in the United States. Mountie Sergeant Jim Brett, a.k.a. Preston Foster, resents the intrusion into his jurisdiction by the southern interloper. This is particularly so once the gentlemanly Texan becomes his main rival for the heart of an angelic blonde nurse, given celluloid life by Madeleine Carroll. Yet, as one suspected from the beginning, all ends well – at least for the white characters – as the Mountie gets the nurse, the Ranger gets the evil whisky trader, and the uprising is suppressed.

For Pierre Berton, *North West Mounted Police* is an aesthetic and political abomination, typifying Hollywood's brazen Americanization of Canada's national image. The popular historian can barely contain his outrage at DeMille's rewriting of Canadian history, such as when the film-maker pretends that it is not the Canadian forces but 'the Métis [who] had the Gatling gun' in 1885 (11). But Berton is even more incensed by the blatantly racist portrayal of what he claims was once Hollywood's favourite renegade, the 'dirty, no-good half-breed' (87). As he writes, DeMille's film is an 'unrelenting libel on the Métis,' which 'can neither be excused by pointing to the tenor of the times in which it occurred, nor explained away by the essential naïveté of the silent films, nor condoned by the need of screenwriters and directors to inject drama and conflict into their stories' (99). In short, Berton charges, the only explanation for the film's depiction of Riel and the Métis is Hollywood's racism.

In the process of excoriating Hollywood for its cultural and racial chauvinism, Berton also blames 'the Canadian educational system' for failing to teach him and his co-citizens about 'our own past.' He states that the second time he watched *North West Mounted Police*, he 'got mad' at himself because he realized not only that he had seen the film years earlier but also that he had 'enjoyed it.' Since he had not learned much about the 1885 conflict in school, he simply assumed the events had occurred the way they were depicted on the screen 'because Mr. Cecil B. DeMille said they did' (11). Berton also contends that the central objective of Hollywood films like *North West Mounted Police* is to help 'perpetuate the easy assumption that there is no essential difference between Canadians and Americans,' an accusation that may have a certain validity. However, he discounts the possibility that the reason Canadians have been so willing to accept Hollywood's 'version' of ourselves (11–12) is not that we are victims of some nefarious foreign conspiracy but rather that we share Hollywood's preconceptions, at least when it comes to the Métis. The fact the Regina Board of Trade lobbied to hold the film's première in the city and then the whole town 'went wild in a three-day celebration,' as Berton notes (164), does not exactly lead one to believe that Canadians were outraged by the film.

G.H. Needler's *The Battleford Column: Versified Memories of a Queen's Own Corporal in the Northwest Rebellion 1885* (1947) certainly suggests that the idea of the 'Wicked Half-Breed' (Berton 89) was alive in Canada well into the middle of the twentieth century. The work, as its subtitle indicates, is the product of a veteran of the Saskatchewan campaign, the

> Last clash at arms on our North Continent
>   Twixt Red and White, the curtain here was rung
> On the long drama: the fading light now spent,
>   Here fell the Red Man's goetterdaemmerung:
> A fitting stage the spreading prairie's sward
> By waters rune-wise whispering 'Battleford.' (47)

In the poet's unambiguous words, this was the historic moment when the relationship between the First Nations of North America and the European Newcomers was finally established, 'one to dictate, / The other bide inexorable fate' (47).

Needler was a respected and worldly literary scholar, a translator and professor of German at the University of Toronto. He was also a native of Millbrook, a predominantly Orange village in central Ontario, some of whose volunteers captured the bell of Batoche and took it home as war booty (Daniels and Winslow).Yet, even though he is writing in the late 1940s, Needler can still produce a poem that is very much in the tradition initiated by Edmund Collins of portraying Riel as a debased religious and political zealot, a 'Fanatic' driven by a 'deluded quest' (5). The poet is especially unforgiving of Riel's alleged attempts to rally the First Nations to his cause, his 'calling the Indian for his culprit's tool' (83), or what the author elsewhere calls 'the unpardonable crime of deliberately inciting the Indians of our Canadian Northwest to join him in a general crusade against the whites' (*Louis Riel* 28). As Needler writes near the conclusion of *The Battleford Column*, his aim is to record for posterity the accomplishments of the young soldiers who 'kept the faith and saved their souls alive, – / Who smote the serpent, kept their country one' (80).

Admittedly, Needler's poem is an anomaly among representations of Riel since the end of the Second World War.[8] The only recent works that even raise the possibility that the Métis leader may have been an enemy of Canada are two poems by Elizabeth Brewster and Frank Davey. Brewster's 'At Batoche' (1982) describes a visit to the Saskatchewan battleground by a group of tourists, including the speaker. More specifically, it details the unexpected discovery by the 'poet,' as she reflects on the bloody struggle over this 'godforsaken country,' that her sympathies are less with the Métis than with the people who defeated them. She finds it surprisingly easy to identify with Gunner Phillips merely upon spotting the young Canadian soldier's grave, even conjecturing that the nineteen-year-old probably believed he was 'saving the West for the settlers, / or avenging Thomas Scott' (50); but the institutional idolization of Riel and Dumont makes her suspicious and uncomfortable, drawing out an unmistakable sense of Otherness:

Folk heroes maybe?
or a parcel of rebels
as my grandfather thought them
and half crazy at that?
(If any relative of mine
fought in this battle,
he was certainly on Gunner Phillips' side.) (51)

For Brewster's poet, the inescapable conclusion is that the current Canadian embrace of Riel and other nineteenth-century Métis leaders as national heroes necessarily requires the vilification of their opponents, her own biocultural ancestors. She even suggests that the government-sponsored reconstruction of the battle site is anything but innocent, stating that at Batoche 'the children of the victors / have appeased bloodguilt / by erecting monuments to the vanquished' (51; H. Adams, *Tortured People* 120).

Davey's poem, simply entitled 'Riel' (1985), also reveals a strong awareness of Canada's political and cultural past. The key to the work, which is part of a long poetic narrative about modern North American myths, is that it has two distinct voices – a seemingly autobiographical male poet and his history-conscious mother. Davey's poet knows that Riel's image is increasingly a positive one. As he states, 'looking at him in 1955 / from the lower Fraser Valley there were so many / nice things about Louis Riel' (49). Yet, because of the knowledge his mother imparts to him, he also comes to recognize that this has not always been the case. As the poet remarks, Riel 'had done something and now it doesn't matter. / He had done something but now it wasn't something' (51). One of the things Riel does, of course, is sanction the death of Scott, the Ontario Protestant 'troublemaker' incapable of abiding by Métis rules or laws:

Even in Fort Garry prison he got himself drunk.
Had once tried to throw the boss of his road crew
into the Red.
Maybe he was an anarchist individualist.
He called Riel a 'dumb frog,' the Metis
'a pack of cowards.'
Maybe he was a fascist running-dog.
He told Louis in colourful Protestant language
to go love the Blessed Virgin.
Louis Riel said, 'He is a very bad man,'
And sent him to a Metis tribunal.
The court found Tom
not up to community standards.
Man, this is one tough city, said Tom Scott. (52)

Another thing that Riel does is keep 'crossing the border,' both the international line between Canada and the United States and all sorts of religious and political borders. Indeed, there is 'something fishy,' the poet says his mother tells him, 'about Louis Real' (56, 51).

There are several significant, if curious, elements in Davey's poem. First, as mentioned in the introduction to this study, he seems fascinated by the concreteness of Riel and his place in Canadian culture. As he describes the 1885 conflict, 'There was no way / you could imagine it & therefore / it had to be a real rebellion' (49). Davey's insistence that Riel is somehow 'real' is surprising considering his assertions elsewhere that there are no 'objective' witnesses to historical events (*Clallam* n.pag.). Equally unexpected in light of the author's postmodernism is his apparent unreceptiveness to Riel's hybridity, the latter's proclivity to disregard boundaries. The most noteworthy aspect of Davey's poem, though, is the way it is situated in a living politico-literary tradition. By juxtaposing the poet and his mother, thus highlighting the discrepancy between Riel's current cultural reception and the way he used to be perceived in the not-too-distant past, Davey underscores the fluidity of accepted truth. That is, he implicitly acknowledges the existence of earlier perspectives of Riel against which his work will have to be situated. Davey's historicity would seem to be unexceptional. However, given the way most other contemporary Canadian writers either disown or deliberately fail to acknowledge the existence of earlier representations of Riel, it is nothing short of radical.

Before concluding this chapter, perhaps I should stress that, their views of the Métis leader aside, the early works on Riel as traitor are not always antagonistic toward his people. The caustic Collins may assert that 'Riel is an impostor,' yet he also states that 'the cause which he has espoused is a holy one' (*Story* 74). While Henham portrays Riel as a nonentity, he has one of the Métis 'most zealous to the cause' explain to his priest that he took part in the uprising because 'the white man has taken all from us, except life. Let him take that also, or give us back that which makes it happy. That is why I fought, my Father' (228–9). Likewise, after Connor's Commissioner of the Mounted Police describes the Métis leader as 'crack-brained Riel,' he tells one of his officers the reason he is worried about the 'restless half-breeds' is that 'they have real grievances ..., real grievances' (256). Bengough's attitude toward the Métis can also be surprising. Only a few days after Riel's hanging, the editor of *Grip* published a cartoon showing the allegorical figure of Justice, her back turned to Macdonald, telling the prime minister that she is not quite satisfied just because 'Riel is gone.' In Justice's words, 'you have hanged the EFFECT of the Rebellion; now I want to find and punish the CAUSE' (pl. 4). Even more unexpectedly, a few months later, at a time when numerous communities across the country were erecting memorials to the volunteers, Bengough sketched a cartoon depicting 'Miss Canada' pinning a 'Redress of Wrongs' medal on the chest of a Métis soldier. In his caption, the cartoonist further elaborates that Ottawa should 'recognize the efforts of the Halfbreeds, by giving them the rights they fought for' (pl. 5; Cumming 145–7).

The sympathy that those writers and artists express toward the Métis, however, is rarely extended to their leader. This is a situation that would change noticeably in the second half of the twentieth century. Davey's and Brewster's poems excepted, very few contemporary works on Riel even reflect an awareness of the discrepancy between his image today and immediately following his execution. There certainly have been no recent vengeful calls of 'blood for blood; / The death of Riel for the death of Scott,' such as in E.J. Pratt's 1952 poem *Towards the Last Spike* (47). Instead, the dominant trend has been on reconciliation, the need, if not always to incorporate the Métis into the larger Canadian family, at least to understand them on their own terms. As Steven Michael Berzensky (writing under the pseudonym Mick Burrs) articulates the new reality, the 1885 conflict was not an uprising but 'a war for independence.' Or, as the same poet asks rhetorically, if you call 'the people's violent act against the government' a rebellion, 'what do you call the government's violent act / against the people' ('Introduction' iii; *Moving* n.pag.). The Métis leader's image has changed so radically since about the end of the Second World War that the very theme of the treacherous Riel has been supplanted by an equally old one, that of the martyr.

3

The Martyr (I)
Riel As an Ethnic and Religious Victim of Confederation

> Un martyr ne meurt pas.
>
> *Louis Fréchette (1885–6)*

Frank Davey's 'Riel,' I argued toward the end of the previous chapter, complicates the contemporary image of the Métis leader considerably by showing that neither the author nor his subject exists in a cultural vacuum. More precisely, by virtue of its two voices, Davey's poem suggests that today's Riel is not necessarily yesterday's. If anything, the reception of Riel is even more problematized by his own writings. With his racial and cultural European heritage, the Métis leader of course makes an ambiguous non-Westerner (Hart 163–4). Nevertheless, it is undeniable that his writings often resist the representations of him, not only by his opponents but also by his presumed allies. Indeed, as one examines the profusion of works that claim Riel as a Canadian, a French Canadian, a Frenchman, or a generic North American – almost anything but a Métis – one cannot help but notice how his poetry and prose contest these affiliations.

Like the initial representations of Riel as a traitor to Canada, the first work on him as a martyr of Confederation was inspired by the troubles at Red River. Early in 1870 the Quebec writer Pamphile Le May published an invective condemning English Canada's reaction to the Métis leader's role in the execution of Tom Scott. Entitled 'À ceux qui demandent la tête de Riel. Crucifiez-le! Crucifiez-le!' Le May's poem begins on an acerbic note, calling sarcastically for the crucifixion of 'ce faux roi, cet infâme,' the perfidious outlaw that 'la canaille acclame / Et qu'elle appelle Majesté!' The scant irony there is in the work soon dissipates, however, as ridicule gives way to open vilification of anyone who expresses a desire to bring Riel to justice, the people the author characterizes as the 'Juifs hypocrites de nos jours' (207).

For Le May, Quebec's 'poète lauréat' and the spiritual guardian of the province's 'âme nationale' (Pellerin 35; Roy, 'Pamphile Le May' 9), the outrage over Riel's treatment of Scott is transparently dishonest since the Orangeman is a 'victime ignoble' who had attempted to 'plonger son fer, la nuit, avec malice / Dans le coeur de son souverain.' Riel, in contrast, is an 'homme franc, juste et noble,' a compassionate individual whose sole ambition is to 'faire régner le bonheur' (207–8). So gentle is Riel's nature that it becomes obvious that the efforts to demonize him and to 'déifier' Scott are not really about the two men (207). As the poet accuses the unidentified pro-Scott forces,

> Ce que vous regrettez, ce n'est point la carcasse
>   De votre ami traitre et vénal,
> Mais c'est le sceptre seul, le sceptre aimé qui passe
>   Dans les mains d'un heureux rival!
>
> Ce que vous demandez dans votre aveugle rage,
>   C'est que le Canadien-Français
> Dont l'esprit généreux partout vous porte ombrage
>   Soit foulé sous un pied anglais!
>
> Ce que vous demandez c'est que le catholique
>   Qui toujours si bien vous traita
> Expire sur la croix, ô secte fanatique,
>   Comme son Christ au Golgotha! (208–9)

In other words, the clamour in English-speaking Canada following Scott's death concerns not so much what Riel has done but what he is. Or rather, perhaps, what he symbolizes, Quebec.

Le May's poem provoked such controversy in the English-Canadian media that a fellow author wondered if one might not end up hanging with 'la même corde' both 'Riel et son poète' (Fréchette, 'Pamphile Le May' 181; Pellerin 39), yet it is the only major work by a Quebec writer on the Métis leader's activities at Red River. While the early theme of Riel as a victim of ethnic and religious prejudice is very much a Quebec one, the man Premier Honoré Mercier in 1885 would call 'notre frère' (328) does not capture the imagination of his Eastern 'siblings' until after the fall of Batoche – Father Charles McWilliams, Riel's former schoolmate and one of the two priests who accompanied him to the scaffold, affirms that as late as September of that year he was unable to persuade even the Métis leader's 'anciens compagnons de collège' in Montreal to show solidarity with the prisoner by signing 'une requête au gouvernement' (53). There are several reasons for this development. First, Quebec society has always been very ambivalent about both Riel and the Métis, uncertain about 'the degree of their relatedness to French Canadians' (A.I. Silver, *French-Canadian* 159). Second, at least in 1885, there were two French-speaking battalions fighting, not with Riel, but against him, volunteers determined 'à subir un insulteur, un drôle, / Un vil menteur payé pour ternir l'auréole' (Desaulniers 9; D. Morton, 'Des canadiens'). Finally, there are the matters of his religious heterodoxy and of his alleged animosity toward Quebec. As the Franco-Catholic clergy in Saskatchewan charged at the time, Riel is not only an 'HOMME NÉFASTE' and 'UN MALIN ESPRIT,' 'notre ANTECHRIST,' but he considers French Canadians 'CANAILLES' (André 7; Fourmond 15; Piquet 24).

Whether influenced by the perception that English Canada was increasingly associating the North-West Rebellion with Quebec or by the 'rôle mobilisateur du télégraphe' (Rens 47), following Riel's surrender at Batoche, Quebec at last started identifying with the 'pauvre fou' who 'était l'âme de l'insurrection' (Beauregard 52; A.I. Silver, 'French Quebec' 95). Like their society, though, Quebec writers continued to exhibit a somewhat schizophrenic attitude toward Riel. They tended to see the Métis leader and his people, not as their brethren, but as 'nos amis' whose destruction would 'humilier' Quebec because of the friendship she bore them. Without fully embracing him as one of their own, Quebec authors turned Riel into their ultimate religious and ethno-racial martyr. He was someone who was victimized basically for his Quebeckness, his French ancestry and language as well as his Catholicism, the faith that the Catholic hierarchy was simultaneously contending he had forsaken in 'SON APOSTASIE' (A.I. Silver, 'French Quebec' 96; André 7).

The most celebrated work on Riel as a victim of Anglo-Canadian religious and cultural chauvinism is *Le dernier des martyrs* (1885–6), a poem by another Quebec 'national poet,' Louis Fréchette – as the critic Camille Roy once remarked, 'le titre [est] facilement attribué chez nous' (*Histoire* 89). Written as part of a subscription drive by the new Montreal newspaper *La presse*, Fréchette's work situates Riel in the long line of francophone and Catholic martyrs. The Métis leader is not 'le dernier des martyrs' but 'le plus récent,' for the 'oppresseurs se sont toujours trompés: le sang / Des héros en produit infailliblement d'autres'(3; Hayne 173). The poem's message seems to be precisely that the 'héros malheureux ..., saint et ... martyr' must not be allowed to perish with his death. As Fréchette concludes, in an envoy addressed to the readers of *La presse*, 'L'an qui vient de finir s'est appelé le Crime; / Que l'an qui va s'ouvrir s'appelle Châtiment!' (7–8).

Fréchette's poet professes to be saddened by the fact that 'l'ère des martyrs n'est pas encor [*sic*] fermée' (8), that fanatical English-Canadian Protestants could still harbour such hatred toward adherents of another Christian denomination. He even mockingly invites 'primitive' nations like the Maoris, Hottentots, Sioux, Fijians, Boers, Zulus, and Comanches to travel to Canada to witness first-hand 'ce qu'on fait quand on est baptisé, / Qu'on est bon orangiste, et bien civilisé!' For the poet, the Orangemen's behaviour is particularly unforgivable since the objects of their venom are a most amiable and industrious group, a 'brave petit peuple' that courageously 'avait planté sa tente / Au désert.' The celebrated buffalo hunters are 'paysans, sans fusils, sans canons' (4–5).

Despite the affability of the Métis and the nobility of their psychologically troubled leader, who 'pour protéger les femmes, les enfants, / Se livra de lui-même aux vainqueurs-triomphants,' there is no placating their foes (5). While the Métis may be a small and vulnerable people, they are Catholic and French, and for their enemies that is all that matters. As the poet articulates the situation in a dramatic dialogue,

> – Mais cet homme n'a fait que défendre ses frères
> Et leurs foyers. – A mort! – Mille actes arbitraires
> Ont fait un drapeau saint de son drapeau battu ...
> – *A mort!* ... – *Mais,* songez-y, cet homme est revêtu
> Du respect que l'on doit aux prisonniers de guerre:
> Vous avez avec lui parlementé naguère.
> – *A mort!* ... – Mais tout rayon en lui s'est éclipsé;
> Allez-vous de sang froid tuer un insensé?
> C'est impossible! – *A mort!* ... Mais c'est de la démence;
> Pour lui le jury même implore la clémence ...
> *A mort!* ... – Un peuple entier réclame son pardon;
> Son supplice peut être un terrible brandon
> De discordes sans fin et d'hostilités vaines ...
> Allons! – *A mort!* – il a du sang français aux veines! (6)

Or, as Fréchette makes even more explicit when he revises the work for his seminal collection *La légende d'un peuple*,[1] '– A mort! à mort! il a du sang français aux veines! / A voilà son vrai crime' (287).

Fréchette does at times acknowledge the national specificity of the Métis. For him, as we have seen, Riel's people are a band of diligent but uneducated pioneers, 'ne lisant qu'au grand livre/ De Dieu' (*Dernier* 5). In a footnote to a segment of the revised version of the poem, he even states that, although the Métis are 'des descendants de Français unis à des Indiennes,' they 'forment une race à part' (*Légende* 343). Nevertheless, the unfailing impression one gets from *Le dernier des martyrs* is that the Riel affair is not really about the Métis but about the French fact in North America; that is, about Quebec. The way the poet throughout the work refers to 'notre peuple asservi,' 'notre foi sainte,' and 'nos enfants, fiers, libres et français' makes it apparent that his subject is not Riel's new American nation, the fusion of the Aboriginal and the European. Rather, it is the more strictly French society on the Saint Lawrence, the 'race' that has earned itself a privileged place in the Americas 'par droit d'aînesse et par droit de conquête' (*Dernier* 3–4).

The same sense that Riel's hanging is just an extension of Quebec's seemingly perpetual struggle in Confederation, especially the concomitant anti-French and anti-Catholic feeling in the rest of the country, is evident in other works triggered by his death, such as the anonymous *À la mémoire de Louis Riel: La Marseillaise canadienne* (1885). Also known as 'La Marseillaise rielliste,'[2] this five-stanza poem on the 'duel des races au Canada' became extremely popular in Quebec schools, reportedly transforming young scholars into 'ardents cocardiers' (Groulx, *Mes mémoires* 36). To quote the initial stanza:

Enfants de la nouvelle France,
Douter ne nous est plus permis!
Au gibet Riel se balance,
Victime de nos ennemis. (Bis.)
Amis, pour nous, ah, quel outrage!
Quels transports il doit exciter!
Celui qu'on vient d'exécuter
Nous anime par son courage. (Anonymous 3, n.pag.)

Or, as the poet adds in a refrain with a recognizably Riellian touch, 'Courage! Canadiens! Tenons bien haut nos cœurs, / Un jour viendra (Bis.) Nous serons les vainqueurs' (Anonymous 3, n.pag.).

The remaining four stanzas of *À la mémoire de Louis Riel*, which members of the Quebec clergy attempted to ban after declaring it 'séditieux' (Blais, '*À la mémoire*' 9), focus on the dreaded Orangemen, the 'tyrans' and 'esclavagistes' who would love nothing more than to eradicate all French-speaking Canadians. They also deal with the three Quebec federal cabinet ministers who remained loyal to Macdonald's government, those political renegades who sold their 'âmes' to the enemy and who 'souillèrent ta noble histoire, / Canada!' Tellingly, the poet always addresses his prospective audience as 'Enfants de la nouvelle France' or 'Canadiens!' In a work ostensibly about the leader of the two North-West conflicts, there is not a single reference to his people, the Métis. Consequently, it does not seem illogical to deduce that when the poet exhorts his listeners to remember the 'Amour sacré de la Patrie,' or when he declares that Riel's name 'souvent répété / Nous parle de la liberté, / Et nous prêche l'indépendance,' he is not alluding to a Prairie homeland, be it on the Red River or on the South Saskatchewan (Anonymous 3, n.pag.)

The centrality of Quebec is also unmistakable in two poems that Rémi Tremblay devotes to Riel. 'Une épopée' (1885) is the more remarkable of the two, certainly the more ironic. Tremblay's poem is the perfect antidote to all the unadulterated poetic celebrations of the 1885 volunteers, including Gonzalve Desaulniers's L'absolution avant la bataille (1886), in which young Quebeckers proudly march off to the North-West to prove to the motherland that 'tes fils d'aujourd'hui sont dignes de leurs pères' (Desaulniers 13). In a disingenuous footnote, Tremblay declares he knows that 'nos braves miliciens se sont couverts de gloire' in the Saskatchewan campaign. But he adds strategically that his 'chanson ne s'applique pas aux intrépides conquérants des Métis, mais seulement à ceux qui ont eu peur' (146). That is, he is not interested in heroes but in cowards, those soldiers for whom

> Fuir est notre affaire
> C'est notre salut, (bis)
> Voilà notre but
> Lorsque nous faisons la guerre.
> Nous serons peureux
> Et peux valeureux. (bis) [146]

In his effort to ridicule the volunteers, Tremblay is even ready to sacrifice Riel himself, turning the Métis leader into a military nonentity utterly subservient to Dumont. As the poet writes of the soldiers, each carries 'sa corde' with which to hang Riel. But when Dumont turns up instead, 'On devient peureux / Et peu valeureux' (147). Indeed, in contrast to the heroic volunteers of much English-Canadian poetry, who for 'kindred and country's sake' intrepidly face the 'Half-breed hell-hounds' (W. Campbell, 267; Mulvaney, 'Our Boys' 74), Tremblay's 'beaux militaires' make sure Batoche has been abandoned before they ever venture into the village (146).

Tremblay's other Riel poem, 'Aux chevaliers du nœud coulant' (1887), is more typical of the late nineteenth-century representations of the Métis leader as a victim of ethnic and religious prejudice. Even more uncompromisingly partisan and belligerent in its language than 'À ceux qui demandent la tête de Riel' or *Le dernier des martyrs*, 'Aux chevaliers' presumably won its author 'l'honneur de perdre un emploi' with the federal government (Tremblay, 'Aux chevaliers' 70), and it is not difficult to discern why. A work of a 'rare violence' (Blais, '*Coups*' 158), it presents all the figures who fail to support Riel, not as his adversaries, but as quislings, 'enfants dégénérés d'une race virile' for whom 'la trahison est un titre de gloire' (70). Yet, in a poem that decries the death of a martyr whose 'sang ... eut rougi l'échafaud,' there is not a word about his people (71). Riel is simply incorporated into another collectivity, not his beloved New Nation, but the larger French-speaking community in North America.

The general tendency to associate Riel with Quebec is evident even in the work of non-francophone authors. In her poem 'Quebec to Ontario' (1885), which is subtitled 'A Plea for the Life of Riel, September 1885,' the Ontario writer Agnes Maule Machar implores the government of Canada to give clemency to the Métis leader, someone whose hatred of injustice led him to take up 'arms, in evil hour, to fight, / For weakness – with the strong' (36). As she entreats Ottawa, it should forgive Riel not only because of his gallantry but also because its triumph is so complete:

> While he who sought his people's weal,
>   Who loved his nation well,
> The prisoner of your fire and steel,
>   Lies doomed in felon's cell!
>
> Pity the captive in your hand,
>   Pity the conquered race;
> You – strong, victorious in the land –
>   Grant us the victor's grace! (37)

Interestingly, while stating that Riel's struggle is 'a patriot cause,' Machar identifies his mission, not with the Métis, but with the people of Quebec. In the words she gives to the Métis leader, he and his people opposed Canada because 'The blood of the old voyageur / Leaps boiling in our veins' and their aspiration was to recover the territory conquered by Cartier and Champlain, 'the land our fathers bought' (36).

The identification of Riel with Quebec is also unequivocal in Mathias Carvalho's *Poemas americanos I: Riel* (1886), the only known South American work on the subject. Written by an obscure Brazilian author whose name appears to have vanished even from the annals of his country's literature, the collection was recently rediscovered and published in a bilingual Portuguese-French edition by Jean Morisset, a Quebec geographer who has written extensively on Riel as an 'écrivain américain' (Morisset, 'Louis Riel'; 'Postface'). Carvalho's poem is simultaneously a republican manifesto, an anti-English diatribe, and a paean to pan-American solidarity. The most original aspect of the work is that it depicts Riel not just as a national but as a New World liberator. As Carvalho writes in his preface, Riel is a 'fearless fighter for Canadian independence' [destemido luctador da independencia do Canadá].[3] He is 'a martyr to the most sacred of causes – the freedom of the motherland' [um martyr da mais sagrada das causas – a liberdade da patria], a patriot who struggles to ensure that Canada, like the author's Brazil, will soon join the ranks of the newly independent nations that constitute the 'gloria' of the Americas (16).[4]

Poemas americanos is set against the backdrop of the U.S. Civil War. At the outset of the clash between the North and the South, what Carvalho calls the forces of 'Good and Evil' [O Mal e o Bem], the slaves over whose fate they are supposedly fighting dream of a haven to which they can escape, a sanctuary where they can regain their humanity. For those 'cripples of the New World' [aleijões do Mundo Novo], there is only one hope, that 'sacred, boreal eminence, / Canada' [essa eminencia boreal, sagrada, / O Canadá] (20, 24). But the slaves are in for a great disillusionment. After they begin their exodus northward, they learn that they will not be able to find shelter across the border, since 'Canada lies in a dreadful prison' [O Canadá – jaz em prisão terrivel]. Rather than being a promised land for the oppressed of the world, Canada is itself oppressed. It is a victim of British imperialism, an unfortunate land into whose 'generous heart' [largo coração] England's 'cursed dragon' [maldito dragão] has sunk its fangs (24, 30).

It is in such a context that Carvalho situates Riel. Aware of the misery that reigns not only in Canada but in the whole of the Americas, the Métis leader comes to the realization that 'he could / Save the motherland through combat' [podia/ Salvar a patria pelo combate]. Seeking inspiration from other New World liberators such as Benito Juárez, and 'asking nature for arms' [armas pedio á natureza], Riel begins to envisage the moment when 'Privilege' [o Privilegio] would finally be vanquished by the 'sons of Reason' [filhos da Rasão] (32, 38). In the poet's words,

He saw ... moving before his dazzled eyes
The image of the Union [Army] – repelling the soldiers,
Defeating the battalions of that English government,
Raising its head at a decisive moment,
Crying out to the continent: 'Charge ... forward!
Raise your arms! It's your turn.'

[Elle via ... passar nos olhos deslumbrados
O quadro da União – repellindo os soldados,
Vencendo os batalhões d'esse governo inglez,
Levantando a cabeça a um ponto culminante,
Gritando ao continente: 'Avançai ... para diante!
As armas empunhai! vos toca a vez.'] (38)

Riel, of course, is ultimately defeated, 'assassinated' [assassinado] by the dastardly British. Yet the resistance by the 'Man of the North to whom nobody gave a thought' [Homem do Norte em que ninguem pensára] is not in vain, since his struggle against foreign imperialism earns him an illustrious place in the pantheon of New World heroes. Indeed, along with the Brazilian proto-nationalist Tiradentes and the U.S. abolitionist John Brown, Riel forms an 'American Triad' [Triade americana].[5] At a time when much of the continent struggles under foreign or local tyranny, they are giants driven by nothing but 'the Love of the Motherland' [o Amor da Patria] (32, 52).

Carvalho's portrait of Riel in Poemas americanos is clearly an idiosyncratic one. In light of the subject's religious and political conservatism – the fact he embodies not only 'a narrative of liberation but also an eruption of the colonial and the feudal' (Hart 164) – it is incongruous to see him depicted as the epitome of republicanism and liberalism. First, instead of always being progressive, Riel was an ardent supporter of the Conservative party, considered himself a direct descendant of

France's Louis xi, and claimed that 'Le Métis comprend que l'église / Est Reine à la tête de tout' (4: 320; Flanagan, 'Louis Riel: Icon' 222–4). Second, the history of republicanism in the Americas is not nearly as emancipatory as both Carvalho and Morisset suggest. As Mario Vargas Llosa has pointed out, 'in countries like Chile and Argentina, it was during the Republic (in the nineteenth century), not during the colony, that the native cultures were systematically exterminated' ('Novels' 35). Or, as the Brazilian novelist João Ubaldo Ribeiro writes, 'Emancipation didn't abolish slavery. The Republic didn't abolish oppression, it created new oppressors' (455). Finally, one cannot help but be struck by the national affiliation that Carvalho ascribes to Riel, who actually fights for Canada. For the poet, who never acknowledges the Confederation of 1867, Canada means essentially Quebec. This is a society dominated by those devious English 'lords' (26), including presumably Macdonald, the founding prime minister whom his editor and translator christens the 'anti-liberator' and even the 'anti-Canadien' (Morisset, 'Conquête' 284; Identité usurpée 15). As Carvalho notes, 'Canada must free itself from English slavery in the same manner that we [Brazilians] must free ourselves from the slavery of the monarchy' [O Canadá ha de libertar-se da escravidão ingleza do mesmo modo que nós nos havemos de libertar da escravidão monarchica] (16). Paradoxically, given the poem's focus on the need of the peoples of the Americas to liberate themselves from oppression, be it imperialism or monarchism, Riel is completely dissociated from his own nation. There is not one reference to the Métis in Poemas americanos. As in most other works on Riel as an ethnic or religious victim of Confederation, the protagonist is simply absorbed into Quebec society. Or, as Carvalho calls it, Canada.

There is only one early poem on the political martyrdom of Riel that consistently identifies his plight with that of the Métis people, Georges Lemay's 'Chant du Métis' (1886). Himself a Métis, Lemay does not minimize the ethnic and religious chauvinism that may have been responsible for the Regina hanging. On the contrary, he writes that after Riel's death a strong wind blows across the prairie, murmuring: '"Les lâches m'ont vendu!"' For the poet, the Métis leader is not just a victim of perfidy; he is also betrayed by his own kin. Riel has been sold by the 'valets des sectaires' to the wicked 'orangistes,' who are now obscenely celebrating 'mon trépas: "Nous marcherons dans le sang des papistes, / Nous foulerons leurs crânes sous nos pas?"' (566). Still, Lemay's Riel remains incontestably part of the Métis nation. As the martyr from Saint Boniface posthumously evaluates his political career,

Ai-je plus fait que défendre mes frères,
Dépossédés par des nouveaux venus,
Que réclamer, sur ce sol de nos pères,
Un coin de terre et des droits méconnus?
Et quand un jour, fatigués d'injustice,
Nos gens émus élevèrent la voix,
On cria: 'Mort à la race métisse!'
On nous traqua jusqu'au fond de nos bois. (566)

In other words, the target of Riel's enemies is not French-Catholic Quebec but the hybrid people who claim title to the strategic centre of the country. However, by killing Riel his foes do not destroy the Métis nation but rather provide it with a vital symbol of national resistance. As the poet addresses his hero, 'Le gibet donne à ta cause un martyr. / Un cri vengeur s'élève de ta bière / Que tout leur or ne fera que grandir' (567).

Lemay's poem, though, is an exception. Riel's Métisness is again subsumed into the larger Quebec world in two plays – both entitled *Riel* – published in response to the Métis leader's fate after Batoche. Written by two French immigrants, Charles Bayer and E. Parage, the first work is a convoluted and tendentious political melodrama. For instance, the leading anglophone character, the Canadian government's commissioner in the North-West and governor of Fort Prince of Wales, is surnamed MacKnave. In contrast, the visiting Franco-American journalist who wins the heroine's heart bears the family moniker of Francoeur.

Despite its title, Bayer and Parage's *Riel* does not focus primarily on the Métis leader but on the aforementioned MacKnave, his wife, Élisabeth, their five-year-old daughter, Nelly, the latter's Blackfoot maid, Takouaga, and the teenaged Nelly's paramour, Francoeur. As the play begins, one learns that MacKnave has travelled to Ottawa, ostensibly to convey to the federal government the numerous grievances of the territory's first inhabitants. But the moment he returns, it is obvious that he is no friend of the First Nations and the Métis, whom he describes collectively as a 'race rouge ... maudite ... condamnée à disparaître' (15). MacKnave's racism becomes even more glaring when

Takouaga informs him that she has learned through her son, a young chief named L'Esprit-Errant, that the Blackfoot have been assembling in the mountains under the leadership of none other than Riel. MacKnave freely admits that he 'méprise les Peaux-Rouges et les Sang-Mêlé [sic]' (16), but he especially loathes Riel, with whom he has been involved in a long and bitter feud. As he relates to Takouaga, his father was a Hudson's Bay Company commissioner during the Sayer imbroglio of 1849, and at the trial Riel's father invaded the court and forced the senior MacKnave to surrender his money and arms. Later at the Collège de Montréal, where they were both pupils, the younger Riel and MacKnave continued the family hostilities, even coming to blows. The latter has never forgotten the familial humiliation and ever since has been plotting his 'vengeance' against his enemy (17).

There are several interesting elements in Bayer and Parage's play or, as Chris Johnson has called it, their 'political tract in dialogue form' (179). MacKnave is consumed by revenge. But his need for retribution is grounded in socio-historical reality, his conviction that he and his family have been grievously injured by the Riels. Untypically for an anglophone representative of the Canadian government, he is also educated at the Collège de Montréal. The last detail inevitably leads one to conclude that, in the context of the work's ideology, a Franco-Catholic education cannot really overcome an individual's genetic and cultural heritage, at least if the individual in question happens to be of Anglo-Celtic stock. As well, although she is ignorant of her husband's character and politics beyond credibility, Élisabeth MacKnave entertains unusually pro-Aboriginal views, at one point describing 'ces pauvres gens' as 'nos frères' (15). But then, perhaps, one should not be surprised. Judging by the spelling of her first name, she is likely a francophone and, in this play, that is synonymous with being compassionate.

Even less commendably, Bayer and Parage's melodrama is blatantly racist and sexist. Its sexism is evident in the characterization of the relationship between Francoeur and MacKnave's daughter, where Providence itself is invoked to help assure the young woman's transition from being her father's chattel to her husband's. The work's racism is equally conspicuous. So negative is the two Frenchmen's portrayal of a Jewish merchant called Abraham and a British journalist by the name of Steward that a critic has stated, if it were not for 'l'anachronisme, on croirait les dramaturges de bons nazis' (Collet 249). Abraham and Steward are perfidious as well as inarticulate, two caricatures whose deformed French seems to be a direct reflection of their moral inadequacy.

After meeting Francoeur, Steward explains that his newspaper 'avait entrepris de regénérer le Angleterre et les colonies de elle, en dévoillant les vices, les tourpitioudes qui infectent les populations de elle' (34). As for Abraham, he brazenly attempts to swindle the Blackfoot, but when he discovers that instead of being easy prey to his schemes, they have been deceiving him, he bellows hysterically: 'Ah ma bar qui est folée aussi ... ah! les chiens! ... les foleurs! ... les Juifs! ... (*Se reprenant*.) pas les Juifs ... les Bcaux-Rouges!' (37).

The playwrights also take considerable liberties with the historical record – or make an elementary error – when they depict the Blackfoot, as opposed to their rivals the Cree, as Riel's main Aboriginal allies. As we saw in chapter 2, notably in the discussion of Connor and Roquebrune, the significance of the role played by the Blackfoot in 1885 was that they did not join forces with the Métis – a decision usually attributed to the influence of either the Mounted Police or Father Lacombe, but which historians now credit primarily to the work of chiefs Red Crow and Crowfoot (Dempsey, *Crowfoot* 167).[6] The historical Riel himself appears to have had a low opinion of the Blackfoot, branding them 'nothing but savages ..., indians in the true sense of the word' (2: 240). Yet Bayer and Parage have the Blackfoot not only supporting Riel but becoming utterly subservient to him and the Métis, a collectivity popularly known as 'the Cree mixed bloods' or 'the French-Cree Red River breeds' (Dempsey, *Crowfoot* 124; Schultz 380). Moreover, the authors compound this confusion by naming Takouaga's son L'Esprit-Errant, which is the same name, Wandering Spirit, as that of the Plains Cree 'war chief' believed mainly responsible for the killings at Frog Lake (Stanley, *Birth* 338).

Most pertinent in terms of the subject of this study, Bayer and Parage's play only deals peripherally with Riel, though the Métis leader is not totally absent from the action. In a scene charged with political symbolism, during his 'procès sans nom,' Riel experiences an 'APOTHÉOSE' in which he anticipates his imminent martyrdom, knowing that he has the full support of his 'fidèles amis du Bas-Canada' if not the whole French-speaking world (53–4). As he waits in jail, his alter ego is shown kneeling before a white-clad '*Liberté*' and surrounded not only by Aboriginal people and Métis but also by '*des Canadiens et des officiers du 65e*,' the French-speaking regiment that had gone to the North-West to fight him (54–5; D. Morton, 'Des canadiens'). Then, just before Riel has a revelation from God and realizes 'le sort qui m'est réservé' – 'Je marcherai calme et tranquille au supplice' – the 'Marseillaise' plays slowly in the background (55). Throughout most of the play, though, Riel is overshadowed by the romance between Francoeur and MacKnave's estranged daughter. Indeed, while the Métis leader may be 'le glorieux martyr canadien' (66), as is stated after his death, the playwrights do not even include him in the last act.

Riel has a slightly more central role in the other play written about him in 1885. The sole dramatic work by the Quebec medical doctor Elzéar Paquin, the second *Riel* is a lengthy and overtly factional historical drama. Its partiality is discernible from the outset. In the list of dramatis personae, the author describes Riel as 'le grand Patriote martyr' and Scott as 'le bandit' (n.pag.). In the stage directions for act 1, Paquin stresses that he will be addressing the 'causes et principaux apercus [sic] du soulèvement de 1869–70, faussement appelé insurrection ou rébellion' (5). Then, in the preamble to act 4, he characterizes Riel as a 'héros politique' and his sentence at Regina as a 'meurtre judiciaire,' a travesty of justice that leaves 'la race franco-canadienne' two distinct choices: 'd'un coté, l'oppression anglaise et le joug orangiste, de l'autre, la politique libérale du parti réformiste ou l'annexion aux Etats-Unis' (93).

The same political tendentiousness is evident in the play proper. Paquin devotes the first three acts of his *Riel* to the politico-military events at Red River and Saskatchewan, making little effort to camouflage his antagonism toward both the government of Canada and the First Nations. He opens his play with a caustic denunciation of the social and spiritual ills that supposedly plague Aboriginal people. Paquin is especially critical of the endemic indolence of the men, who allegedly sit around smoking and drinking while their women 'travaillent tant qu'elles peuvent, font tout l'ouvrage' (5). In the process of dramatizing the malaise afflicting the First Nations, which culminates in their fervently embracing Catholicism, the 'religion [qui] fait des hommes et des saints' (13), he also identifies the parties responsible for their plight, the Canadian government, in particular, and Anglo-Saxon civilization, in general. Actually, the reason Riel becomes so important is that he is the first individual who realizes that Ottawa's central objective in the North-West is nothing less than to destroy the Métis and the First Nations. As he confides to a fellow Métis, 'j'ai découvert le dessein pervers que nourissent ... tous ces émigrants et tous ces arpenteurs d'Ontario. Tous, ils ont la même idée, les mêmes intentions; tous, ils veulent nous exterminer ou nous chasser de nos maisons' (19).

The fourth act, however, focuses almost exclusively on the controversial aftermath of the Métis leader's trial. Furthermore, in an attempt to absolve his hero of any blame for the blood shed in the two North-West conflicts, Paquin denies him a political role. As depicted in the play, Riel is not accountable for the troubles of 1869–70 because his actions are 'la plus noble revendication nationale contre la plus noire et la plus basse conspiration militaire.' His only crime is that, like Joan of Arc, he has 'jeté la terreur dans la nation anglaise' (103, 105). As Dumont asserts, 'Riel n'avait aucun contrôle, aucun droit de vote ou de sanction relativement aux décisions du conseil de guerre, sous le gouvernement provisoire. Riel n'était que le président de ce nouveau gouvernement' (111). Similarly, the Métis leader is in no way implicated in the Frog Lake Massacre. Despite the historical Riel's explosive words to 'Métis et ... Sauvages' to rise up against the Canadian forces – 'Soulevez-vous. Faites face à la Police ... [P]renez le Fort Bataille. Détruisez-le' (Riel, 3: 79) – he bears no culpability for the incident in which Big Bear's Cree killed nine people, including two Catholic priests and a Métis (Stanley, *Birth* 339). In Dumont's words, 'Responsable de ce massacre! Comment? Pourquoi? Il a eu lieu à son insu! Gros-Ours et sa bande seuls en sont les auteurs. Riel était à Batoche bien loin de ses sauvages, n'ayant aucune communication avec eux' (111). That is, Riel is so little involved with the events of 1885 that one begins to suspect that perhaps there is something to the thesis propounded by people like Henham and DeMille that he was merely their nominal leader.

Even more conspicuously, Paquin ends his play by alienating Riel from his own people. After declaring his protagonist's trial 'l'homicide politique de Regina' (127), the playwright evaluates the impact of the Métis leader's death, not on his nation, but on Quebec. Paquin's *Riel* actually concludes with two characters discussing the advantages and disadvantages of Quebec's annexation to the United States, and there is little doubt which side the author favours (142). A certain Senator Trudel, presumably the ultramontane journalist and politician the historical Riel once called 'un de mes bons amis' (Riel, 2: 20), contends that, 'sous la Couronne d'Angleterre, si nous le voulons, nous pourrons devenir le plus grand peuple de l'Amérique.' A Franco-American, however, claims that 'l'annexion aux Etats-Unis est une question de temps' (142–3). For the symbolically named Jean-Baptiste, the benefits of such a union are not only economic and political but also spiritual and ethical. As he closes the play, 'Les préjugés disparaitront, la vérité reluira, et on comprendra que sous le rapport religieux comme sous le rapport matériel, le peuple canadien aura tout à y gagner' (143).

While politically intriguing, Paquin's *Riel* is obviously a flawed work. One critic considers it 'the most boring play' ever written about the Métis leader (Osachoff, 'Riel' 131). Another states that the author 'a beaucoup à dire, mais il ne sait pas comment le dire' (Bélanger 662). Still another asserts that the characters are not individualized figures but 'des porte-parole de l'auteur, des personnages-mannequins évoluant à travers un espace théâtrale mal défini' (Doucette 128). Paquin's dramaturgical ineptitude is certainly difficult to ignore. This is seldom more evident than near the end of the play. As several characters read verbatim the reactions to Riel's hanging in Quebec newspapers, one of them comments, 'J'ai lu dans *La Vérité* de Québec, quelque chose d'aussi fort et d'aussi beau! Malheureusement, j'ai perdu les extraits que j'en avais faits' (131). In an essay contrasting Paquin's *Riel* and Bayer and Parage's, the theatre historian L.E. Doucette makes some cogent observations. Doucette, who finds both works 'dramatisés mais peu dramatiques,' claims that the main differences between the plays by the two French immigrants and by the 'Québécois de vieille souche' are national (130, 123). As he writes, Paquin's 'défauts ne sont pas moindres, mais cette fois ils sont bien canadiens et proviennent surtout d'un respect trop soucieux des données historiques' (127). Even the Quebec playwright's xenophobia, it seems, is home-grown. According to Doucette, Paquin is no less bigoted than Bayer and Parage, but he is 'raciste aussi à sa façon,' stressing the social and moral superiority of the Métis over the First Nations. Thus, instead of 'l'anti-sémitisme *gratuit* des Français ..., le racisme ici vise un but important: il s'agirait de rehausser la nation métisse vis-à-vis des Amérindiens, en soulignant sa supériorité fondamentale due à une culture canadienne-français [*sic*]' (128). Indeed, one of the most notable aspects of Paquin's play is the way the author co-opts Riel and the Métis. By minimizing the Aboriginal portion of their heritage, he is easily able to incorporate them into the larger Quebec family. They are simply Quebeckers who happen to live in Western Canada.

Riel is claimed by yet another collectivity, France, in Joseph-Émile Poirier's *La tempête sur le fleuve* (1931). First published under the self-consciously anti-Voltairian title of *Les arpents de neige* in 1909, the Frenchman's novel focuses chiefly on the 1885 events in what a Quebec critic calls the '"chez nous" lointain de la Saskatchewan' (Poirier, *Arpents* 11; Roy, '*Arpents*' 311). The work's ideological identification is established early, when Riel's people are described as the 'métis franco-indiens du Nord-Ouest' and 'ces demi-Français' (*Tempête* 8, 89). Their enemy too is not the Canadian government but 'le gouvernement anglo-canadien,' which provokes the clash at Batoche by – among its 'incessantes vexations' – selling to the 'Sociétés de colonisation et à des Syndicats agricoles, une paroisse métisse tout entière, celle de Saint-Louis-de-Langevin' (8). The focal point in *La tempête sur le fleuve*, the first novel by a writer best known for his poetry and with an 'âme de poète' (Roy, '*Arpents*' 311, 315), is the relationship between two Métis brothers, Pierre and Jean La Ronde. Their conflict is both personal and political. Jean, who at twenty is two years younger than his brother, is extremely insecure about his mixed heritage. For example, upon being informed after a freighting trip of recent Métis military successes against the Canadian forces, he remarks curtly to his father: '... tu sais ben que les journaux anglouais nous traitent déjà de sauvages! ... On veut donc qu'ils ayent raison ... Si les Cries et les Pierreux se mettent avec nous ... ' (17). So, when circumstantial evidence suggests Jean supports the English settlers, the community immediately begins to suspect him of treason. Pierre is especially critical. After confiding to a French visitor that Jean 'a pas le cœur d'un Bouais-Brûlé,' he even refuses to shake hands with his sibling, saying, '... je ne touche pas la main aux amis des "Vestes-Rouges!"' (46, 51).

Pierre's suspicions regarding his brother's treachery seem to be confirmed when several Métis notice Jean's horse in the possession of a British-born gentleman farmer named Hughes Clamorgan and his twenty-year-old daughter, Elsie. The younger La Ronde had saved the Clamorgans from 'une mort certaine et probablement horrible' during the burning of Fort Pitt and then lent them his horse to reach safety at Battleford, but all he tells his brother is that he is aware of the fort's 'prise et l'incendie' (50). Described as an 'anglo-saxon de pure race,' Clamorgan is an inveterate racist who disdains both of the country's dominant cultural and linguistic groups. As the narrator states, 'il estimait les Anglo-Canadiens fort inférieurs aux gens de la métropole; les descendants de Français lui semblaient tout à fait négligeables.' Worst of all, Clamorgan abhors the Métis, whom he dismisses as a 'race dont il ne convenait pas de faire le moindre état' (26). Yet Pierre is more disturbed by the romantic implications of his brother's involvement with Elsie than by the political ones. He simply cannot fathom how a true-blooded Métis male could become emotionally involved with 'une Anglaise, une hérétique, quand il y avait parmi les Bois-Brûlés et à Batoche même tant de filles gracieuses et séduisantes élevées dans les principes de vérité' (54). In any case, any lingering doubts that Pierre may still have regarding his brother's duplicity vanish when he witnesses Jean bearing a message to a Canadian officer. Elsie, knowing that she is 'passionnément aimée par un homme qui lui est indifférent,' has persuaded Jean to carry letters to her 'frère dans l'armée canadienne, un frère qui ignore ce que son père et sa sœur sont devenus, qui les croit morts, sans doute massacrés par les Indiens' (59, 61). The young woman's 'frère' turns out to be her fiancé, Edward Simpson, a lieutenant with the 90th Battalion. Pierre is unaware of the reasons for Jean's clandestine visits to the Canadian camp. Thus, believing his brother to be a 'traître,' a 'Judas' who 'voulait nous livrer aux Vestes-Rouges,' he declares himself a 'justicier' and shoots Jean in the back, wounding him severely (102–3).

The seemingly incontrovertible evidence that Jean is collaborating with the enemy leads Dumont to order him to appear before a Métis council to defend himself of the accusation of treason. When confronted by Riel's 'implacable' lieutenant, Jean finally reveals the circumstances that brought him in contact with Elsie, maintaining that he has not betrayed his people and that he 'n'avait agi ainsi que sûr de la loyauté de cette femme' (137). Like everyone else present, Dumont accepts the young man's account, saying that it was 'cette fille aux "cheveux jaunes" ... qui était la cause de tout ce trouble. Jean La Ronde n'avait été qu'un instrument entre ses mains; son honnêteté, sa bonne foi étaient hors de cause; seules, sa grande jeunesse et la séduction de cette femme l'avait induit en faute' (137). Before closing the proceedings by absolving the accused, Dumont demands that Jean swear 'sur la croix' to the truth of everything he has told the council and to pledge 'sur le Sauveur que tu ne chercheras jamais à revoir cette fille anglaise' (138).

Dumont's exoneration of Jean becomes a critical event not only in the life of the younger La Ronde but also in that of his brother. Soon after leaving the meeting, Pierre encounters Rosalie Guérin, a 'belle fille de dix-sept ans' he pines for, who turns on him violently: 'Assassin! Caïn! ... qui a voulu tuer son frère' (65, 144). Totally unprepared for Rosalie's outburst, Pierre begins to envy those 'hommes que la mort emporterait dans quelques heures, peut-être' (144). This is an opportunity that does not take long to materialize. In the impending clash between the Canadian forces and the Métis at Batoche, he distinguishes himself in the defence of the village. Following Pierre's heroic retrieval of the Métis flag from the church's steeple, Riel himself entrusts the older of the La Ronde brothers with the safeguard of their people's national emblem (191). But after Pierre saves the flag two more times, he perishes in a battle with the Canadians, his 'yeux fixés sur ce drapeau qu'il avait trois fois sauvé' (234). Jean has a more pleasant fate. He is gravely wounded as he helps his brother fetch the flag, a misfortune that leads to his being nursed by his not-so-secret admirer Rosalie. Meanwhile, his romantic feelings for Elsie have undergone a dramatic transformation. As the narrator analyses Jean's emotions during the younger La Ronde's convalescence, 'maintenant, une honte, une confusion si inexprimables d'avoir joué un tel jeu de dupe l'envahissaient que le seul souvenir de miss Clamorgan lui devient subitement odieux.' Jean's thoughts are now devoted solely to Rosalie, the 'brave et jolie fille de Bouais-Brûlé' and 'Travailleuse numéro un' who loves him unconditionally (212). Before the end of the novel, to highlight the continuity of Riel's people, the couple produces a child of its own (250).

As should be evident from the above description, Riel stands very much on the periphery of the events depicted in *La tempête sur le fleuve*. Still, his portrait is a unique one. Poirier's novel is narrated from the perspective of Vicomte Henri de Vallonges – the author sometimes gives Vallonges's first name as Henry, which is the spelling used in the original edition of the novel – a French adventurer who searches for 'expériences d'élevage' in the 'territoires presque sauvages du nord-ouest' (13, 18, 47; *Arpents* 7). Vallonges, one of whose ancestors was killed by a 'balle anglaise' during Wolfe's capture of Quebec in 1759, sees Riel as a major historical figure. For him, the Métis leader is a man 'd'une taille supérieure à la moyenne, avec un visage ouvert, dont une barbe noire accentuait encore la chaude pâleur' (12, 11). Unlike his people, who speak a 'langage archaïque' that reminds the visitor of the coarse speech of his own Norman compatriots, Riel expresses himself in 'le plus pur langage français' (13, 11). He is also one of the elect, an individual with a 'face tour à tour souffrante et illuminé comme celle d'un prophète' who has created around himself 'une atmosphère de loyauté en vérité presque naïve' (57).

Regardless of Riel's enlightenment, though, the most significant aspect about the Métis leader for Vallonges is that he and his people are definitely French. Thus, when Riel first meets the Frenchman, he introduces himself as the 'président du gouvernement provisoire de la pétite France de la Saskatchewan' (11). The narrator, too, identifies the North-West conflict as the repetition of the battle of the Plains of Abraham over a century later. As he affirms, March 26, 1885, is the 'date mémorable où un petit peuple de descendants de la vieille race française venait de reprendre, au fond du Canada, la lutte interrompue plus d'un siècle auparavant par la mort de Montcalm' (18). Similarly, the Métis flag that Pierre La Ronde retrieves is described as the 'drapeau fleurdelisé' and he as a hero 'dont le sang rougit les fleurs de lis' (227, 231). In fact, at Batoche the Métis are defending 'tout le passé français,' and what their confrontation with the Canadian government reveals is 'la vitalité de notre sang et la permanence de nos traditions' (230, 252). As a local old man tells Vallonges after the latter announces that a group of 'compatriotes' will soon arrive from France to help preserve the area for the Métis, 'M'sieu, le vicomte, dans ce pays-cite, on est de pauvres Français sauvages, mais on est de ben bons Français tout de même.' The two men then drink to 'l'avenir de la vieille et de la jeune France!' (342).

Notwithstanding the heartfelt expressions of solidarity between the French and the Métis, the French-speaking world would subsequently exhibit remarkably little interest in Riel and his people. Excepting Poirier, and the one-time Canadian resident Maurice Constantin-Weyer, French writers were never really captivated by the Métis leader. Even Quebec authors would soon cease to devote much attention to his plight, a development for which Adjutor Rivard may provide an explanation. In his introduction to the first edition of Poirier's novel, the Quebec linguist contends that a 'Canadien français' could never have written such a work:

> Écrit par l'un des nôtres, ce roman serait pris pour une thèse, on chercherait à y voir l'expression d'une opinion politique. La révolte des métis a trop profondément ému la population du Canada, le nom Riel a été mêlé à des luttes trop violentes, et le souvenir est encore trop vif, pour qu'un Canadien français puisse, sans ranimer certaines polémiques et des haines presque éteintes, pour cadre d'un roman les événements de 1885. (v–vi)

Another reason why Quebec writers were not likely to write about Riel, one infers, was not their emotional proximity to the subject but their spatial and cultural distance from him. As Rivard notes, contradicting Camille Roy's earlier statement about the affinities between Quebec and the North-West, Poirier's novel is 'rempli des choses du Canada; – je ne dis pas "des choses de chez nous," parce que "chez nous," c'est plutôt la province de Québec, qui se trouve à quelque trois mille kilomètres du nord-ouest' (v). Or, as he adds even less equivocally, although 'les Canadiens français se sont trop passionnés de la cause des métis,' the reality is that 'la scène ne se passe pas dans notre vieille province, nous ne sommes pas les acteurs du drame, et les mœurs décrites ne sont pas les nôtres' (vi). In other words, the early rhetoric aside, Quebeckers have come to the realization that Riel's cause belongs to another collectivity.

Indeed, within a few years of his hanging, Riel virtually disappears from the consciousness of both French- and English-speaking Canadians (Owram, 'Myth' 316–17), suggesting that neither group truly embraced him as its own. Significantly, when the Métis leader does emerge again in the mid-1940s, he does so, not in Quebec, which would soon begin to plot out its potential future as a separate nation, but in the predominantly English-speaking parts of the country, including the old Orange heartland of Ontario. The post–Second World War Riel, however, is radically different from the ethno-religious martyr of the end of the nineteenth century. Perhaps because most of the authors writing about him are anglophones as well as Protestants, they tend to emphasize, not the religious aspects of his struggle, but the racial, regional, and cultural ones. As Rudy Wiebe has the Métis bard Pierre Falcon state at the end of *The Scorched-Wood People*, an influential novel that will be examined in detail in a later chapter, 'There's no white country can hold a man with a vision like Riel ... Canada couldn't handle that, not Ontario, and not Quebec, they're just using him against the English. They all think he was cracked, mad' (351). The new Riel is taken outside not only the Catholic-Protestant prism but also the Quebec-Ontario one. Instead, he is embraced as an ancestor, an Aboriginal maverick who valiantly opposes both the Eastern-dominated vision of Canada and the homogenization of Western civilization. In Leslie Monkman's perceptive analysis, Riel becomes increasingly seen as 'the potential mediator between red and white cultures.' He is the go-between whose 'mystical visions led him to dream of a peaceable kingdom in the west and himself as a prophet of the new world' (120).

4

The Go-Between
Riel As a Cultural Mediator

He was the leader of the people,
And the father of our west;
He led the battles of the settlers,
When their voices were suppressed.
Martin Heath (1952)

The theme of Riel as a mediator among different religious, racial, ethnic, and regional groups is a relatively recent one. As we have seen in the previous two chapters, whether English- or French-speaking, most early writers on the North-West conflicts do not display much empathy with the First Nations. Whatever identification they have with the country, it seldom seems to include its first inhabitants. Consequently, they could not possibly envisage the need to be reconciled with peoples they are convinced are not only doomed but have already finished 'de mourir' (Roquebrune, *D'un océan* 9). This is a situation that does not change until well into the twentieth century, especially after the Second World War. In the aftermath of the cataclysmic events in Europe, English-speaking writers in particular appear to undergo a radical geo-cultural transformation, shifting their collective allegiance from the Old World to the New. Through what Laura Murray, in a different context, terms 'the aesthetic of dispossession' (212), they ever more forcefully begin to portray the First Nations, not as an impediment to their possession of the land, but as an integral part of it, as 'a new set of ancestors' (Kroetsch, 'On Being' 76; *Lovely* 23). In Robert Kroetsch's words, the North-West Rebellion is no longer an 'uprising' but 'a necessary revolution of the perceiving self' by which Riel and Dumont 'showed us that we are a new people in a new landscape.' Indeed, for the Alberta novelist, the two Métis leaders have become nothing less than 'the poets of place, telling us what to see' ('Canada' 34).

In *The Flying Years* (1942), a panoramic novel about Western Canada that deals briefly with the pervasive 'panic' felt by white settlers in the Calgary area during the 1885 crisis, the Scots/Canadian writer Frederick Niven has a Cree chief state that the Canadian landscape will eventually convert all its occupants into indigenous dwellers. In Buffalo Calf's words, 'this is Indian country and it turns even white men to Indians in time' (171, 123).[1] Most Euro-Canadian writers, though, have been far less confident that residency alone will be enough to metamorphose them into full citizens. Instead, they suspect that some sort of spiritual affiliation with the First Nations is also required, that they will only be able to find themselves 'by finding the Indian' (Livesay, 'Native People' 22). As the poet John Newlove asserts, the country is 'crammed / with the ghosts of indians' and 'they are all ready / to be found, the legends / and the people' (106–7). Interestingly, this nativist genealogical embrace tends not to be effected directly, but through that foremost of European-Aboriginal hybrids, Riel, who had long anticipated the task.

In his writings, Riel often depicts himself and his people as the natural mediators between their two ancestral groups. The Métis leader suggests that the New Nation was created precisely to exercise such a function, stating as early as 1870 that 'le peuple de la Rivière Rouge a été formé à même ces deux grandes divisions pour leur servir d'intermédiaire' (1: 92). Or, as he notes over a decade later, it is the better educated 'Halfbreeds who have always up to themselves plaid the most conciliatory role between their white parents and their indian relatives' (2: 374). Needless to say, Riel's vision of the Métis as a human bridge between the First Nations and the European settlers is not without complications, particularly from the former's perspective. For the one-time divinity student, the standards to which a people should aspire and by which it ought to be judged are invariably European. This is quite apparent in his ethno-cultural hierarchy. As Riel writes, it is by 'their constant communication with the whites [that] the Half-breeds are getting every day more civilized' (2: 272). In turn, the reason the 'crees are the most civilized indians of the Canadian Northwest,' and superior to the Blackfoot or the Bloods, is that 'they have been for a good many years in constant communications with the halfbreeds' (2: 240). The fact the Métis are not yet as sophisticated as the Europeans, of course, does not preclude them from being destined to take possession of the North-West and, in the process, absorb their two parental groups.

In other words, Riel's combination of Eurocentrism and Métis nationalism condemns the First Nations to 'disparaître sans secousse et degré
par degré' not only biologically, like the Europeans, but also culturally,
for the new confederation of Métis nations will be alien to them in both
language and religion (2: 409).

The first significant aesthetic representation of Riel as a cultural
mediator, Roquebrune's *D'un océan à l'autre*, is rather critical, decrying
the adverse impact of biocultural *métissage* on the First Nations. As I
discussed in chapter 2, the 1924 historical novel is an unusual work.
Unlike the vast majority of Quebec texts on the subject, it is overtly pan-
Canadianist in its sympathies, being in fact a paean to the construction
of the Canadian Pacific Railway, the historic engineering project that
another Quebec writer calls the culmination of 'le rêve de nos ancêtres
français qui ont traversé l'océan pour trouver un passage vers Cathay'
(Roux 92). Similarly, it also favours the First Nations over the Métis.
The ethnologist narrator Augustin Ménard freely admits that he is
professionally interested only in the 'vrais Indiens,' not the Métis, who
have 'dégénéré jusqu'à avoir du sang français ou anglais dans leurs
veines' (18). As he declares, he has no intention of even visiting the
Métis during his field trip to the North-West, since they are for him a
people 'sans intérêt ... qui n'offrent au savant aucun sujet d'étude
sérieuse' (67). Ménard's antipathy toward Riel's people, like Roquebrune's, reveals simultaneously a fear of miscegenation and a desire to
prove to Europeans that Canadians are ethnically pure, that 'il n'y a
jamais eu d'unions entre les Canadiens et les sauvagesses' – or, at most,
'une demi-douzaine' (21). But it also reflects his conviction that the
cultural and religious assimilation of the First Nations is detrimental to
them, since it supposedly destroys their spiritual values without incul-
cating into them new ones. To quote Ménard, whose prospective study
of the mores and customs of the First Nations of North America is a
'monument considérable d'érudition et d'observation,' he is a 'bon
catholique' who believes the missionaries were right to 'convertir autrefois ces sauvages' (161, 17). Yet, based on his scientific research, he
cannot help but feel that the converted 'Indiens ... n'ont plus aucun
caractère,' having 'perdu leur antique cruauté et leurs mœurs pitto-
resques' without becoming 'civilisés en aucune manière' (16–17).

Another negative aspect of Aboriginal-Caucasian miscegenation
stressed in *D'un océan à l'autre* is the propensity of the products of those
unions, the Métis, to embrace the ways of their European ancestors.
Certainly the harshest accusations that the Cree chief L'Ours[2] levels at

Riel and his people is that they are always betraying their Aboriginal forebears. As L'Ours berates a Métis guide before shooting him to death, 'Quant à toi, métis, traître qui s'attache aux pas des étrangers, tu seras puni comme le seront tous ceux de ta race qui préfèrent la lâcheté à la liberté de nos ancêtres' (93).[3] The same ethno-cultural antagonism is evident in his exchanges with Riel, including an animated one in front of Ménard. During a clandestine visit to Quebec City, likely precipitated by his being pursued by the law for 'divers crimes,' L'Ours sells the ethnologist his family's coat of arms, which has been tattooed on a piece of 'peau humaine' (42). Later, in the North-West, as the two men examine 'le double emblème du Soleil et de l'Ours,' Riel gazes at it with 'une espèce de terreur.' Noticing Riel's reaction, L'Ours turns to the Métis leader and scornfully tells him that he has sold the amulet to Ménard because the Quebecker 'aime les dieux de notre race que tu dédaignes, toi qui leur préfères des dieux étrangers' (114).

The conflict between L'Ours and Riel is less linguistic or political than spiritual. L'Ours, described in the text by Bishop Vital Grandin as an 'ennemi de notre religion' who 'déteste les missionaires' (97), is positive that only through the intercession of New World deities will the First Nations and the Métis be able to arrest the march of European civilization across the North-West. As he asserts, 'C'est par le Soleil que nous vaincrons ... Et toi, Riel, si tu veux remporter la victoire sur les étrangers, il faut que le Soleil soit avec toi. C'est le plus puissant des dieux' (115). But Riel is never truly able to share his Cree ally's cosmology. While he ponders how to 'concilier ces antiques croyances avec la foi catholique,' it is apparent that he is bound to fail, since he still believes 'en Dieu et à tout ce que les Pères m'ont enseigné' (116). Regardless of the Catholic Church's reservations about his religious orthodoxy, Riel is incapable of transcending his Christianity. Thus, after L'Ours tells him that as 'un Indien ... tu dois croire au Soleil' and that the 'évêque et les robes noires te trompent,' an indignant Riel calls the Cree chief a liar and forbids him to ever speak like that again about the Catholic clergy. Even more significantly, Riel then abruptly ends the debate by dismissing L'Ours as 'un païen' (116), suggesting that he has been so alienated from the faith of his Aboriginal ancestors that he does not even consider it a genuine religion. Later, when Archbishop Taché refuses to bless him on the eve of the Batoche campaign, Riel agrees with L'Ours to chase 'les étrangers de notre pays.' But when the Cree leader questions if 'tu chasseras aussi les Pères,' Riel conveniently gallops away before providing an answer (184–5).

Riel betrays no such ambivalence about his Aboriginal heritage in his next representation as a cultural mediator, John Coulter's *Riel* (1950), a play with a largely inter-Christian focus. The work usually credited with having initiated the 'Riel industry' (Coulter, *In My Day* 238, 268; Moore, *Reinventing Myself* 174), Coulter's epic drama had an inauspicious beginning. It opened on February 17, 1950, at Toronto's Royal Ontario Museum Theatre, a basement lecture hall with almost no stage. Although the multi-character chronicle was produced diligently by Dora Mavor Moore's New Play Society, which touted it as 'the first important drama our country has produced out of its own history' (New Play Society n.pag.), the pioneering troupe possessed limited resources. Consequently, it was forced to entrust the command of the piece to a first-time director, a young actor and writer named Don Harron, who would not be 'persuaded ... to direct a play again' for almost another fifty years (M. Harron 116). The cast, which comprised such future luminaries of the Canadian stage as Harron, Robert Christie, and Moore's son and helpmate Mavor, was also largely inexperienced. In addition, for such a multicultural enterprise, it was predominantly of Anglo-Celtic stock. As Mavor Moore notes, 'our francophones were not francophone, our Natives were not native' (*Reinventing Myself* 177).

Coulter's *Riel* is an ambitious project. In the memoir he published just before his death, the playwright states that he decided to write about Riel because in the story of an individual who comes to believe God has anointed him the protector of his marginalized people, 'I saw the shape of a Canadian myth.' However, his play is not merely the author's way of dramatizing an obscure chapter of Canadian history but also of incorporating himself into that history, his means of self-Canadianization (Coulter, *In My Day* 261; Garay 283, 309). Born in Belfast in 1888, Coulter immigrated to Canada in 1936 upon marrying the Canadian journalist Olive Clare Primrose. He was already an established author in England and Ireland, having written several radio plays and worked as 'managing editor' of John Middleton Murry's influential journal *The New Adelphi* (Coulter, *In My Day* 79). So, soon after settling in Toronto, he 'threw himself into the Canadian cultural scene,' becoming a zealous advocate of the idea of a national theatre (Moore, *Reinventing Myself* 167). Still, as a writer who transplanted himself to a new country at the relatively mature age of forty-eight, he found his efforts to contribute to its emerging theatre constantly foiled by his inability to capture the idiosyncracies of the local language. As Coulter acknowledges, 'the dialogue I wrote on one day, thinking it truly imagined in Canadian speech of current idiom, invariably seemed to me next day to be concocted and false.' In order to circumvent the problem, he resolved to 'go back in time and write about some Canadian who had been pivotal in a dangerous revolutionary crisis and turning-point in Canadian history,' a search that led him to Riel (*In My Day* 260).

Despite Coulter's valiant effort to help make Canadian theatre 'specifically Canadian,' the most striking aspect of *Riel* is what has been called its 'Irish accent' (Coulter, 'Canadian Theatre' 505; Cohen 4; C. Johnson 187). This Hibernian inflection is evident both in the play's unrelenting emphasis on Catholic-Protestant sectarianism and in the prominence it gives to the Fenian William O'Donoghue, an Irish-born mathematics teacher at Saint Boniface College who actively promoted the annexation of Red River to the United States (Stanley, *Birth* 164–6). *Riel* is divided in two parts, the first dealing with the events of 1869–70 and the second with those of 1885. The first section opens at Riel's home. The young Métis has gone riding on the prairie, as his mother says he is wont 'when he must decide something,' and several armed supporters impatiently await his return. While they do, an unidentified Priest appeals to O'Donoghue, as 'one of the few men of education here,' to attempt to curb his leader's rhetoric and 'restrain this madness.' But the Fenian promptly informs the cleric that he is not the ideal person to control Riel or any other would-be revolutionary, since 'I'm the maddest of the mad myself – if any of us *are* mad!' Indeed, O'Donoghue elaborates, his only disagreement with Riel is that the latter's 'madness isn't mad enough. He's for holding the North-West but under protection of the British flag. I'm for holding it under the protection of our own flag, our own arms' (1–2).

The conflict between Riel and O'Donoghue, which dominates the Red River portion of the play, is precipitated less by any event in the Settlement's history than by the two men's disparate perceptions of Great Britain. Shaped by his national history, O'Donoghue is incapable of trusting his homeland's oppressors. As he tells the Priest why the Canadian surveyors must be stopped, 'If we tolerate them Canadians will swarm in after them in thousands. They'll grab both us and ours. They'll lay us under tribute. Tax us! Bleed us white! ... We won't let Canada do to us what England did to Ireland ...' Riel, in contrast, has a far less visceral view of the Empire and superpowers in general. Unlike O'Donoghue, he does not believe that what 'any big over-blown nation in history does to a small neighbour [is] – grab it! Gobble it up!' (3).

Quite the opposite, the reason he is so confident about Red River's ability to withstand any attacks by its rapacious neighbours to the east and south is that it has the political and military support of Great Britain, which he regards, not as a predator on his land and people, but as their protector (26).

Considering the ideological chasm between Riel and O'Donoghue, it is not surprising that they would have a major confrontation, which they do over the flying of the Union Jack. After the Métis capture Fort Garry from the Hudson's Bay Company, O'Donoghue decides to mark the occasion by pulling down the British 'rag' and replacing it with 'our own flag – fleur-de-lis and shamrock' (23). The moment Riel learns of the Fenian's unauthorized action, he becomes enraged over the 'non-sense' for which 'I should have you put in irons.' Even after O'Donoghue attempts to justify himself by saying that he raised the green-and-white banner to mark 'our independence and integrity as a people,' Riel does not relent in his criticism (24, 25). While agreeing that the people of Red River are not British, he contends not only that they are British subjects but '*must* be.' As Riel states, echoing the colonial dependency of Macdonald's famous farewell to the people of Canada, 'A British subject I was born – a British subject, I will die' ('Sir John Macdonald's Last Address' 777),

> Do you know why? So three million British will have the honour of protecting us when we cannot protect ourselves.
> ...
> To protect us against whoever would march in to grab and conquer even if the would-be grabber is Canada – or the U.S.A. That is why we call England – Mother Country. (25–6)

O'Donoghue remains unconvinced, and when he persists that it is for the Métis Council and not Riel to decide which flag should fly over Fort Garry, the latter replies unequivocally, 'It is decided. I am the Council' (26). Then, as if to underscore his authority, Riel orders that the green-and-white flag be lowered and the Union Jack raised in its place and that everyone join him in shouting, 'God save the Queen' (27).

With O'Donoghue finally silenced, if not quite neutralized, Riel seems destined to emerge victorious in his quest to lead the people of Red River. That is certainly the impression created when even Macdonald characterizes him as an 'extraordinary person ... willing to enter Con-federation with us and become a province of Canada – on Riel's terms, of course' (43). But the Métis leader's prospects suffer a fatal setback as a consequence of another aspect of the Catholic-Protestant warfare, his treatment of Tom Scott. Described in the stage directions as a '*surly, aggressive, fanatical-looking man*,' Coulter's Scott is a demonic figure. In the first scene in which he appears, he calls a group of Métis 'a pack o' mongrel Papishes' and challenges all of them to fight (11–12). Later, when he meets Riel, who is surrounded by guards, he promptly assaults his adversary. But even more puzzling than the Orangeman's behaviour is Riel's response to the man his mother calls 'the devil, the devil' (15). After Scott refuses 'to swear an oath of full loyalty,' Riel has the Ontarian tried and executed for the apparent crime of being 'a windbag' (34; O Broin 137). Another possibility is that Scott is killed, not for political, but religious reasons. As Riel confides to the Priest, 'He is evil. Evil. I tell you ... Satan is in him. He *is* Satan. He is Anti-Christ.' Or, as the Priest retorts, more ominously, 'Perhaps having you execute him is Satan's means to wreck your – mission' (35).

Although Riel does not recognize it immediately, or perhaps ever, his role in the execution of Scott will have grave repercussions for his political career. Responding to public opinion, particularly in his home province of Ontario, Macdonald sends a military expedition under Colonel Garnet Wolseley 'to keep order' at Red River until a new lieutenant-governor replaces the Métis provisional government. A surprisingly naïve Riel prepares to welcome the soldiers, even organizing a 'reception' in their honour (46, 50). But when he learns that Wolseley's troops have not come to maintain the peace but to avenge Scott's death, he realizes that he has been outmanoeuvred by his foes. Feeling a tremendous sense of betrayal, the 'noble patriot' for the first time arms himself and vows not to be taken by the enemy. After defending the British Empire so fervently to O'Donoghue, Riel concedes that he was wrong, declaring: 'I am not now a – loyal subject of Her Majesty' (54, 59). Yet, even in the midst of his greatest public humiliation, he accepts Taché's advice that the best way he can serve his people is by leaving the country and waiting for 'God's time' in exile (60).

Fifteen years later, now married and with two children, Riel is still in exile when he hears of his people's continuing troubles in the Canadian North-West and of their desire to have him 'lead them' again (68). Despite his wife's opposition to his leaving their Montana home, Riel decides to heed his people's call for help. Or, more precisely, he is commanded to do so. As he informs Marguerite, 'God has told me. I have asked God. I have waited fifteen years and now it is God's time. I am to go' (69). But Riel's mission is short-lived. Almost as soon as he incites the Métis and their Aboriginal allies to 'take up arms' against the Canadian forces, he surrenders to those same forces (71). Most of the second part of Coulter's play is devoted, not to the confrontation at Batoche, but to the battle's aftermath and Riel's trial, which he believes will provide him with a forum to disseminate 'the just demands and grievances of my people' (82). It is from his testimony to the victorious General Frederick Middleton that one learns that Riel's order for his supporters to attack and disarm the Canadian volunteers was merely a political ploy, an attempt to force 'those politicians there in Ottawa at last ... to listen and deal honourably with us' (84). Likewise, it is then that Riel explains that he has come to the Saskatchewan Valley as a mediator committed to defend the rights of all local inhabitants, since 'Métis and whites, all have grievances, foul, festering, suppurating sores of grievances that *smell*, and poison the body of society!' (85). Paradoxically, the collectivity Riel succeeds in unifying is not the Métis people but the group that has just defeated them, the Canadians. In Macdonald's words, 'this wretch Riel is actually forcing us to take responsibility and govern Canada. How odd! The outlaw once more shapes the law. Henceforth, Louis Riel's name is scribbled across a chapter of our Constitutional Law!' (130–1). Or, as the prime minister adds, his antagonist will go 'down to history as ... one of the mortal instruments that shaped our destiny!' – a sentiment somewhat quali-fied by the fact that he has just announced Riel's execution with the comment 'he's a gone coon' (131).

There are several interesting elements in Coulter's *Riel*, not the least of which is the play's dramatization of the problematic nature of the Métis leader's place in Canadian history. Mavor Moore has commended the playwright for portraying 'Riel with Jovian impartiality' (*Reinventing Myself* 177), but this is not quite so. As one can see from the characteri-zation of the Riel-O'Donoghue relationship and the demonization of Scott, *Riel* is transparently biased in favour of its eponymous hero. It is true that Coulter does not completely ignore Riel's intolerance, his propensity to brand anyone who does not support him a 'traitor' and to threaten to strike his opponents 'down – without warning or mercy' (19). That being said, there is no avoiding the author's determination to accentuate his protagonist's positive qualities, even at the price of re-versing the historical record. In the flag incident, for instance, the historical Riel did not oppose O'Donoghue but joined him in replacing the Union Jack with the Métis standard (Stanley, *Louis Riel* 77). Similarly, as we have seen, both his writings and his political aims suggest that he was not overly enthusiastic about joining Confederation. Yet the overall picture Coulter paints of Riel is that of a patriotic and peaceable leader, a pious individual who embraces violence only after every other option has failed. Particularly when juxtaposed to the Fenian O'Donoghue and the Orangeman Scott, with their distinct but equally extreme visions of the world, Riel emerges as the personification of common sense and moderation, the born conciliator who would unify even traditional enemies.

Perhaps reflecting Coulter's awareness of being a Protestant writing about a Catholic – 'the covert resentment of my intrusion' on another religion (*In My Day* 265) – the playwright is rather partisan toward the Catholic Church. The most blatant effect of this partiality is his conflation of the Church's asymmetrical responses to the two North-West conflicts. The Catholic clergy played an ambiguous role in 1885, both championing Riel's cause and fearing his theological unorthodoxy, his 'indigenized' or 'sauvage' Catholicism (Huel 15; Morisset, 'Louis Riel' 62). That, however, was not the case during 1869–70, when the Church strongly supported the young leader to the point of forming his only 'true constituency' (Ens 116). Still, Coulter portrays the Red River clergy as a pacifying force, spiritual advisors who constantly strive to persuade Riel to moderate his rhetoric and to recognize that the forcible seizure of the colony's government is bound to have 'the most serious consequences' (2). Tellingly, in a play with such a profusion of characters, Coulter does not include Father Noël Ritchot, the politically engaged Saint Norbert pastor whom the young Riel considered his spiritual guide, a 'nouvel Aaron' (2: 81; Siggins 91–2). As well, when Coulter does address any controversial aspect of the Catholic clergy's involvement in the North-West crises, he fails to pursue it in any detail. Thus, he ascribes Riel's decision to travel to Saskatchewan mainly to a letter he receives from Father Alexis André, telling the Métis leader that he is 'the most popular man with all the people here' and that there 'will be great disappointment if you do not come.' But two short scenes later, without depicting any clash between Riel and the clergy, the playwright has a Priest urging the Métis leader to lay down his arms and abandon his 'blind folly' (68, 73). Indeed, one cannot help but deduce that Coulter's conscious or unconscious fear of being perceived as anti-Catholic contributes immeasurably to his play's most debilitating flaw, its lack of drama.

Coulter's *Riel* has elicited two dominant responses. For some critics, such as Moore at the time of the original production, it is 'the most important Canadian play to date' (quoted in M. Harron 113). Herbert Whittaker, too, deems it a major theatrical and political 'achievement ...', especially impressive to Canadians who have seen their history only through clouds of dust' (22). Other critics, though, find Coulter's work excessively static, lacking in point of view. As Vincent Tovell charges, 'The play presents many opinions about Riel and a good deal of evidence concerning him; it records him fully; but it does not interpret him' (273–4). Or, as Doris Mosdell contends, *Riel* is not a historical tragedy but a pageant, 'a series of disconnected tableaux; no dramatic theme emerges, no fusing, driving conception behind the collection of vignettes and narrative bridges' (15). Even Moore, who from the beginning had some reservations about the text for ignoring the 'private' Riel, ultimately judges it theatrically wanting (Coulter, Letter). The polymath actor, writer, and cultural bureaucrat states that he agreed to write a libretto for an opera about the Métis leader because he felt that Coulter's play 'lacked the incandescence to serve as a metaphor for Canada.' But he somewhat self-servingly attributes this failure not so much to the playwright as to his work's genre, since presumably 'only an operatic treatment could do justice to the soaring theme' (*Reinventing Myself* 312).

Chris Johnson writes that Coulter's 'deficiencies in characterization' are partly explained by the fact that he was 'addressing an audience ... not particularly familiar with the story he was telling' and so had 'to devote a good deal of time to acquainting his audience with the sequence of historical events' (186). Without discounting the insight in this observation, I would suggest that another possibility is that the author's equivocation about Riel reflects both his profound ambivalence about his subject and his work's conflicting aims, the celebration of Canadian history through someone who is either a victim of Canadian expansionism or an enemy of Canada. In a revealing letter to Dora Mavor Moore in 1949, attempting to persuade her to stage some of his plays, Coulter describes *Riel* as 'a theatre piece on the public life' of the Métis leader. Yet, even as he strives to rectify the 'intolerable situation' of being a playwright in Canada and not being able to contribute to the nation's developing theatre, he acknowledges that 'Riel's private life may be more interesting.' He even admits that he is 'already busy trying to make a simplified version, with a good deal of Riel's private complexities interfused' (Letter 1–2). Coulter's apparent discomfort about the Métis leader's public life is twofold. First, while he considers

Riel's story an archetypal Canadian one, he believes 'that but for the accident of history, which found him where he was, when he was, he should have lived and died and never again be heard of, an irascible, discontented, religious and political fanatic' (*In My Day* 261). In the words of another writer, Riel is not an intrinsically dramatic or significant figure; he does not move history, but is 'moved into it' (Davey, 'Riel' 51). More significant, Coulter seems to realize that his protagonist is at war with the country whose past the author wishes to celebrate. If there is a predatory power in Coulter's play, it is obviously Canada, and for that reason Riel has to oppose it. In short, Riel is a problematic Canadian icon, a negative hero who, at best, becomes a patriot by opposing Canada and forcing it to define itself (Morisset, 'Cents ans'; D. Morton, 'Reflections' 49).

Curiously, Coulter tends to downplay Riel's Canadian patriotism in the two other plays he devotes to the Métis leader. Several years after the landmark production of *Riel*, the author received a Canada Council grant to write two more dramatic works about 'two other Canadian subjects of historical and theatrical importance,' thus forming a trilogy. Since he found no other figures 'with anything like the dramatic potential of ... my half-mythical, rebel half-breed, my John Brown of the North,' he decided instead to adapt them from his earlier work (*In My Day* 271). The first of these plays, *The Crime of Louis Riel* (1966), appears to be the 'simplified version' of *Riel* that Coulter mentions in his letter to Dora Mavor Moore, yet it has a distinctly international flavour. As Coulter writes in the preface, the piece 'is about the degree to which I see the Metis leader and the rebellions which he led as precursors of later and present uprisings all over the world, particularly the so-called Third World' (Letter 2; *Crime*, n.pag.). The second play, *The Trial of Louis Riel* (1967), which has been called 'the first true documentary in Canadian theatre' (Filewod 12), is a strategically edited version of the Regina judicial transcripts. Staged annually since 1967 in the Saskatchewan capital, whose Chamber of Commerce commissioned it 'as a tourist attraction' (Coulter, *In My Day* 271), the work focuses primarily on Riel's mental state toward the end of his life.

In contrast to Coulter's later plays, there is little question about either Riel's Canadianness or his place in history in Martin Heath's 'Louis Riel' (1952). Published in the popular Communist magazine *New Frontiers*, the song constitutes the first unadulterated apotheosis of the subject as a pan-Canadian hero. To quote its opening stanza:

In our early western story
Riel fought to have men free,
Shared his heart with white and Metis,
In the cause of democracy.
His the voice of the Red River,
His the spirit of our folk,
When they banded all together
To defeat a tyrant's yoke. (9)

Heath does not merely exalt Riel, who has won 'a people's fame,' but also indicts his opponents. As the poet writes in a chorus that is repeated three times, those individuals who hanged the Métis leader for 'the crime / ... of standing up for justice' today are 'forgotten men, / But to those who fight for freedom, / Louis Riel lives again' (9).

The matter of Riel's status as a Canadian hero, though, is central to Jean-Louis Roux's *Bois-Brûlés* (1968). Written by a distinguished actor and theatre director – as well as a political figure whose term as lieutenant-governor of Quebec ended prematurely following his admission of having worn a swastika during his university years (Chartrand 17) – it was originally staged by Montreal's Théâtre du Nouveau Monde. *Bois-Brûlés*, which is subtitled 'reportage épique,' bears numerous similarities to Coulter's *Riel*. Like the earlier play, it is divided in two parts, the first exploring the troubles at Red River and the second those at Batoche. It also has a multitude of characters and incidents, as befits a play that is not just about Riel but the whole Métis nation. As Roux writes in the foreword, the reason he gives his work a collective title is to 'indiquer que si la figure centrale en est Riel, ses compatriotes, son peuple, "son sang" n'en constituent pas moins un des personnages principaux. Je ne veux pas que raconter l'histoire d'un homme, mais également chanter la saga de la nation métis [*sic*]' (10).

There are also major differences between *Bois-Brûlés* and *Riel*. The most obvious of these is the fact Roux has his play partly narrated by Pierre Falcon, a strategy Rudy Wiebe would emulate a decade later in *The Scorched-Wood People*. Falcon, who lived from 1793 to 1876, is not reported to have played any significant role at Red River and was dead long before the crisis on the South Saskatchewan erupted (Complin 51–2). His inclusion in a work about the two conflicts is thus necessarily anachronistic. Yet Roux's 'exercise of the dramatist's licence' is not without merit, for it enables him to contextualize his play (C. Johnson

188). It is through the revered Métis bard, the first poet to sing 'la gloire de tous les Bois-Brûlés' (Falcon, 'Bataille' 7), that Roux is able to inform his audience about the then largely unknown Plainsmen and their unique way of life. As the playwright has Falcon explain, the Métis are a nation whose love of 'la chasse aux buffles' and of 'la liberté de la vaste plaine,' as opposed to agriculture and other sedentary pursuits, makes them 'le peuple le plus heureux de la terre' (19). Or at least it did until recently. In the minstrel's somewhat romantic words, both internal and external forces are now conspiring against his people:

> ... petit à petit, nous avons appris les charmes de la civilisation blanche: l'appât au gain, l'envie, le sense jaloux de la propriété. Les Blancs nous ont appris que nous étions leurs inférieurs. Ils nous ont appris que la liberté connaissait des frontières. Et depuis, nous ne sommes plus le peuple le plus heureux de la terre. Nous ne sommes même plus maîtres de notre destin. (21)

Falcon vividly conveys the calamitous changes in his people's fortunes, their loss of control over their collective fate, by having the Hudson's Bay Company, England, Canada, and the United States haggling over the Métis as if they were cattle: 'Qui dit mieux? Qui dit pire? Une fois; deux fois, trois fois ... Vendus!' (21).

Another notable difference between *Bois-Brûlés* and *Riel* is in their asymmetric portraits of Scott. Roux has been praised for his 'remarkable fairness to the English-speaking side' (C. Johnson 189), but this definitely does not include the controversial Ontarian. Like most other post-Second World War writers on Riel, Coulter deals with the always sensitive Scott episode by demonizing the Irish-born settler as some sort of Orange devil. Roux goes further. Not content to depict Scott as evil, he also makes him a cold-blooded murderer. After the Métis takeover of Fort Garry, several members of the Canadian party congregate at John Christian Schultz's store to plot strategy against the 'gouvernement rebelle' (56). As they do, a mentally handicapped Métis youth named Norbert Parisien wanders toward the compound, and Scott shoots him to death, on the pretext that Parisien is a spy. The Orangeman, who loudly proclaims, 'Jamais un sang-mêlé oserait toucher à un cheuveu d'un Anglais,' is soon arrested, and promptly punches Riel in the face (66). A Métis soldier responds to Scott's insolence by threatening to kill him, but his leader intervenes and orders that even such a brigand 'doit être jugé légalement' (67). However, Riel's action is not as magnanimous as it seems, for before long he too begins calling for Scott's head, but not for the reasons one might expect. While deliberately rewriting history to transform Scott into a killer, Roux characterizes Riel in a way that suggests the Métis leader's motivation for having Scott executed is only tangentially connected to his foe. Coulter's Riel candidly states that the Orangeman must die because 'it is necessary to have acceptance here of our authority' (36). Roux's makes a similar admission, declaring: 'Il faut un exemple; sinon plus personne n'aura de respect pour moi' (71). But Riel then traces his need for retribution to another event, an earlier trauma whose scars clearly have not yet healed. As he tells his mother,

> Quand j'étais à Montréal, je suis tombé amoureux d'une jeune fille. J'ai voulu l'épouser; mais, lorsque ses parents ont appris que j'avais du sang indien, dans les veines, ils ont refusé leur consentement. Un Métis! Un sale Métis! Ce n'était pas assez bon pour leur fille à peau blanche. Je me suis juré qu'un jour, je forcerais le respect des Canadiens pour les Métis. Les sales Métis! Les sales Métis, tout le monde apprendra à les respecter: Thomas Scott, le premier. (72)

That is, Riel is determined to ensure that Scott will die, not because the Orangeman is a 'meurtrier sanguinaire' (67), but in order to show the world the Métis people will no longer acquiesce silently to their oppression. Or, to phrase it differently, regardless of his guilt, Scott is a scapegoat for both Anglo-Protestant and Franco-Catholic chauvinism, notably what Riel considers his racially motivated rejection as a prospective son-in-law by Marie-Julie Guernon's parents.

Yet another unique aspect of *Bois-Brûlés* is its treatment of the Catholic Church. Roux's Riel is not nearly as pious as Coulter's, who, before he even appears on stage, is reported to be having one of his 'solitary pow-wows with the Almighty' (1). By contrast, the Quebec playwright makes his protagonist a far more political figure, first introducing him as the leader of the group of Métis that stops the Canadian surveyors (31). Besides, when the Church at last makes its presence felt, it does not do so very favourably. As Bishop Taché leaves his residence after returning from an apostolic visit to Rome that had kept him away from Red River during the seizure of Fort Garry, he is informed by an armed Métis posse that 'vous êtes confiné à l'intérieur de votre Palais. Ordre du Président' (75). With some effort, the prelate manages to secure an audience with his one-time protégé, but the meeting is unsuccessful.

While Taché reprimands Riel for taking 'armes contre l'autorité établie' (77), the latter seems unimpressed. At first, Riel states that he is uncertain whether he is addressing a religious representative or a 'délégué' of the Canadian government. But then he goes further and tells the visitor unequivocally, 'Je ne veux pas vous traiter en ennemi, Monseigneur; je veux seulement établir clairement qu'il n'y a – ici – qu'un seul chef politique des Métis: c'est moi' (76, 80). Indeed, what the encounter between Taché and Riel encapsulates is the essentially political nature of the conflict between the young politician and the clergyman, the fact they are fighting less for the souls of the Métis than for their hearts and minds.

There are contradictions in Roux's characterization of the relationship between Riel and the Catholic Church. For instance, at the same time that the Métis leader keeps Taché's residence under 'garde,' one of Taché's own priests, Father Ritchot, is negotiating with Ottawa on behalf of the Red River government (82, 88). Yet what one cannot help but notice in *Bois-Brûlés* is that Riel and the clergy are engaged in a power struggle in which spiritual concerns play a rather inconsequential role. This political strife becomes especially pronounced in 1885. Almost from the moment Riel arrives in Batoche, Father André denounces the visitor as a negative influence whose 'présence ne peut qu'exciter la population, la pousser à commettre des actes de violence irréparables' (133). The French missionary's reasoning is that the legal-political conditions have changed in fundamental ways since 1869–70, for the Métis are no longer organizing a 'résistance contre une invasion étrangère' but are now 'bel et bien en territoire canadien.' Therefore, André duly informs Riel that, if he persists with his 'propos incendiaires,' 'le clergé de la Saskatchewan se verrait dans l'obligation de vous combattre' (133).

One of the ways in which André opposes Riel is by negotiating directly with Ottawa, a tactic that amounts to a repudiation of the Métis leader. André, who claims that his sole objective is 'de voir notre peuple tranquille et satisfait,' begins by informing Macdonald about Riel's activities and warning the prime minister that his government's general unresponsiveness to the Métis grievances is bound to make the returnee ever more popular with his people. Then, at Macdonald's instigation, he attempts to bribe Riel to return to Montana, where he could best serve his cause. But the latter refuses the 'fourbe,' declaring somewhat ambiguously that 'Louis Riel vaut plus de mille dollars par année!' (137). André once again contacts Ottawa, but, when he fails to persuade the prime minister to pay the 'cinq ou six milles dollars' he believes 'régleraient la question' (144), he denounces Riel as an apostate, a false Joshua. In André's fiery words to his parishioners, 'Vous êtes aveugles! Regardez-le! Regardez-le bien: c'est l'antéchrist; nul autre que l'antéchrist; l'antéchrist en personne!' (151).

In an effort to gain control of the situation, André threatens to excommunicate anyone who agrees to take arms against Canada, a warning that Riel dismisses derisively as evidence of clerical jealousy of his political influence, the fact 'Dieu m'a confié le salut de la nation Métis [sic].' Most of the Métis appear to agree with the former exile, and soon respond to his call to 'défendre nos droits par les armes – s'il le faut' (152, 157). Rejected by the people he has crossed half the world to serve, a people whose 'sang,' Dumont pointedly reminds him, he does not share (155), André watches helplessly as his flock prepares to face the Canadian forces. Certain this is a confrontation the Métis cannot win, he concludes that the wisest course is to 'écourter la bataille. Plus l'engagement sera rapide et décisif, moins il y aura de sang répandu' (168). To that end, he asks Charles Nolin to go to the Canadian camp and inform General Middleton that 'on est moins de cent cinquante' (175).

Whether André's decision to reveal the number of Métis fighters to the enemy constitutes treason, as members of the community's political and intellectual elite would charge decades later (Comité historique 427; Adams, Prison 30, 33), depends largely on how one judges the events of 1885. For Roux's Riel, the decision to arm the Métis is simply 'une démonstration. Rien d'autre qu'une démonstration' (149). André, however, perceives the strategy as a suicidal mission whose only possible outcome is not just the destruction of a people but also the abandonment of 'les chemins de la vérité' (169). Its morality aside, what the missionary's action at Batoche also underlines is the unequal relationship between the Catholic clergy and the Métis. This political disparity is seldom more manifest than near the end of the play. After Riel's trial, as the Métis leader awaits word of an Ottawa clemency that will not arrive, André visits him in his cell, and a reconciliation of sorts takes place. Fearing that his death is imminent, Riel makes overtures to André about returning to the Church but is unwilling to admit that he is guilty of any 'hérésies.' The priest, though, insists that Riel must abjure his 'erreurs,' in writing, and at last Riel assents, declaring solemnly: '"Je désire, de tout cœur, retourner dans le sein de notre Mère, la Sainte Eglise catholique et romaine, qui m'a vu naître et grandir ..."'

(194–5). Moreover – as in history, although administered by a different priest – Riel's recantation is not uttered directly by the penitent but is dictated to him by André.[4] That is, even the contents of the dying man's confession of faith are determined by the Catholic Church.

Bois-Brûlés is not without structural flaws. Like Coulter's Riel, it attempts to examine the whole of its protagonist's career, and inevitably fails. Since there are so many characters and incidents, they are often mere sketches (Dassylva 136). Even the Métis leader's behaviour at times seems psychologically unmotivated. For example, Riel is quite lucid throughout most of the first part, explaining that he must stop the Canadian surveyors because if the Métis allow Canada to take possession of their land without any conditions, this will be simply the first of many losses. As he asks, 'Nous déloger de nos terres? Pourquoi pas, ensuite, nous défendre de parler notre langue maternelle et d'exercer la religion de notre choix? Pourquoi pas nous obliger à changer notre façon de vivre?' (37). Later, he decides to keep Taché under house arrest not only because he believes there can be only one leader of the Métis but also because he suspects the bishop of duplicity, of being an agent for Ottawa, a suspicion that appears to be confirmed when Taché conspires with Macdonald to send him into exile. Yet, by the end of the segment, Riel suddenly begins to shout that he has no fear of his enemies, for he is under the protection not just of God but also of the 'comte de Chambord, de France' and of 'Don Carlos, d'Espagne' (112).

Again like Coulter's Riel, Roux's play also betrays a discernible authorial doubt about its central character, an uncertainty whether he is 'fou ou visionnaire' (Nutting 192). As shown earlier, the playwright depicts the Catholic Church as overtly antagonistic toward Riel. But the clergy's attitude becomes understandable if the Métis leader happens to be an apostate, which the text suggests he probably is. Thus, when Father André refuses to allow armed Métis to gather in 'assemblée' at Batoche, Riel breaks ranks not just with the missionary but with the Church itself, setting himself up as an alternative institution. In Riel's words to his community, 'les prêtres ne font pas la religion. Il [André] vous refuse les sacrements? Venez à moi! La vieille Eglise romaine vous rejette de son sein? Venez à moi! Je suis votre prophète; je suis le prophète du Nouveau Monde! Venez à moi!' Or, as he adds immediately after, 'Je serai le prêtre de votre religion' (150, 152). Similarly, Roux also seems equivocal about his protagonist's politics. The playwright begins with an openly pro-Riel stance, portraying Riel as a natural ruler acclaimed almost unanimously by his people as 'chef,' therefore minimizing the diversity of political views within the Métis community at Red River (38; Ens 121–3). Yet, gradually, indications appear in the text that Riel may not be the utterly positive figure the work first suggests. To begin with, he is devoid of irony to the point of hypocrisy. Only moments after condemning Scott to death for rather tenuous reasons, he says that the North-West will become a beacon for all 'les peuples opprimés du monde,' a place where 'on sait faire respecter la liberté' (73). Despite his frequent assertions about being motivated solely by the welfare of his people, he is also intolerant of any questioning of his authority, since he sees himself as 'mon peuple. Je parle pour mon peuple.' Perhaps most critically for a political leader who steers his nation into an armed confrontation with a mightier force, Riel may not be rational, having no expectations of defeating the enemy except through 'un miracle' (72, 177).

Nevertheless, one of Roux's achievements in *Bois-Brûlés* is that his play respects Riel's national specificity as a Métis. The playwright is not averse to emphasizing his protagonist's supposed desire to unify Canadians, such as when he drafts the unlikely message of welcome to the first lieutenant-governor of the new province of Manitoba, expressing the hope that 'Canadiens de toutes origines pourront y vivre paisiblement, dans un accord parfait et dans une union prospère' (103). Still, Roux's Riel remains unmistakably Other, an alterity that has not always been appreciated, especially in Quebec. As one critic protests, with his ambiguous portrait of the 'héros de la liberté et illuminé,' Roux fails to enable Quebec audiences to 'lire leur propre histoire à travers celle des Métis' (Greffard 108). Yet, judging by the story enacted in *Bois-Brûlés*, this seems to be less the playwright's failure than a fair recapitulation of a not so glorious historical reality. Even from a Quebec perspective, Riel is either a rebel against the Church or a victim of anti-Aboriginal racism, not just Anglo-Protestant racism but also Franco-Catholic. The Métis leader simply cannot be easily incorporated into the larger Canadian family, including Quebec, for his presence necessarily highlights negative aspects of its collective past.

If Dorothy Livesay ever had any question about Riel's Canadian patriotism, or about the possible conflict between Canadian and Métis nationalisms, she shows little awareness of it in 'Prophet of the New World: A Poem for Voices' (1972). In her influential essay 'The Documentary Poem: A Canadian Genre,' the Manitoba-born author writes that the Canadian long poem could be characterized as a writer's 'conscious attempt to create a dialectic between the objective facts and the subjective feelings of the poet.' She also states that the genre has a strong didactic component, aiming less to narrate a tale than to 'illustrate a precept' (267, 269). The opening stanzas of 'Prophet,' sung by a chorus, leave little doubt as to the 'precept' the author wishes to exemplify:

> Who is he that comes, treading on hope
> Indian footed? Remembering how
> when the lean rock pulls winter on its face
> natives of the plains know time is near
> to hunt the buffalo for hides, for meat
> and in thin bush to trap the beaver skin?
>
> Who is he with Ireland in his name
> and Scandinavian humour in his veins?
> What poet, or what dreamer, caught
> in music of his own imagining? (148)

The answer is of course the devout and filial Riel, 'with French vowels on his tongue / *l'amour de dieu* [sic] within his heart,' the model young man that his mother proudly calls 'a hunter, yet a dreamer' (148).

Livesay's identification with Riel is so complete that it has been suggested he is her 'spiritual kinsman' and that poet and subject 'speak as one.' It is certainly difficult to conceive of a more adulatory portrait of the Métis leader than the one painted in 'Prophet,' a work begun in the mid-1940s and based on two radio plays, 'Red River – 1869' and 'Flags for Canada' (Tiessen and Tiessen 325, 315; Livesay, 'Prophet' 147). While Livesay's Riel is a political figure, he is driven mainly by spiritual concerns. More specifically, he is an individual torn between two dreams. In one dream, a celestial voice tells him that his rudderless people have anointed him as their leader, and that he is to represent not just them but also God. As the voice informs him, 'From the flock you must go out, there where my children are / as speechmaker and peace-maker; you must be voice / for them, for Me' (149). In the other dream, Riel imagines that he wrestles in a wood with God, 'my Lord / with flaming tomahawk, his mind afire,' and 'I, crying to be known / by him, delivering fierce blows for truth.' Riel is positive that he sees the Almighty's 'blood spurt and bruises burst like flowers' but ultimately succumbs to his adversary. Yet, in a way, he emerges victorious, for as a consequence of his bout with God he discovers the purpose of his worldly mission: 'Here on this earth to fight for freedom's light, / here in this flowered land to end the hate' (150).

According to Livesay, the reason Riel is able to decipher his dreams is that he is spiritually and poetically inspired. Even his dementia is a reflection of his artistic creativity – or, possibly, of his mixed heritage – since

> ... Madness is
> the meat of poetry; and every poet's mad
> who has a message burning in his bowels.
> Say I am mad; say that the slowly turning world
> rifled with hate, red skin against white
> fathers perverting sons, and all of nature made
> into a kitchen midden for man's wasteful heart –
> call these things *sane*? and their existence, *bliss*?
> Still I am mad, who would destroy and burn
> the shame of racial hate; I, the half-caste
> neither white nor brown, am therefore mad:
> more human, less possessed of bigotry
> nearer, I feel, to the great God who came
> to be amongst us, flesh, to feel
> the animal passions of this creature, man. (151)

To the poet, Riel's possible insanity is a positive force. This is made explicit when she has her protagonist end the stanza by asking God to make him even more mad, so that he can transcend 'the barriers of everyday' and his soul 'forever be on fire / a comet flashing faith upon the world' (151).

Livesay's picture of Riel in 'Prophet of the New World' is obviously an idealized one. Her object in the poem is not just to narrate a tale about the architect of the two North-West conflicts but to rehabilitate his image, which she is able to do by providing a rather idiosyncratic view of history. For instance, Livesay has Riel abandoning his sacerdotal studies the moment he learns that his father has died and that his people wish him to lead them. She ignores not only the Guernon affair, which forms the kernel of Roux's interpretation of the Métis leader in *Bois-Brûlés*, but also the fact two years elapse between the death of Riel's father and the young man's return to Red River. As well, she seems to attribute Riel's leadership during 1869–70 to divine forces, glossing over both her hero's political ambition and the roles played by other individuals and institutions in the community, not least the Catholic Church. Most conspicuously, when Livesay alludes briefly to the Scott incident, she creates the impression that it is not the Orangeman but Riel who is the victim. In the words she gives to Julie Riel, her firstborn was elected as a member of Parliament in 1873, 'But instead of being allowed to take his seat / he, my son / was charged with the killing of Thomas Scott.' The poet adds cryptically that the 'rights and wrongs of *that* / will be argued for many a year ...', 'yet she herself will not pursue them (152). But then her authorial 'purpose,' to echo her views in 'The Documentary Poem,' perhaps does not allow her to dwell on the more controversial aspects of her subject's life ('Documentary Poem' 274). After all, Livesay's Riel is not a theocrat who cannot tolerate any opposition to his ideas but a humanist who fights on behalf of all groups, 'the native-born / and newcome [*sic*] pioneer' alike. He is the epitome of Christian selflessness, the ethno-cultural mediator who knows 'how to set forth our rights / yet offer, still in peace, the other cheek' ('Prophet' 153).

A similarly exalted view of Riel also informs Adele Wiseman's *Testimonial Dinner* (1978). Set in Winnipeg, the play focuses mainly on an extended Jewish-Canadian family, an immigrant grandfather, his civil servant and university professor sons, and his journalist grandson. But the author occasionally has Riel enter the scene, often sitting on Macdonald's shoulders. As the family deals with its intergenerational conflicts, the two historical antagonists bounce imperviously about, reflecting on what might have been. Thus, the prime minister tells Riel that he and his people should be thankful that Canada acquired the North-West, since 'THE AMERICANS WOULD HAVE SWARMED ALL OVER YOU' had they got there first. To this the Métis leader, voicing what appears to be the author's point of view, replies that 'WE COULD HAVE BUILT TOGETHER HAD YOU RECOGNIZED OUR RIGHT TO EXIST, IN OUR WAY, AS EQUALS. HAD YOU KEPT THE FAITH ...' (18).

Wiseman's depiction of Riel, like that of Macdonald, is heavily symbolic. For the author, Canada's most famous immigrant represents the pragmatic newcomer who believes in 'land grabbing, building an empire no matter what it costs. No matter what it costs somebody else.' Riel, in contrast, typifies 'the visionary' or 'madman' who dreams of 'a more humane society' (quoted in Belkin 159). In the play proper, Macdonald's position is associated with the grandfather. The foreign-born patriarch is a real estate developer with an uncanny ability to divine land prices who, after an extremely successful business career, attempts to build a bridge to his grandson and the future by buying land and returning it to the First Nations. The central aim in both sets of relationships, the fictional and the historical, is thus to achieve a fusion between the material and the spiritual, between the 'immigrant' values of Macdonald and the 'indigenous' ones of Riel. As Wiseman writes in the introduction to *Testimonial Dinner,* her play explores what it would be like 'if Sir John and Riel could somehow, at some time, have been integrated, and Riel given his place in the land instead of endlessly suffering the same apparent defeat' (n.pag.). Or, as she tells an interviewer, 'I'm not saying what would have happened if Riel had won and Macdonald lost. That never comes into question, but what would have happened if Macdonald and his side had been more humane' (quoted in Belkin 159). Wiseman's dramatic exploration, though, remains largely abstract. The play's two concurrent narratives never coalesce, giving the work an experimental aura, which the author judges as a sign of its 'textural density' (n.pag.).

Although Wiseman has stated that she 'conceived the physical and symbiotic relationship' between Riel and Macdonald independently, she admits to having been subsequently influenced by a Bengough cartoon she discovered while writing the play (58). Entitled 'A Riel Ugly Position,' the 1885 caricature shows the prime minister, with the Métis leader perched on his shoulders, riding two horses moving in opposite directions. One horse is named 'French Influence' and the other 'English Influence' (pl. 6). Wiseman's objective in evoking such a charged image of Canada's French-English dualism is clearly political. As she notes in the introduction, her aim in *Testimonial Dinner* is not just to dramatize her belief that 'the past ... is alive and functioning in the present,' that Macdonald still carries Riel 'unassimilated on [his] spiritual back,' but also that the country's social and political reality could have been otherwise (n.pag.). Curiously, one finds very little of this optimism in her precursor. Judging by Bengough's sequel to 'A Riel Ugly Position,' which Wiseman does not cite, the cartoonist is much more fatalistic about any future national rapprochement between the forces represented by the two rivals. In the second cartoon, Riel is still sitting on Macdonald's shoulders as the prime minister rides two horses, but the animals have moved so far apart that Macdonald seems about to split in half, before tumbling with Riel to the ground. One of the horses, too, is no longer called 'English Influence' but simply 'Orange' (pl. 7).

Considerably more complex than the portrait of Riel sketched by

Wiseman, or Livesay, is the one drawn by Margaret Laurence. A native of Manitoba, like the other two writers, Laurence writes only indirectly about Riel. But contemporary Métis play a critical role in her work and, as she examines their lives, she cannot help but deal with their nineteenth-century leader. In texts like *The Diviners* (1974), a novel in which she consciously tried to draw attention to the 'injustices' against Riel's people ('Best Wishes'), Laurence suggests that there is a direct connection between the reality faced by today's Métis and what transpired in 1885. As she has the songwriter Jules Tonnerre describe the effect of the Batoche defeat on his grandfather and namesake, a fighter with Riel,

> He took his Cross and he took his gun,
> Went back to the place where he'd begun.
> He lived on drink and he lived on prayer,
> But the heart was gone from Jules Tonnerre. (283, 374)

The impact of the Batoche tragedy on the younger Jules is so pervasive that it affects him even linguistically. He is a songwriter who, 'with two languages lost, retaining only broken fragments of both French and Cree,' speaks 'English as though forever it must be a foreign tongue to him' (200). Yet, through him, Laurence is able to dramatize the fact that the Métis people did not perish in the Saskatchewan Valley. As Jules asserts, 'the dead don't always die' and his grandfather is not destined to be forgotten, for 'His voice is one the wind will tell / In the prairie valley that's called Qu'Appelle' (283, 375).

Laurence is particularly apt at elucidating how contemporary Métis are touched by white racism, some of it instigated by the memory of Riel. For example, when Jules's sister Piquette dies in a house fire, the novel's white protagonist and Jules's subsequent lover, Morag Gunn, writes in her report for the local newspaper that Piquette's grandfather, the aforementioned Old Jules Tonnerre, had 'fought with Riel in Saskatchewan in 1885, in the last uprising of the Métis.' Morag's white editor promptly deletes the line since, as he explains to his reporter, 'many people hereabouts would still consider that Old Jules back then had fought on the wrong side' (130). When Jules begins to sing the song about his grandfather, white audiences not only laugh at it but demand that he present something more to their taste, 'stuff like "Roll out the barrel"' (229). Even more blatantly, Morag and Jules's teenaged daughter, Pique, is called 'a dirty half-breed' by a schoolmate who cannot believe that she is not promiscuous, for '*halfbreed girls can't wait to get fucked by any guy who comes along*' (344).

Anti-Riel, and anti-Métis, racism is also at the core of Laurence's 'Letter from Lakefield' (1980). A seemingly autobiographical sketch, written in dramatic form and addressed to her long-time friend Wiseman, 'Letter from Lakefield'[5] describes a bus trip from Peterborough, Ontario, to Toronto. Since the bus is crowded, Laurence is forced to share a seat with an older woman named Bertha, who is 'sloshed' (358). Bertha at first takes issue with the fact Laurence is reading a book, an ostensibly subversive activity that marks her as some sort of alien. Perhaps because of Laurence's physiognomy, what the author describes as her 'high cheekbones and slightly slanted eyes inherited from my long-ago Pictish and Celtic ancestors,' Bertha assumes that her travelling companion is a boat-person, 'one of those damn people from Vietnam or Taiwan!' Laurence informs Bertha not only that 'I speak English pretty well' but also that 'I'm from here, Canada' (359–60). When she adds that she hails from Manitoba, Bertha deduces that Laurence must be Métis and explodes in a tirade against 'those goddamn halfbreeds.' In her words, 'Okay then, whatcha think of Louis Riel, then? A devil. A devil. The worst. Part Indian, I ask you. Whatcha think of *him*, then? I was born and raised on the prairies, myself. Saskatchewan.' To this, Laurence responds that she considers Riel 'a great man.' But, she acknowledges, 'to my shame, I did not say this *loudly*' (360).

There is one other important representation of Riel as a cultural mediator, Adrian Hope's 'An Ode to the Metis' (1987). Relatively short, the poem is a veritable love letter to the progeny of the 'stalwart' European pioneers and 'Indian maidens,' especially their innate largesse of spirit (iv). As the poet writes,

Democracy was their byword,
Equality for all.
Having access to both cultures
They were made to learn them all.

They taught the missionaries
To speak the Native tongues;
They also taught the natives
Of things that are not done.
They brought the great explorers
To the lands up in the west,
And showed them where to travel,
On the routes that were the best. (iv)

Hope concedes that the Métis have suffered for their biological and cultural hybridity, which at times has led to their 'not [being] accepted / By the Indians or the whites' (v). Still, he believes that they should seek inspiration from their glorious past. He is especially proud of the example set by Riel, the 'educated' leader who was 'hung [sic] for some misdeed' but is now regarded as a Canadian patriot by 'all the world ... / By all men that are free' (vi–vii). As Hope ends his ode to the 'true sons of the west,' today's challenges may be different from those in the old North-West, but 'We know that we will conquer – / We are the great Metis' (vii).

Hope's poem is noteworthy not just because it is one of the rare works by a Métis on the mediating role played by Riel and his people but also because the poet is so unequivocally proud of it. The few other Métis writers who have explored the subject seem to do anything but revel in their biocultural in-betweenness. As Laure Bouvier describes her protagonist's hybridity in *Une histoire de Métisses* (1995), concluding with an apparent allusion to Bengough's cartoon of the two-horse rider,

> Ni Blanche ni Amérindienne, les deux ensemble sans être l'une ou l'autre; vivant et travaillant depuis toujours au milieu des Blancs sans en souffrir mais sans jamais pouvoir être moi-même totalement, et quasi étrangère à la vie des premiers habitants de ce pays, je suis un être de frontières. À cheval sur deux mondes. Métisse, soit, mais à l'insu de tous presque. Comme si je vivais amputée d'une partie de mes origines. (186)

The discomfort felt by recent Métis writers about their mixed heritage becomes most pronounced when a real 'Indian' draws attention to the fact that 'we / are not one or the other   but a shaded combination' (Scofield, 'Answer' 82). Or when Aboriginal people, with their own land and official status, scorn the Métis and treat them like 'the poor relatives, the *awp-pee-tow-koosons* [half-people]' (M. Campbell 25).

Even non-Métis writers appear to be becoming increasingly wary of depicting Riel mainly as an intermediary between Canada's Natives and Newcomers. The reasons for this development are perhaps best articulated in the work of the Franco-Manitoban novelist Ronald Lavallée, the author of what is arguably the most popular work on the Métis existential condition. Lavallée's *Tchipayuk, ou le chemin du loup* (1987) is not technically about Riel but about a Métis named Askik Mercredi. But Askik's life parallels the Métis leader's to such a degree that one critic has called him a 'Riel anonyme' (Joubert, 'Askik' 176).

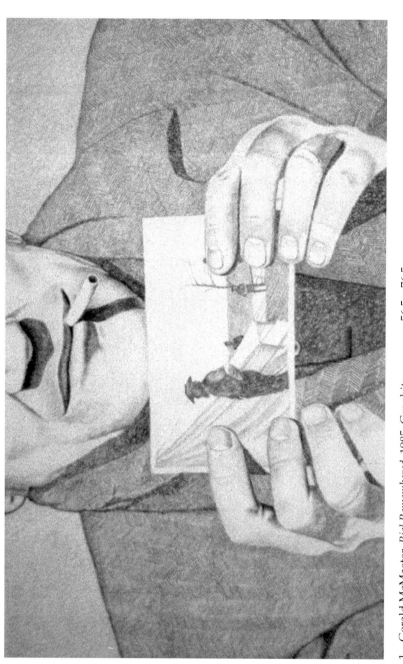

1 Gerald McMaster, *Riel Remembered*, 1985. Graphite on paper, 56.5 x 76.5 cm.

2 J.W. Bengough, 'A Case of Riel Distress!' *Grip*, 25 Oct. 1873, n.pag.

COMBINATION STATUE IN BRASS OF RIEL AND
SIR JOHN.

THE *Mail's* funny man has invented the idea that Mr. Edgar
means to collect funds for a monument to Riel in Queen's Park
—of which monument it gives an ideal picture. The *Globe's* side-
splitter comes out with a companion monument to Sir John. We
submit our combination design to both committees, in the belief that
it would commemorate transactions thoroughly typical of the career
of both heroes. The party Irish which whipped the ultra loyal into
line after those events we have modified into the form in general use
by those who wear the costume represented.

3 J.W. Bengough, 'Combination Statue in Brass of Riel and Sir John,' *Grip*, 27 Feb. 1886, n.pag.

4 J.W. Bengough, 'Justice Still Unsatisfied,' *Grip*, 21 Nov. 1885, n.pag.

ANOTHER DECORATION NOW IN ORDER.

THE GALLANT VOLUNTEERS HAVING RECEIVED THEIR WELL-
EARNED MEDALS, MISS CANADA WILL PROCEED (IT IS
HOPED) TO RECOGNIZE THE EFFORTS OF THE
HALFBREEDS, BY GIVING THEM THE
RIGHTS THEY FOUGHT FOR.

5   J.W. Bengough, 'Another Decoration Now in Order,' *Grip*, 22 May 1886, n.pag.

6   J.W. Bengough, 'A Riel Ugly Position,' *Grip*, 29 Oct. 1885, n.pag.

7   J.W. Bengough, 'Something's Got to Go Soon!' *Grip*, 14 Nov. 1885, n.pag.

8   John Nugent, *Louis Riel Memorial*, 1968. Bronze, 238.1 x 84.1 x 71.4 cm.

9   Marcien Lemay and Étienne Gaboury, *Louis Riel*, 1971, Collège universitaire de Saint-Boniface.

10   Miguel Joyal, *Louis Riel*, 1996. Manitoba Legislature, Winnipeg.

Like his historical compatriot, Askik is born in the North-West, educated in Montreal, and suffers a romantic rejection in that city for what appear to be racial reasons. That is, despite his coming to perceive himself as a Quebecker, he learns that his educational and social achievements ultimately count for little in his host society. As he confesses before deciding to return to the Prairies, 'Il n'y a pas un seul ivrogne du Québec qui ne me soit supérieur. Je suis, et je serai toujours, pour les Canadiens, un sauvage' (399).

What Lavallée illustrates in his novel is the essential Otherness of the mixed-race people of the North-West. As another Franco-Manitoban, the poet Paul Savoie, writes in *Bois brûlé* (1989), the Métis may be the quintessential intermediaries, a collectivity 'à mi-chemin / entre le nouveau monde/ et une ancienne promesse' (101). But whether personified by Riel or Askik, they remain alien because of the inability or refusal of Canadians to accept them as equals. The Plainsmen, writes R.G. Everson in his poem 'The Métis' (1969), 'founded two countries / and fought two wars against Canada.' They are 'Canada's countrymen / murdered by Canada' (20). Consequently, it becomes extremely difficult to celebrate Canadian history through them. This is especially true of Riel, whose story cannot help but reflect negatively on Canadians. The Métis leader is either the country's sworn enemy or a constant reminder of its racism toward the First Nations. So it is not surprising that many recent Canadian writers on Riel have elected not to stress his role as a cultural go-between but rather his spirituality or his victimhood.

5

The Martyr (II)
Riel As a Sociopolitical Victim
of Confederation

Entre le rêve et lui surgit l'Anglais.

Maurice Constantin-Weyer (1925)

The essential Métisness of Riel, I argued in the previous chapter, accounts for the most flagrant contradictions in the representations of him as a cultural mediator. At least since the end of the Second World War, the Riel project has become an increasingly English-Canadian enterprise, with the anti-Confederation rebel of 1869–70 and 1885 being transformed into the very 'symbole' of Anglo-Canadian nationalism (Morisset, 'Cents ans'). But because Riel is so unqualifiedly Métis, any portrayal of him as a Canadian patriot is bound to be seriously compromised by his Métis nationalism. Even those authors who portray Riel as a victim of the sociopolitical forces that culminated in Confederation find it difficult to deal with his national specificity as a Métis. Some writers may begin by decrying the consequences of the predominantly Anglo-Celtic drive to expand Canada's western frontier, but, seemingly embarrassed by the apparent archaic lifestyle of the Métis, they often conclude by celebrating that development. Others, in contrast, circumvent the problem altogether by turning Riel and his people into proto-Canadians. That is, they not only distance themselves from their own bicultural ancestors but also deny the Métis their identity as a nation.

One of the most curious representations of Riel as a sociopolitical victim of Confederation is Maurice Constantin-Weyer's novel *La bourrasque* (1925). Born in 1881, Constantin-Weyer was a Frenchman who spent the years between 1904 and 1914 farming in southern Manitoba. After he returned to his native land to fight in the Great War, he began a series of romanticized fictions inspired by his experiences in the New World that is credited with having introduced the Canadian West into French literature (Frémont, *Sur le ranch* 44; Motut 11, 164; Knutson 260). Known collectively as the 'Épopée canadienne,' Constantin-Weyer's Canadian works were very well received in France, one of them being honoured with the Prix Goncourt in 1928. But in Canada the situation was quite different, particularly concerning *La bourrasque*. While the French acclaimed the one-time settler as a 'Jack London français' (Motut 98), French Canadians felt insulted by what they considered his caricature of their community, a reaction that suggests French people can distance themselves emotionally from the Métis in a way their North-American cousins cannot. The Métis and their supporters were especially incensed by the unflattering characterization of themselves and, above all, their cherished leader (Motut 89–139). So negative has been the response to Constantin-Weyer's depiction of Riel in *La bourrasque* that an English translation of the novel was banned from Winnipeg's municipal libraries in the 1930s. To this day, the author's daughter refuses to allow the French original to be republished, since 'son contenu se situe aux antipodes de l'image que veut projeter la nation métisse' (Frémont, *Sur le ranch* 58–9; Saint-Pierre 12).

The most damaging criticisms of Constantin-Weyer's portrait of Riel and the Métis in *La bourrasque* are his seemingly wilful disregard for the historical record and an irreverence bordering on racism; and neither accusation can easily be refuted (Frémont, *Sur le ranch* 90–1, 103–4). The author's nonchalance toward historical and geographic facts is evident in the novel's opening paragraph, where he writes that the Red River 'prend sa source ... dans le Wisconsin,' as opposed to Lake Traverse on the border between South Dakota and Minnesota (9; Waters 109–10). Elsewhere in the work, he juxtaposes the commercial and cultural differences between the 'English' Hudson's Bay Company and 'la Compagnie (française) des Pelleteries du Nord-Ouest,' a Montreal-based firm that was 'dominated by men of Highland Scots origin' (14; Van Kirk 12). Also, in the novel, he has Protestants celebrating William of Orange's victory over King James at the Boyne, not on July 12, but on Canada's own national birthday, July 1 (38). Perhaps most unforgivable for the Métis and their sympathizers, Constantin-Weyer takes tremendous liberties with the historical Riel, presenting 'le plus intelligent et le plus instruit des gens de sa race' as a frontier bonvivant far more interested in conquering female hearts than in defending the welfare of his people (Frémont, *Sur le ranch* 72).

Constantin-Weyer's Riel is still opposed primarily by English Canadians, or 'Anglais,' a disreputable lot of the Protestant persuasion whose existence appears to revolve around the need to humiliate Catholics. The author traces Riel's political awakening to an incident at an Orange parade in a small Ontario town. When the then sixteen-year-old is overheard speaking French, on Protestantism's 'jour sacré,' he is first insulted and then physically attacked by a group of irate Orangemen (38). The episode leaves an indelible imprint on the youngster, who in future years bolsters his confidence by recalling the day when 'il avait si rudement châtié l'impudent agresseur.' From that moment on, Canada too 'lui devint odieux,' and, on behalf of his people, he resolves to fight the covetous and bigoted enemy (39). But there is another reason Riel comes to believe he is destined to lead the Métis – his family history. According to Constantin-Weyer, Riel is 'la proie d'une ambition démesurée,' having inherited from his father the 'insatiable désir de domination, que le père n'avait pu réaliser, mais que le fils se promettait d'accomplir en entier' (36). The senior Riel, the author writes in an earlier work, is frustrated in his dream of becoming the 'roi' of the Métis by his lack of formal education and, upon the birth of his son and namesake, decides to 'abdiquer ses espoirs en sa faveur' (*Vers l'Ouest* 14, 141). He thus inculcates into his offspring the conviction that the latter was born to conclude his mission and become the supreme chief of the Métis people, which is not just a familial ambition but 'le rêve invraisemblable de sa race!' As the younger Riel tells himself later, 'Lui, Riel, soulèverait les métis exaspérés par les spoliations britanniques. Il les dresserait, centaures invaincus, contre l'envahisseur ... Puis, vainqueur, il se ferait couronner roi!' (*Bourrasque* 41, 40).

Riel soon manages to rally most of his people, if not their spiritual leaders, to his side. The Catholic hierarchy, to whom the senior Riel had strategically entrusted the education of the would-be monarch, is divided about the young man's activities (37; *Vers l'Ouest* 14–15, 245). While the current bishop hopes that the pre-emptive actions by the Métis might help protect his diocese from 'l'invasion orangiste' (60), he is mortified by the idea of rebellion, his knowledge of French history reminding him how the social revolution in 'l'infortunée mère-patrie' in 1789 led to a 'rébellion envers le droit divin' (88). The one exception among the clergy is Father Ritchot, who sides openly with the Métis and, each Sunday, 'fulminait en chaire contre "les cochons de l'Ontario"' (92). Encouraged by that 'partisan en soutane' and 'fanatique ennemi des Anglo-Saxons' (130), Riel leads the Métis to capture Fort Garry. But Riel's success is short-lived, as his role in the execution of the 'meurtrier'

Tom Scott forces him to relinquish his position and to flee to Montana (178).

After spending several years teaching in the United States, Riel returns to the Canadian North-West when Gabriel Dumont and a group of Saskatchewan Métis solicit his help in fighting the wicked 'Anglais,' who 'profitaient de leur connaissance de lois injustes' (208). Yet he is not destined to be of much assistance to his afflicted brethren. When a group of English-Canadian Protestants meets the Métis in the middle of the prairie, both parties are convinced that 'tout se passerait en paroles.' However, the symbolically named and dashing Reverend Mac-Donald, who sports large golden glasses and 'un parapluie neuf (luxe inusité),' for some mysterious reason opens his umbrella. Riel's supporters interpret the display of that 'monstrueux produit de la civilisation ... comme une provocation,' and an armed confrontation erupts. This is a clash that becomes increasingly more preposterous – even if inspired by a historical incident at Frog Lake (224; Cameron 20). The Métis respond to the reading of a summons by the Canadian commander by aiming their guns at the enemy, and the soldiers immediately drop their arms. Still, the final outcome is inevitable. With the continual arrival of reinforcements on the new transcontinental railroad, the Canadians are able to repel the outnumbered Métis, who 's'égaillèrent de tous côtés' (228).

Riel once again manages to seek refuge in the United States, but he is forced to leave his wife and children on Canadian soil. Thus, when he learns that his family has been taken hostage by 'général Littletown' (229), as Constantin-Weyer calls General Middleton, he decides to return to Canada. Riel is confident that he will be given a fair hearing by his foes, but he soon discovers that he is to be tried, not by an impartial judge and jury, but by 'les mannequins justiciards' (240). His own spiritual adviser does not provide him with much solace, either. Father Ernest, a.k.a. Father André, appears to be less God's earthly representative than Satan's. He is a modern-day inquisitor who compels Riel to hand him a letter in which the prisoner 'rejetait sur le Père Ernest l'idée première de l'insurrection' and, under the threat of an auto-da-fé, forces him to 'promettre de prendre sur soi tout le poids de la révolte' (233). Indeed, it becomes obvious to everyone that no justice is possible under the circumstances. As another defendant, a Cree chief, encapsulates the process, 'C'était la vision de la Justice des Blancs, qui, derrière son masque de fausse respectabilité, cache la laideur de son âme' (239). This is a verdict shared by Riel. Upon hearing his fated death sentence, he demands to be hanged 'la figure tournée vers le nord, "du côté où il y a le moins d'Anglais"' (248). The conclusion of *La bourrasque* is powerful but quite misleading. Except for the last few pages, after the action shifts momentarily from Red River to Saskatchewan, Constantin-Weyer's Riel is never a truly tragic figure. The Métis leader and his people may well be victims of Anglo-Protestant racism, targets of the dual Orange desire to 'délivrer l'Ouest canadien de la superstition catholique et de la langue française' (31). Yet it is not self-evident that they are deserving of the reader's sympathies. They certainly appear not to have earned the author's. A mere twenty pages or so from the end, Constantin-Weyer actually has his narrator describe the second North-West conflict as a 'farce réellement gauloise' (225). Riel himself is shown to be inordinately self-centred and manipulative, the sort of person who assumes 'le titre assez singulier d'*Exovède*, voulant montrer sans doute qu'il se tenait hors du troupeau' (223). He is also someone who, when he realizes that he is about to be defeated by the Canadian forces, flees not just 'sans trop savoir pourquoi' but also 'comme s'il avait réellement participé à la rébellion' (228–9). Even more damning, Riel is an irresponsible leader, a Lothario who never allows the well-being of his people to interfere with a potential sexual tryst.

The most conclusive proof that Constantin-Weyer does not take his protagonist seriously is the fact his Riel is not a politician, a mystic, or even a madman, but a lover. The historical Riel is reported to have had some romantic relationships with women, albeit not very felicitous ones. First, there was his secret engagement to Marie-Julie Guernon, which her parents supposedly terminated because of his mixed racial heritage (Stanley, *Louis Riel* 33). Then, there was his courtship of Evelina Barnabé, the sister of the Franco-Catholic priest of Keeseville, New York, at whose home Riel convalesced after his release from the Beauport asylum, and the subject of some of his most intimate lines:

O bonne Evelina! Vous que je trouve aimable
Et pour qui je désire un sort vraiment heureux!
Si vous mangez souvent le pain très délectable;
    Si vous aimez la sainte table;
Je demande au bon Dieu qu'il exauce mes voeux
En daignant nous unir, au plus tôt, tous les deux. (4: 214–15)

Finally, there was Marguerite Monet, the Montana Métisse for whom he would undiplomatically forsake Evelina because, as he writes to the latter after the fact, 'le prêtre mon confesseur m'a conseillé de me marier' (2: 265). There may have been a fourth woman in Riel's life, his sister Sara. Extrapolating mainly from Riel's advocacy of polygamy and incest (2: 144–161), scholars such as Thomas Flanagan have asserted that the Métis leader entertained deep incestuous desires for his younger sister, who later became a nun. Their case would seem to be corroborated by Sara's ambiguous letters to her brother, in which she sends him 'le baiser d'une soeur, dont la plus grande privation en ce moment est la séparation de son cher Louis!' (S. Riel, 122–3). Or, no less suggestively, 'Je demande au Sacré Coeur de te dire pour moi que tu m'est cher – te d'assurer que je t'ai jamais plus aimé que depuis le jour où je me suis arrachée de tes bras' (S. Riel, 167–8). But considering that the two siblings 'were widely separated almost all their lives,' even Flanagan admits that any sexual feelings Riel may have had toward Sara, and vice versa, 'must have remained purely in the realm of imagination' (Louis 'David' Riel 93).

In any case, excluding the highly hypothetical relationship with Sara, Riel does not appear to have engaged in any unethical sexual practices, much less to have been a Don Juan. Yet that is how Constantin-Weyer portrays him. The Riel of La bourrasque is especially irresistible to Métis women, of all ages. Part of his attraction lies in his family name, the fact he is the son of a man who even the clergy concedes is the 'chef temporel de la colonie' (37). Another portion resides in his complexion, his being 'étonnament blanc pour un métis.' With his 'barbe blonde frisée,' Riel is even 'plus blanc' than the local Scots, French Canadians, or French (63). It is definitely difficult to ascribe his success with women to any exceptional gallantry. For example, he beckons the voluptuous Véronique Lapointe to come to his side at a dance with 'un simple et impérieux clignement d'œil' (50). Later, he concludes the seduction by telling the young woman, 'T'as des beaux tétons, Véronique!' a compliment that goes right to Véronique's 'cœur' and impels her to succumb to her suitor's designs (55).

Riel's romantic liaisons, though, are not restricted to Métis women, or even Catholic ones. His most significant conquest in the novel is actually an 'Anglaise' named Madame Hamarstyne, a beautiful but pious Presbyterian who, as one critic rightly suggests, 'deserves a novel of her own' (Osachoff, 'Louis Riel' 64). Very loosely modelled on the historical Annie Bannatyne, the Halfbreed woman who horsewhipped Charles Mair for his derogatory comments about the rivalries between mixed-race and white women at Red River (Mair, Letter 396; Dumas 27–8), Hamarstyne is both violently attracted and repelled by the young Métis. The couple first meets, accidentally, at her store. Remembering that he had once seen a Frenchman kiss a woman's hand, Riel decides to do the same with Hamarstyne.[1] This is a gesture that she seems to fail to appreciate, telling him bluntly: 'Je vous déteste.' Her real feelings toward Riel, however, are far more complex, and contradictory. She is mortified by the idea of falling in love with a man other than her husband, but she dreads even more that the man in question happens to be an impious Catholic. In her words about God's potential judgment of her behaviour, 'Qu'est-ce qu'Il va penser de Sa créature ... Et un catholique encore (*Le rémords trembla plus poignant dans sa voix*) ... Un catholique ... c'est une honte ... une grande honte' (71). Yet, despite her genuine fear of damnation, Hamarstyne is unable to resist her desire for the alluring stranger. As she addresses Riel just before he leaves her shop, 'Partez, lui cria-t-elle entre deux sanglots ... Partez et ne m'induisez plus en tentation ... Mon mari ne rentrera que demain ... Revenez ce soir ... tard' (71).

Hamarstyne's schizophrenic relationship with Riel, which wavers ferociously between lust and remorse, reaches frenetic highs during lovemaking. One moment she is in tears, fearing the divine ramifications of her sexual transgression. The next, she abandons herself to her lover's caresses. Such is the sexual attraction between Hamarstyne and Riel that, even though she is fully aware of the religious and cultural divide between them, she soon 'lui fit jurer de l'aimer toujours, et de revenir au premier signe qu'elle lui ferait' (75). Still, while the body may at first seem to triumph over the spirit, the liaison is ultimately destroyed if not by religion at least by politics, two subjects that admittedly are not always separable in the history of Catholic-Protestant relations. After Scott is sentenced to death by the Red River court martial, Hamarstyne begs her paramour to spare the Orangeman, even at the cost of her own life. Or, as she dramatically puts it, 'Prends-la Riel ... mon âme, prends-la, mais sauve Scott.' Riel promptly accedes to his lover's request, merely asking that she let him give 'les ordres ... Il n'y a plus qu'une demi-heure à peine.' But in her rush to show her appreciation for Riel's magnanimity, Hamarstyne throws her arms around him, murmuring: 'nous avons le temps ... Oh! ... Oh! ... Oh! ... Riel ... Prends-moi ... prends-moi tout de suite' (183–4). Lost in ecstasy, the two lovers become oblivious to the world, until they hear a short order in the courtyard below. Riel runs to the window, but, by then, guns have been discharged and 'une tache immobile' lies on the ground. He and Hamarstyne glance at each other and, instinctively, know that whatever held them together has suddenly dissipated. As the narrator notes, 'Ils savaient maintenant devoir se haïr mutuellement à jamais, et que l'énoncé même du nom de l'un serait pour l'autre une douleur inguérissable' (184). Moreover, it is not only their relationship that dies with Scott. Along with the Ontarian with the 'jeune figure de demi-dieu' also perishes Riel's political career, for English-speaking Canada will not permit the killer of one of its own to attain power (127).

Judging by Constantin-Weyer's portrayal, Riel thus owes his downfall to his libido. Yet the novelist goes further, suggesting that the Métis leader's sexual adventurism is a reflection not so much of his personality as of his biocultural background. Throughout *La bourrasque*, Riel's conduct is attributed to his 'âme indienne,' his 'sang indien,' or some 'atavisme indien' (58, 69, 186). This association of the protagonist's behaviour with his Aboriginal roots has been decried by critics, who find it especially perplexing in light of the source. After all, the author was married to a Métis woman, whom he reportedly abandoned when he returned to Europe, and his own children were 'plus indiens que ne l'était Riel' (Frémont, *Sur le ranch* 32–3, 104). But what is often ignored is that Constantin-Weyer can be as disparaging of Riel's French heritage as he is of his Aboriginal one. As the author has one character state, 'chez les métis, ce n'est pas le sang indien qui fait le sauvage, mais bien le sang français.' Or, as his narrator explains why the Halfbreeds disdain their French-speaking cousins, 'Pour eux, les métis français étaient issus de deux races vaincues' (169, 168). In fact, the reason Riel fails in his quest to become king of the Métis is that he is largely a product of Franco-Catholic civilization, a metaphysics-laden culture that purportedly lacks the vitality of the more pragmatic Anglo-Protestant civilization the author both abhors and admires.

One of the more intriguing aspects of *La bourrasque* is that its most positive character is not Riel, or some Frenchman or Quebecker, but that celebrated exponent of Anglo-Canadian expansionism, Donald A. Smith. Although the future Lord Strathcona plays a relatively minor role in the novel, he is about the only figure who is consistently depicted in favourable terms. An avid imperialist, Smith is not just a director of the Hudson's Bay Company and of the Canadian Pacific Railway but the very embodiment of what Constantin-Weyer elsewhere calls the 'poème de l'étonnante réussite anglo-saxonne' (*Manitoba* 75–86). The Scottish-born magnate is a 'poète,' a 'créateur,' who proclaims that it is 'le lyrisme qui fait les nations, c'est l'analyse qui les défait. Que serait l'Empire sans le chant des poètes.' Typically, Smith does not derive his poetic inspiration from the work of Shakespeare, Milton, or even Robbie Burns, but from what he terms the greatest of all poems and the 'plus beau manuel d'impérialisme,' the Bible (145). For Smith, the Bible, or more specifically the Old Testament, is his sole guide on matters spiritual as well as on matters material. It is from his assiduous reading of the Scriptures that he discerns the English are God's 'peuple élu' and Canada the 'terre de Chanaan.' The author writes that when most people look at Canada, including Smith's Methodist secretary and the French, they tend not to see past Voltaire's proverbial 'arpents de neige,' the 'immensité monotone' of endless frozen wastelands (146; Voltaire 188). Smith, however, senses both the country's untapped natural riches and its unique beauty. As he declares in a sexually charged encomium to the new Promised Land, Canada is 'une jeune vierge cachée sous ses voiles blancs ... une jeune vierge en robe de noces, et qui dort ... Et moi Smith, comme dans les contes de fée, je viens éveiller cette jeune vierge, je vais la baiser sur la bouche, je vais la féconder' (149). Or, as he remarks later, 'Une perle, ce pays. Une perle chatoyante en hiver ... Une couronne d'épis d'or en été ... Beau joyau pour l'impériale collection' (151).

Smith's vision of Canada, and of the world, is an explicitly social-Darwinian one, in which he and the English seem to have been elected by Providence to take possession not only of the country's territory but also of its inhabitants. While he foresees the Canadian landscape 'couvert de champs de blé qui onduleront au vent sur les mêmes rythmes que les plis du pavillon de l'*Union Jack*,' he states that the 'gentils sèmeront ce blé, et les fils du peuple élu le récolteront' (149). Still, there are few indications in the text that Constantin-Weyer disapproves of this raw imperialism. On the contrary, judging by his portrait of the peripatetic Highlander, the author appears to fully endorse Smith's evolutionary view of history. As the Métis once vanquished the 'premiers propriétaires du sol' and introduced their 'anarchie bienheureuse' (13), Constantin-Weyer writes, they are now being displaced by a more dynamic civilization. The only regret one discerns about this development on his part is that Canada's new rulers will not be his beloved French but those Bible readers, the English. As he notes ruefully, after La Vérendrye's explorations in the first half of the eighteenth century, France controlled 'un bon tiers des États-Unis et du Canada' (14). But by the end of the following century, all those possessions had been squandered, a loss he blames chiefly on the pernicious impact on French culture of Catholicism or the New Testament, which appear to be one and the same. For Constantin-Weyer, the French, in contrast to the English, have not yet liberated themselves intellectually from 'toute la sensibilité du Nouveau Testament.' Thus, instead of embracing only the 'enseignements virils' of the Old Testament, they fall for the love-thy-brother fantasies of the New (149). This prevents the French from grasping the reality of human nature and the need for long-term planning, such as is required in the development of new lands. More germanely, it explains their failure to control North America. As he has Smith assert, 'L'Évangile, c'est un rêve socialiste. Que serait l'Angleterre si elle était catholique? ... Un pays d'utopies humanitaries. C'est-à-dire rien' (150).

Curiously, despite Constantin-Weyer's patent exaltation of Anglo-Protestant culture in *La bourrasque*, at least one English-Canadian publisher did not deem the work Anglophilic enough. In 1930, five years after the publication of the original text, two anonymously translated English-language editions appeared in North America, one in Canada and the other in the United States. Entitled *The Half-breed*, the U.S. translation is generally faithful to the French original. The Canadian version, which carries the more judgmental title of *A Martyr's Folly*, is virtually identical to the U.S. one except for the section dealing with Riel's trial. Thus, 'le mannequin-chef' (236) is rendered by the U.S. edition as 'the puppet-chief' but by the Canadian as 'the stipendiary magistrate-judge' (*Half-breed* 295; *Martyr's Folly* 294). Likewise, 'les mannequins justiciards' (240) is translated in *The Half-breed* as 'the legal puppets' (299) but in *A Martyr's Folly* as 'the court' (299). More critically, in the latter work, two whole sections on the politics of the trial are deleted and two new ones added. In one of the new segments, Riel expounds on his belief that 'I have a mission' and on the testimony of 'the glorious General Middleton.' In the other, 'after Scott's avengers [have] no difficulty in condemning Riel to capital punishment,' the counsel for the Crown discusses the potential ramifications of the proceedings at Regina (*Martyr's Folly* 300, 302). One of the lawyers is concerned that the federal Liberal leader will be 'thundering out his indignation at the notion of a mere stipendiary magistrate trying a case of such nation-wide importance.' His colleague, however, is more anxious about the likely 'appeal to race prejudice' by another Liberal politician, 'the honey-tongued' former minister of justice – and future prime minister – Wilfrid Laurier (*Martyr's Folly* 304). The first lawyer also reveals what he thinks is the real reason Riel must die. While the Métis leader was 'a kind of Joan of Arc in a mild way,' the attorney asserts, his religious heterodoxy has cost him the support of the Catholic community. This is fortunate because 'the Orangemen won't let us forget Scott. It is that folly that will hang him in the end, though it can never be brought forward as the prime reason' (*Martyr's Folly* 305).

A *Martyr's Folly* also bears an illuminating introduction by one of Canada's best-known early-twentieth-century intellectuals, Pelham Edgar. A former professor of both French and English at the University of Toronto's Victoria College, Edgar was the mentor of such distinguished literary scholars as E.K. Brown, Douglas Bush, Kathleen Coburn, and Northrop Frye, the last of whom christened him the 'Dean of Critics' (Frye, 'Dean' 169). He is very complimentary toward Constantin-Weyer, lauding him for his novel's 'essentially foreign truth,' which is nevertheless 'compacted of values that are eminently worth while, and which a native writer might have missed by excess of saturation' (v). Edgar does chide the author for focusing disproportionately on the events at Red River and for having 'swerved from historic fact in permitting Riel to escape into the United States after the Batoche episode' (v–vi). Still, he is effusive in his praise of Constantin-Weyer's Rabelaisian characterization of the Métis, a people the Canadian academic describes as 'illiterate, superstitious, sensual, deliriously drunken, and as incapable of organization as a horde of Bedlamites' (vi). Edgar is especially impressed with the Frenchman's impartiality, his obvious respect for Anglo-Protestant enterprise:

> The drama of nation building is always an imposing spectacle. When the obstacles to success are merely physical the play lacks the full virtue of the clash of opposites. Here we have at least some element of the human conflict, and if the author permitted himself to dwell with sympathy on the futile dreams and aspirations of a little people, he gave also, in the empire vision of the young Donald A. Smith, the necessary counterpoise. (vi)

Ironically, while commending the translator for his 'reproductive skill,' Edgar regrets that the use of the Crown counsel in the novel is 'meager if ingenious,' seemingly unaware that the two lawyers are mainly the creation, not of the author, but of either the translator or some ghost-writer (vii; Knutson 274).

The portraits of Riel in *La bourrasque* and *A Martyr's Folly* are clearly eccentric, yet they are representative of their time at least in their negativity toward the Métis leader. As I stated earlier, Riel would not be widely depicted as a hero until after the end of the Second World War. The rehabilitation of his image, or what a less generous critic calls his 'facelift' (Dowbiggin 171), actually begins in the 1930s. Such works as Jonas Jonasson's 'The Riel Rebellions' (1933), A.S. Morton's *A History of the Canadian West to 1870–71* (1936), and George F.G. Stanley's *The Birth of Western Canada: A History of the Riel Rebellions* (1936) provided an increasingly balanced perspective on Riel and his people. But all of the above were academic studies and had little impact on the wider Canadian public, Jonasson's doctoral dissertation never even finding a publisher (Owram, 'Myth' 323–34). In the words of Stanley, who would later emerge as the dean of Riel scholars, 'To interpret Riel as the defender of a Native culture rather than as a rebel against constituted authority was to imply ... a degree of sympathy unacceptable at that time to many Canadians' ('Last Word' 11). Or, as he quotes the response by the historian Donald Creighton when Stanley told him in the 1950s he was writing a biography of Riel, 'Not that man! Never!' ('Foreword' xxii).[2] This was a situation that would not change until 1952, with the publication of *Strange Empire*, by the Alberta-raised Montana writer Joseph Kinsey Howard.

Strange Empire, which was published posthumously – the first U.S. edition is subtitled *A Narrative of the Northwest*, and the first Canadian one, *Louis Riel and the Métis People* – is a difficult work to categorize. In the foreword he wrote for the manuscript, which he would manage to complete but not revise before his death, Howard claims that 'even the words spoken by the people in this book are taken from the record ... There is no interpolated fictional dialogue' (19; DeVoto 3–5).[3] Yet his text, which bears no footnotes, is very subjective, a situation that usually results in historians classifying it as a historical novel (Payment 34; D. Morton, 'Reflections' 52) and fiction writers as a work of history (Gutteridge, 'Riel' 11). Although *Strange Empire* makes no notable contribution to Riel scholarship, it has emerged as a landmark in the history of the reception of the Métis leader in Canada, influencing not only most contemporary writers on Riel but also painters and sculptors (Mattes, 'Whose Hero?' 16–17). There are several reasons for this. First, Howard is a gifted storyteller, as is evident in his reconstruction of the life of someone like the 'conspiratorial cripple' Enos Stutsman, a U.S. customs agent, lawyer, and journalist who would play a significant role at Red River despite being born without legs (81–3). Second, he is a writer-activist, a partisan who openly celebrates Riel as a gentle 'dictator, who adored God and feared and hated bloodshed,' and who excoriates Canada for its 'bigotry and imperialistic visions' (17, 144). Finally, notwithstanding his unabashed continentalism, Howard seems to have appealed to Canadians not so much because of his 'poetic love of the land' (Doyle 181) but because his hybrid work signalled the discovery of a Canadian historical figure by a U.S. writer, a parochial response that Canadian Riel scholars have long resented (Owram, 'Myth' 323–6; Stanley, 'Last Word' 11–12).

Contrary to the general impression created by his many detractors, Howard does not paint a one-dimensional portrait of Riel. Mixed with its adulation of the 'erstwhile poet, almost priest' (147), *Strange Empire* also carries the seeds of his possible unmaking as a hero, particularly as a Prairie hero, his supposed untypicality. As Howard describes Riel,

> He was a mediocre horseman. He was clumsy and his hands were undexterous; many men of his race caught in prairie blizzards with no tool save a knife could survive, but he would have committed his soul to God and died. He could not shoot straight: he knew nothing of firearms and he dreaded and shunned them all his life. Living among people who drank to excess whenever they could, he used liquor sparingly; he had enemies who claimed they had seen him drunk, but as many friends swore he was a teetotaler. As for women, not even his enemies could make out a case against him. Either he had resigned himself to the priestly vow of chastity or he was unusually discreet, and he was nearly forty when he married. (147–8)

Constantin-Weyer aside, Howard's Riel is an ascetic individual. He is not just un-Métis but un-Western, a Montreal-educated intellectual who seems utterly out of place on his native soil. As even Riel's hagiographic biographer Maggie Siggins states, he is 'something of a prig and a momma's boy' (32). Indeed, it is not difficult to imagine why Howard would anticipate that the 'John Brown of the Half-Breeds' might be destined to be superseded as a Western hero by the 'prince of the prairies,' Gabriel Dumont (331, 358).

Still, Howard's hopelessly urbane if not effete Riel remains the undisputed leader of the Métis, the personification of their 'dream of a strange empire in the West.' He is both their 'brain' and 'their voice: the only man they had ever produced ... whose eloquence could become a sort of alchemy, transmuting frontier expedients into eternal human values, shaping standards out of habits' (18, 148). More importantly, Riel is not just the Métis chief but the potential leader of all Prairie First Nations. He is a nativist visionary who ignores the 'wholly artificial boundary' between Canada and the United States and who, had he triumphed at Red River, would have transformed the North-West into an 'organized native state' (49, 251). As both Howard and his editor Bernard DeVoto emphasize, Riel is an 'American primitive' (DeVoto 9). Or, to phrase it differently, Riel is not an adversary but an ancestor, undoubtedly the aspect of *Strange Empire* that had the most impact on other writers, on either side of the international border.

The first author to be influenced by Howard was a fellow U.S. citizen, the North Dakota playwright Frederick Walsh. First staged at Fargo's Little Country Theatre, Walsh's *The Trial of Louis Riel* (1963) deals chiefly with the Regina proceedings of 1885. The most important aspect of the two-act drama is its unrelenting focus on the political nature not just of Riel's trial but of history in general. The action is partly narrated by six talesmen, which the *Oxford English Dictionary* defines as either storytellers or substitute jurors, as if the playwright wishes 'to remind us that Riel's jury was deficient in numbers' and that we, too, must become 'talesmen, called upon to make up the deficiency' (C. Johnson 191). In the narrator's words, 'Treason was the charge, but treason is a word, and it is always the victor who defines the term' (19).

Walsh's Riel is a gentle if innocent mystic, a political leader who even one of his opponents asserts believes 'religion should be based on morality and humanity and charity' (75). Against him are the rapacious governments of the United States and Canada, especially the latter and its wily leader, Macdonald. Early on, Walsh has one character claim, 'Whoever builds the railroads will control the whole Northwest,' a thesis the author then proceeds to demonstrate (15). The central premise of *The Trial of Louis Riel* is that the prime minister himself deliberately provokes the second North-West conflict in order to get public support to finance the transcontinental railroad. Macdonald learns from one of his cabinet ministers that if the railroad does not reach the Pacific soon, Canada is bound to lose part of its territory to its southern neighbour, since 'many of our people out in Manitoba are talking about pulling out of the Dominion and joining the United States' (59). Not surprisingly, Macdonald is distressed by the prospect of witnessing his dream of a transcontinental country vanishing the moment he seems about to realize it. However, another minister instantly devises a strategy to preserve Canada's territorial integrity, by completing the railroad. As the second minister outlines his plan, 'We order the army to move against Riel. The army will need to be provisioned and supplied. Hence we need the railroad for the war effort. A few taxes here and there ought to do the job and everyone's happy' (61). Or, as Walsh's narrator concludes, 'And so the dream of a transcontinental railroad was married to the dreams of a few rebellious half-breeds' (62).

A distinct portrait of Riel as a sociopolitical victim of Confederation emerges in the opera *Louis Riel* (1967). Often considered the first major achievement in the history of Canadian music theatre, the three-act opera was composed by Harry Somers, then the nation's 'leading composer' (Schafer 5, 17). Its multilingual libretto, which in addition to English and French contains some Cree and Latin, was written by Mavor Moore, with the assistance of the Quebec playwright Jacques Languirand – 'who improv[ed] my French scenes' (Moore, *Reinventing Myself* 332). Curiously, for a Centennial project, *Louis Riel* follows Howard in its overt demonization of Canadian expansionists, from Tom Scott to Macdonald. The work opens with the arrival at the Minnesota/North-West border of William McDougall and his entourage, including his daughter, with whom he is 'BORNE ONSTAGE [*sic*] IN A LITTER ALMOST AS PRETENTIOUS AS A SEDAN-CHAIR' (2).[4] Red River's lieutenant-governor designate was a science-promoting politician 'respected by his contemporaries as gifted with extraordinary intelligence' (Zeller 257). Yet he is portrayed as both a pseudo-aristocrat and a bigot, as we can see from his reaction when he learns that the Métis have blocked his way by lowering a gate across the road:

Damn half-breeds have been at it again.
Hallo! Is anyone there? (NO REPLY)
Alright [*sic*]!
We'll show them who's master here:
We'll show the rebels what is what!
We'll teach them to be civilized
If we have to hang the ruddy lot!
Fire a shot! (2)

Similarly, following Scott's execution, the militant Canadian nationalist John Christian Schultz is shown inflaming passions in his native Ontario in a 'holy crusade' against Riel and the Métis, the people who purportedly murdered the Orangeman for 'his faith!' Schultz not only 'POCKETS THE HATFUL OF COINS' the outraged Ontarians have donated to the cause but then confesses to his associate Charles Mair that 'Thomas Scott alive / was a pain in every ass / but his corpse'll be a hero by and by' (24–5).

Riel and the Métis, by contrast, are depicted as a most humane and pacific group. Even after Scott shouts at Ambroise Lépine, 'Speak English, mongrel!' and calls him a 'Papish half-breed,' Riel's Red River commander 'STANDS BY WITH GREAT DIGNITY' (3, 5). Riel's political demands, too, seem eminently reasonable. As the Métis leader informs the Easterners, he is not 'starting a prairie fire' but 'stopping one from breaking out.' Moreover, no one has the 'right to take away our rights! / This land was ours before you came: / it is not yours to sell' (6). Particularly in the second North-West conflict, Riel, who has an 'INDIAN WIFE' rather than a Métis one, is supposed to be acting on behalf not just of the Métis but of all First Nations. Thus the Saskatchewan Valley contingent that travels to Montana to ask him to go to Batoche, in addition to Dumont, includes the 'ENGLISH-SPEAKING HALF-BREED' James Isbister and 'POUNDMAKER, CHIEF OF THE CREES ' (34–5). Poundmaker, of course, is not reported to have gone to Montana, and his insertion reveals the librettists' deliberate attempt to highlight the existence of a Métis–First Nations alliance in 1885, a solidarity that incidentally is decried as a pernicious 'myth' in the first history of those events from an Aboriginal perspective (Stonechild and Waiser 1, 240).

Moore and Languirand's partiality is also echoed in the opera's music. As the composer R. Murray Schafer has noted, 'Somers has set most of the Prime Minister's lines in *Sprechgesang* to contrast with Riel's passionate and lyrical singing. A sort of atonal vaudeville is evoked for Ottawa.' Somers creates 'the work's most poignant moments' in the mostly unaccompanied arias he gives to Riel and his wife, a technique employed 'to evoke the loneliness of Canada's pioneer life'; whereas Macdonald is presented as 'a rather silly figure. The prelude to Act II has a staggering, intoxicated lilt which is an obvious reference to the Prime Minister's alleged alcoholism' (19). It is worth noting that when the Canadian Broadcasting Corporation (CBC) televised the opera two years later, in 1969, the one 'significant characterization change' the producer felt compelled to effect was to make Macdonald look and sound 'a little less farcical' (Schafer 24).

Their undisguised antipathy toward individual Canadian expansionists aside, Moore and Languirand – like Somers – appear to be sympathetic to the idea of Confederation itself. They may not subscribe to Macdonald's nationalistic determinism, the conviction that Canada must either become a transcontinental nation or collapse, yet the librettists are not indifferent to the fate of Confederation, as is indicated by the words they give to the prime minister:

Nothing can stop this country now.
There may be local obstacles,
jealousy and hate and pride:
but the wheel, my friends, is turning and
we are only flies upon the wheel.
Nothing can stop us. Nothing will.
If we unite from sea to sea
we shall become a mighty power:
if we do not, we'll all be naught ...
shouting unheard in French and English both. (11)

Indeed, in light of Moore and Languirand's divergent depiction of the Métis and their Canadian adversaries, the most unusual aspect of their work is the parallel they draw between Macdonald and Riel. The two leaders seem to be less visionaries than mere politicians, two short-sighted and opportunistic individuals who hide behind the state in order to justify the elimination of an opponent, and who use precisely the same words in doing so. Thus, Riel asserts that Scott must be executed because 'I cannot let one foolish man / stand in the way of a whole nation!' Macdonald, in turn, proclaims that Riel must die, since 'I cannot let one foolish man / stand in the way of a whole nation!' (21, 52). Despite its scepticism about certain facets of Canadian nationalism, if not nationalism in general (Hutcheon and Hutcheon 4, 8), *Louis Riel* in the end both condemns and celebrates the ideals of Canadian nationhood. It ultimately owes less to Howard's continentalist Riel than it does to the Riel of Coulter, the playwright Moore says first recognized the Prophet of the New World as 'an ambiguous Canadian legend' and whom Moore describes as 'a great progenitor' (*Reinventing Myself* 176, 354).

Howard's influence, however, is pervasive in a later Canadian representation of the Métis leader, Don Gutteridge's *Riel: A Poem for Voices* (1968). An Ontario writer who specializes in long poems about prominent individuals in Canadian history, what he calls 'private poems about public figures' ('Riel' 8), Gutteridge is even more unabashedly pro-Riel than his model. Whereas Howard extols Riel as 'the Métis's only prophet of nationalism,' he has profound reservations about the

formal education that makes that role possible, for it supposedly alien-
ates him from his land and people. Howard (himself Caucasian) is also
ambivalent about both Riel's religious ideas and the European part of
his biological and cultural heritage, commenting that 'Louis was more
white than red, and consequently he was a worrier' (501, 337).
Gutteridge, though, seems to have no doubts about his protagonist's
oneness with his world. As the Canadian poet depicts the young Riel's
last meeting with his father before leaving for Montreal,

> They were walking: as a Métis always walked
> Because a man could feel the Mother Earth through the palms
> Of his feet, and know the firmness of her flesh
> And the great unturning heart at the centre of her,
> Were walking because walking told in every stride
> Of man's moving over the earth in a passing as brief
> As a footprint, and because a Métis found
> In walking a togetherness of spirit,
> Of flesh knowing the same earth at the same turning
> Of the sun or the season, and a man moving
> Was like the wind's loving of the deep grasses,
> And did not stand like the rocks and die with stillness
> In the bones, and because a walking made spring
> Out of muscle and limb, and a man could feel
> His body lean as a willow in its long greenness,
> And because there was joy in a Métis walking
> With himself or his brother. (2)

Even though Riel is about to embark on a spiritual and intellectual
journey devoted to the study of Western theology, he is certain of his
communion with his natural surroundings because 'These things had
been told / To him by his elders, and he had felt them' (2).

Given its subtitle, *Riel* is to be seen as a polyphonic work. Combining
fictional discourse with letters to newspapers, government reports,
commercial advertisements, journal entries, and popular songs, the
poem is narrated from a variety of perspectives, including those of Riel,
Macdonald, Scott, Evelina Barnabé, and an anonymous Canadian soldier. But there is never much question which voice the poet privileges –
the Métis leader's. For Gutteridge, the promoters of Canadian expansion into the North-West are not simply misguided but evil, a fiendish
horde whose utter amorality is surpassed only by its innate stupidity.

As he has Schultz describe his vision for Red River, 'One had to believe in some "cause"; and the West / Would be caught up in the Orange thrust and commercial / Sweep, as it were, of Ontario.' Likewise, Macdonald, that 'ragamuffin Glasgow boy / With soot-stained palms,' dreams of a transcontinental nation without ever 'knowing what the reality was, nor when' (9, 17). However, Gutteridge reserves his most acrid vitriol for the volatile Scott and Mair, the 'buffalo-rimer and sometime epic bard' (8). Mair was a much maligned but complex individual, an apostle of Anglo-Canadian culture who could also write that the greatest crime 'in the natural history of America' was 'the reckless and almost total destruction of the bison,' by 'that great enemy of wild nature, the white man' ('American Bison' 93, 95; Braz, 'Wither'). Yet, betraying an apparent poetic Oedipal complex, Gutteridge dismisses the earlier writer as a colonial and a fraud, an 'ass' who suffers from an 'acute constipation of the brain' and whose political ideas are even 'less successful than / His importunate iambicizing' (7, 9). Scott, too, is not just intemperate but a pervert, a torturer of animals. He is a beastly dullard who thrills on driving a herd of buffalo over a bluff, 'bones stickin out like a bunch a felled trees, all splintery, an the blood squirtin every which way.' As the recent Ontario migrant, and thus most unlikely buffalo hunter, gleefully recounts the slaughter to his fellow prisoners at Fort Garry, 'By God, fellas, I tell ya, I ain't had so much fun since ... I tell ya, that there half-breed antichrist, is gonna end up just like them bulls at the bottom of some cliff, an the only thunder's gonna be me laughin, just laughin an laughin ... ' (25–6).

The violence of Gutteridge's portrayal of the Canadian politicians and settlers elicited a swift censure by the poet Edward Lacey, which in turn triggered an even more combative essay by Gutteridge. Canada's '"first homosexual poet,"' as well as a tormented soul who wrote under his own name but pretended it was a pseudonym (Lacey, *Magic Prison* 104; Beissel 10), Lacey makes a series of criticisms. The first is that, in his foreword to *Riel*, Gutteridge confuses the Métis with the French Canadians and erroneously constructs his poem in terms of 'the French-English problem.' More germanely, he chastises the author for 'the evident bias with which Mr. Gutteridge treats Riel's opponents and mingles fancy with history' ('Poetry' 130–1). An Ontarian who spent most of his adult life as an expatriate in the tropical climes of South America, North Africa, and Asia, Lacey was not exactly a supporter of Canadian nationalism. He rejected both the 'culture & climate' of his native land (*Magic Prison* 48), which he describes as an unformed country 'whose only rebels fled, / when defeated,' and 'whose only heroes were hanged or exiled failures, or decorate boxes of / chocolates' ('Saudade' 60; Beissel 6, 10). Still, he is incensed by Gutteridge's characterization of people like Schultz and Scott, asking where is the poet's 'authority for considering the latter a sadist to animals (except, of course, Canadian cultural traditions) or for causing him to speak an unauthentic, subliterate garble?' ('Poetry' 131).

Gutteridge's response to Lacey's 'barbarous' and 'ungentlemanly charges' was 'Riel: Historical Man or Literary Symbol?' a fascinating essay in which he expresses his views both of his poem and of poetry about historical figures in general. Gutteridge begins by making a marked distinction between poetic history and historical poetry. Poetic or poeticized history, he asserts, is poetry whose central 'purpose is to make history "come alive," as it were, by rendering it in more accessible forms of literature' (3, 6), whereas historical poetry is simply poetry 'with history as its organizing metaphor.' The latter is the sort of poetry in which a poet uses historical materials the way Keats uses the nightingale, 'as symbol or structuring principle in order to make a personal statement of his own, or put another way and more pompously, to reveal the universal in the particular' (4, 7). Since Gutteridge considers his poem historical poetry, not poetic history, he feels free to create a Riel in his own image. As he repudiates Lacey's criticism, 'a work of art which interprets historical events in the light of their symbolic or mythical meanings obtains any validity it might have,' not by respecting the external reality of its sources, but by being '"true"' to their spiritual reality and 'by being simultaneously "true" to the imaginative needs of its author at the time of the writing' (10).

Whatever merit Gutteridge's essay may have as literary criticism or theory, it is invaluable for making explicit what at times is only suggested in his poem. For example, in *Riel*, the poet has his protagonist explain why he 'had *had* to kill' Tom Scott:

> Scott had deserved death; for he was a symbol
> Of all that stood in the way of their hopes, the vision:
> Canadian, Orangeman, bigot, blasphemer,
> A man without root, with no touch of the soil
> In him or wind on him. (26)

In his essay, Gutteridge goes further and declares that the Orangeman has to be executed, not for what he has done, but for what he is, for his unnatural relation to the land, his 'Europeanness.' In Gutteridge's words, 'those strange men like Macdonald and Scott' did not merely oppose Riel but 'pitted themselves so foolishly and ignominiously against the flow and circularity of Nature herself' (15). That is, their actions constitute not so much a crime as an abomination, a sin.

'Riel: Historical Man or Literary Symbol?' is also important for the light it sheds on Gutteridge's sense of his relationship to Riel, a relationship mediated largely through Howard's *Strange Empire*. For the poet, Howard 'makes the white man feel ashamed, and fills the sensitive reader with a feeling of tragic loss.' The Montanan 'sides' with the First Nations and the Métis because he is captivated by their 'mystical, humane, constructive, and socially harmonizing' idea of the land, a world-view 'so powerful that it dissolved racial and language barriers in a way which from our present vantage-point seems marvellous' (13). It is also his deep appreciation of the Aboriginal 'philosophy of land' that leads Gutteridge to empathize so unequivocally with Riel, and his people. He writes that 'I am not Metis, do not speak French, am intractably presbyterian [*sic*], and have no plans to effect a revolution,' yet such are his national affinities with his protagonist that they enable him to 'render Riel's feelings because I conceived them partly as my own.' Curiously, this is the same ethno-cultural transcendence that he does not grant to someone like Coulter. As Gutteridge asserts, the reason the Irish-born playwright failed to grasp Riel's true significance was that he 'was not a native Canadian (I mean here that he was not only not born here, but more seriously does not think or feel like a Canadian).' Therefore, even though Coulter 'had researched his material thoroughly (much more thoroughly than I ever could, or would), he had missed what Riel really was in Canadian terms. He had got his history straight ..., but he had missed the meaning' ('Riel' 10, 11).

While Gutteridge's identification with Riel appears to be a most positive development, it is actually quite problematic. It could be considered nothing less than a form of appropriation, a refusal to respect the Métis leader's national specificity, his Otherness. Gutteridge candidly admits that his work on historical figures is the direct result of 'my desire to re-discover the peculiarly Canadian myths of my historical past' ('Riel' 9). However, as the Métis art historian Catherine Mattes asserts, there are many dangers in using 'Riel's image for movements that he himself did not believe in,' notably 'the creation of Canada' ('Whose Hero?' 4, 77). The most obvious of these pitfalls is that, since Riel cannot be fully incorporated into the Canadian mythology without doing much violence to his own national story, Gutteridge is able to envisage the Métis leader as a fellow citizen only by denying him.

Still, despite its obvious contradictions, Gutteridge's genealogical embrace of Riel is far from being an anomaly in Canadian letters. Several other writers have also produced similar versions of the two North-West conflicts, representations in which they make little attempt to conceal their solidarity with the Métis leader and their contempt for the politicians and settlers who opposed him. One of the more riveting of these is *Moving In from Paradise* (1976), a series of interlinked (and unpaginated) short poems by Steven Michael Berzensky. A U.S.-born Saskatchewan poet who used to write under the name Mick Burrs, Berzensky portrays Riel, not just as a hero, but as a Canadian hero and, more specifically, a Western Canadian hero. He is the trans-ethnic political leader who fights

> for a new order on the prairie
> beneath the dancing lights of heaven
> with the singing spirits of God and earth
>
> while other Christian strangers
> more conscious of the fashions of the day
> tried you at last for the murder of Scott
>
> and called it treason against Her Majesty
> called it Insurrection
> and sentenced you
>
> to spend your last moments of dignity
> under a white hood – on their
> dark gallows. ('Civil Service')

In brief, Riel is the sort of patriot who sanctions the execution of Scott not only because of the Orangeman's defiance of the Métis provisional government, 'for insulting your leadership,' but also 'for hindering the peace with Canada' ('Red River').

Berzensky's Riel is clearly a victim of racism. This is evident in the poet's depiction of Jack Henderson, the one-time Fort Garry prisoner who 'swore vengeance / for his compatriot Scott's execution' and 'slept with hate his lover / these fifteen years' for the simple satisfaction of putting 'the hangman's knot under your ear' ('The Volunteer'). But

Berzensky suggests that no one person is responsible for his protagonist's fate. As he writes of the anonymous civil servant who is never
available to meet with Riel, 'His name doesn't matter. / It never has'
('Civil Service'). Berzensky does not go as far as another Saskatchewan
writer, Kim Morrissey, who contends that there was no 'deliberate
villain' at Batoche, that it was really 'a bureaucratic bungle' ('Art of
Rebellion' 12–13). Yet he appears ready to absolve everyone of culpability in Riel's downfall, including the country's first prime minister, who
'died / calmly in bed' after 'Riel was martyred, hung [sic] in Regina'
('Toward an Epic of the Rebellion That Was a War'). As the poet states,

> It was a war
> > a war declared
> > > by the government in Ottawa
> > > against the people of the West
> > > whites metis indians
>
> The enemy is and was and will always be
> no single individual
> no one you can put your finger on
> no even wily John A Macdonald ('Toward an Epic')

Actually, for Berzensky, Riel is victimized not just by the Canadian
government but by Western civilization itself. Even after acknowledg-
ing his hero's role in the execution of Scott, he asserts that the Métis
leader is killed solely 'for serving your vision' ('The Beast'). This is not
surprising, since we live in a science-dominated culture that has alienated us from our traditional ways of seeing ourselves and the world
and 'sentences our poets to death / for visions' ('The Horizon'). Nevertheless, Berzensky remains confident about Riel's eventual rehabilitation, for 'hanged men are always reprieved / one century too late'
('Toward an Epic').

An even more firm belief in Riel's ultimate redemption informs a
song written about the same time, Willie Dunn's 'Louis Riel' (1976). A
Mi'kmaq/Métis writer and singer, Dunn depicts Riel as a noble leader
who returns to Canada when he learns that the 'people are hungry, the
people need food.' His community wishes him to destroy 'the traders
and the buffalo skinners,' and he humbly obliges. However, Riel is
undermined by external forces. Suspecting that he is 'putting down the
system,' Ottawa decides to 'beat him, defeat him, roll him in the jail

house right now' (48, 49). Yet, despite the opposition to Riel by the local priests, who are 'upset' about his activities, there is no question that the 'brave and ... bold' Métis leader is doing God's work on earth. He may well be not just a political liberator but also a spiritual one, a second Christ, who gives 'his life, working for the people' (49).

The deification of the Métis leader, along with the vilification of his adversaries, continues unabated in Janet Rosenstock and Dennis Adair's 'novelization' *Riel* (1979). Based on a screenplay of the same name by Roy Moore, Rosenstock and Adair's work has been described as an attempt 'to Harlequinize the West' (Swainson, 'Rieliana' 295). As a historical fiction, it is certainly perplexing. One has little difficulty situating a satire like Eric Nicol's *Uninhibited History of Canada* (1969), with its mordant irreverence:

> After being hanged, Riel had been elected to parliament but was disquali-
> fied on the grounds that, being deceased, he was only eligible for the
> Senate. This left Riel bitter towards the government, and he seized the
> opportunity to lead a rebel force in a running retreat from law and order.
>   Riel was caught again and hanged at Regina. This time it took. He never
> ran for public office again. (n.pag.)

One also does not face much of a challenge locating a self-consciously postmodern poem like Luc Bégin's *L'abitibien-outan*, in which a machine-gun toting Riel cruises the Quebec countryside in the 1960s with his spiritual confrère Che Guevara in a Renault Major (37–8). Rosenstock and Adair's *Riel*, however, is a different story. On the one hand, the novel's realism seems to invite a straightforward reading. But, on the other hand, its idiosyncratic attitude toward the past suggests that it cannot really be trusted. Indeed, the only justification for not dismissing the work out of hand is that it is the textual incarnation of a lavish but largely uninspired CBC TV production and has some cultural significance. The two-part CBC series was an 'extraordinary success' with the public, drawing almost five million viewers. More significantly, it bears the imprimatur of a Crown corporation, thus revealing how a number of influential Canadian artists and bureaucrats felt that Riel – and his adversaries – should be portrayed at the end of the 1970s (Klooss 19).

The CBC *Riel*, which is directed by George Bloomfield and whose stellar cast includes Don Harron, Leslie Nielsen, Christopher Plummer,

Jean-Louis Roux, and William Shatner, never disguises its political sympathies. In the written preamble to the film, either Moore or Bloomfield states that 'prime minister Macdonald looked forward to the day' the Hudson's Bay Company relinquished its title to the North-West to Canada 'so that he could further his plans for a railroad and for Confederation.' The prime minister's obsession with the transcontinental railroad is accentuated when an inebriated Macdonald is introduced playing with a model train (Bloomfield, n.pag.). Riel, in contrast, is shown as a sober and God-fearing young man, a 'civilized' leader whose only aim is to ensure that his people will be able to live in 'freedom and dignity.' As he addresses the various communities of Red River after his return from Quebec, 'There's enough land here for all of us, and no need to fight over it.' To accent Riel's ostensible Canadian patriotism, the screenwriter and the director even transfer his religious epiphany from Washington, DC, to Montreal. As they have Macdonald declare, Riel is 'a fascinating man – fascinating. He has vision, determination; he cares for his people, and has their trust.' Typically, when the recently elected Riel sneaks into Parliament to sign the members' register, it is the obtuse Macdonald himself who escorts the renegade MP for Provencher out of the building (Bloomfield, n.pag.).

The Bloomfield/Moore *Riel* provoked a barrage of responses, including a forceful one by Kenneth Coutts-Smith. In an essay for the media magazine *Centerfold*,[5] the art historian agrees with the multitude of voices that have drawn attention to 'the blatant distortions of historical accuracy throughout the screenplay' (229).Yet he contends that much more significant than the historical distortions are the 'implications' of those distortions, the film's 'coded message' (229, 233). Coutts-Smith tends to overemphasize the multicultural harmony that prevailed at Red River, in which 'Riel's authority' is resisted only by fanatical Ontario Orangemen. He also charges that the characterization of 'Riel's millenial [*sic*] sense of mission' immediately establishes for a secular audience 'the implicit anticipation of Riel's mental disturbance,' something which is not self-evident to me (230, 232). That being said, there is much insight in his observation that the reason *Riel* is such an abysmal failure is not that it is 'a total trivialisation of history' but that the film is not really about the two North-West conflicts but about French-English relations, particularly the October Crisis of 1970. It is certainly difficult to dispute his thesis when he quotes Macdonald's response in the film upon learning Riel has formed a provisional government at Fort Garry:

'God, man! This means *Separation!*' As Coutts-Smith notes, Red River 'can hardly "separate" from a confederation to which it does not yet belong' (232–3).

Harry Daniels, the then president of the Native Council of Canada, also denounces the TV film in no uncertain terms. In a letter to the head of the CBC, he suggests that the public broadcaster 'should realize the inevitable; that "Riel" is an artistic and financial flop and should be buried in the archives with less notable works.' Interestingly, Daniels's dissatisfaction is not so much with the film's portrayal of Riel as of his people, asserting that the work 'showed a flagrant disregard for the valuable contributions that the Metis have made in the development of Canada.' In fact, part of his indignation seems to lie in the centrality the work gives to Riel, especially the apparent impression that the Métis were 'buffalo hunters who only found a cause with the arrival of the literate Riel' (Daniels).

Like Bloomfield and Moore, Rosenstock and Adair establish their work's tone early. As they write in their preface, they wish to transcend history, since it is not the history of a figure or event that is real but 'the spirit of the history.' The authors thus dedicate their work 'to all historians, who know better than anyone that history is the greatest of all fictions' (7–8). Although they do not expand on their belief in the inherent fictionality of history, it perhaps explains their casual approach to the archival record. For instance, Rosenstock and Adair have Riel fighting not just for the Métis but for all Prairie First Nations. The self-styled Prophet of the New World, who planned to move the Holy See from Rome to Saint Boniface, is also 'dedicated to his church' (7). Similarly, the authors depict Dumont as Riel's commander at both Red River and Saskatchewan, displacing in the first conflict the once much admired but now largely forgotten Ambroise Lépine (26–33; H. Adams, *Tortured People* 119).

Even more conspicuous than Rosenstock and Adair's idealization of Riel, and the liberties they take with the historical past, is their overt contempt for Anglo-Canadian figures, particularly Macdonald and Scott. For the authors, the Orangeman is not just a racist and a bully but an unredeemable retrograde, 'an uneducated labourer and surveyor, who ran whisky to the Indians for a living.' Unlike the other Canadian settlers, Scott is fairly versatile. No less a figure than Dumont says that 'Scott was different. Scott did know how to survive [on the land]. The man was a rattlesnake, fast and dangerous' (50, 97). But despite his physical prowess, the Orangeman remains a rustic who cannot master even his native language. As the narrator comments, Riel not only spoke French with 'the kind of accent a cultured Frenchman might have' but his 'English was superior to Scott's. Scott, Louis knew, had been born to his English, but he was uneducated' (63–4). Furthermore, in light of Scott's dream of becoming 'one of the largest landowners' in the North-West once Canada acquires the territory, he is more interested in romance than in politics or real estate. Like Constantin-Weyer's Riel, he is first and foremost a lover (49).

The object of Scott's desire is Elizabeth Schultz, the (Catholic) wife[6] of the Canada First militant and future lieutenant-governor of Manitoba, John Christian Schultz. A woman who seems to belong more in the 1970s than the 1870s, Elizabeth is a pragmatist who bears allegiance to no one but herself. She purportedly married the older Schultz because he is 'a man of influence' and now cavorts openly with Scott while her husband is 'busy making us rich' (49). It is Elizabeth who incites Scott to shoot Riel, which he does ineptly, hitting an 'oil lamp just above Louis' head' (92, 80). After Scott is arrested by the Métis, while making love to her, Elizabeth meets with Riel, but not on behalf of her sexual partner. As she explains to the Métis leader, '"Mr. Riel, I'm not here to plead for a lover, though he was hardly that. A little diversion, perhaps, but Tom Scott a lover?" She shook her head' (100). Her concern is not that Scott might be executed but rather the impact that his killing might have on the English-speaking community. In her analogy between her private life and Red River's political reality, 'Marriage is an unnatural state. ... We are the only species of God's creation that insists on such confinement. Without compassion, without recognizing one another's needs, that state can become imprisonment. If your people and mine are destined to that kind of marriage, may God have mercy on us!' (101). Elizabeth's words, though, fail to move her righteous interlocutor. Offended that such a 'woman could so easily invoke the name of God,' Riel goes to church that evening and prays for hours to the Lord, whose heart he knows 'opened to all of them – the Métis, the Indians, even the English' (101).

Rosenstock and Adair's Macdonald, too, is a most venal individual, a politician who is less interested in people than in business, especially railroad business. The prime minister provokes a confrontation with Riel and the Métis in order to be able to conclude the transcontinental rail line that he believes will unite 'Canada from sea to sea' (36). As he callously addresses Donald Smith after news reaches Ottawa of an 'Indian and Métis uprising' in Saskatchewan, 'We will get our railroad, won't we?' Moreover, he is washing his hands of the situation, for 'we need the railway and now Parliament will vote us the funds! It's just making the best of a bad mess!' (161–2). As he acknowledges later, 'I'm an opportunist too. I've used this to move the railroad farther west' (175).

So intent are the authors on ensuring that Macdonald does not emerge unscathed from his clash with Riel that they have him lose a member of his immediate family at Batoche, even if they have to completely disregard the historical record in the process. The retribution they reserve for the prime minister is the death of his son Hugh John, a volunteer with the Canadian forces who supposedly perishes of 'scarlet fever' in 1885 (183). To give Rosenstock and Adair credit, Hugh John did enlist in both North-West conflicts (Wilson 9–14, 23–6). The younger Macdonald, who was the only one of the prime minister's children to survive to adulthood, was also not very sympathetic to the Métis or their leader. As he expressed his regret that Riel surrendered to the Canadian scouts, 'Had our fellows taken him he would have been brought in a coffin and all trouble about his trial would have been avoided' (quoted in Wilson 26). In fact, the rabidly Anglocentric Hugh John did not seem to look favourably on many people of non-British origin, striving to keep 'Canada for Canadians' by, among other measures, curtailing 'Slavic immigration' (Wilson 37–8). Nevertheless, Hugh John's death at Batoche is outrageous since he would not only become premier of Manitoba but also the province's police court magistrate, a position that enabled him to combat the 'dangerous foreign "Bolsheviki"' during the Winnipeg General Strike of 1919 (Wilson 36–45).

The partisanship of Rosenstock and Adair's *Riel*, or Bloomfield and Moore's, becomes especially noticeable when one compares it to the portrayals of the Métis leader in the recent CBC TV series *Canada: A People's History*. In *From Sea to Sea* (2000), the ninth episode, writer and director Jim Williamson is quite sympathetic toward the Métis leader. Thus, he de-emphasizes the political opposition to Riel at Red River, except by Ontario Orangemen. He also does not depict, or even acknowledge, the ghoulish disposal of Scott's body. Yet even as Williamson holds Macdonald largely responsible for Riel's prominence, since it is 'provocative acts by the government of Canada' that prompt the would-be priest to return to Red River to lead his people, he does not dehistoricize the prime minister. Indeed, one of the singular aspects of *From Sea to Sea* is the way it shows that Macdonald's attitude toward Riel is shaped by an extremely traumatic event in the early days of Confederation, an incident usually glossed over in representations of Riel – the killing of Thomas D'Arcy McGee. According to the film, the assassination of Confederation's most passionate orator causes 'a hardening at the top levels of government.' This is especially true of Macdonald, who is 'deeply affected by his friend's death' and will no longer 'tolerate those who seek to change society by a barrel of a gun' (Williamson, n.pag.). In other words, Williamson suggests, Macdonald's views of Riel may reflect not only a personal animosity toward the Métis leader but also a most harrowing episode in his and the country's political life.

A similar balance is evident in episode ten of the series, William Cobban's *Taking the West* (2000–1). Cobban's film is openly divided in its politics. As the title implies, it is a celebration of the settlement of the West. Yet it is not insensitive to the impact that the influx of outsiders has on both the Métis and the First Nations. Still, there is one crucial difference between Cobban's portrayal of Riel and Williamson's. As depicted in *Taking the West*, by the time Riel arrives at Batoche, he is mentally ill. He is obsessed with religion and spouts 'increasingly bizarre' ideas that alarm even his closest allies, such as Will Jackson. Moreover, while Cobban's film shows that the Métis have many legitimate grievances against distant Ottawa, it does not camouflage its support of Confederation. As we are told, 'taking the West is the key to completing a country that will stretch from sea to sea' (Cobban, n.pag.). Actually, what Cobban never quite resolves is how you settle the West with immigrant farmers without dispossessing the region's first inhabitants, whose economy and culture revolve around hunting and gathering.

Rosenstock and Adair's *Riel*, like Bloomfield and Moore's, or Gutteridge's, epitomizes not only the lionization of the Métis leader as a Canadian patriot but also the demonization of his opponents as imperialists and chauvinists. In his book on Duncan Campbell Scott, Stan Dragland expresses his dissatisfaction with a previous study of the Confederation poet by stating that its author exhibits 'no sense of sharing, however uncomfortably, Scott's mind-set' (9).That criticism could also be made about the vast majority of writers on Riel since the end of the Second World War. Contemporary Canadian writers seem at pains to establish their kinship with the country's original inhabitants and to distance themselves from the Euro-Canadian politicians and settlers, the people who first secured the cultural and political hegemony that their descendants still enjoy. But given the status of the First Nations and Métis in Canada today, one suspects that those writers share much more with their nineteenth-century forerunners than they care to acknowledge. In fact, it may not be inappropriate to echo Mario Vargas Llosa when he questions the Latin American tendency to blame the Europeans for what 'they did to the Indians. Did they really do it? *We* did it; we are the conquistadores' ('Novels' 35).

In any case, the idea of Riel as a selfless national hero vanquished by petty politicians has not ended with Rosenstock and Adair but persists to this very day. In works like Kevin Roberts's short poem 'Riel' (1985), it is not just the hero's adversaries who are unnatural but Canada itself. In the poet's words, 'Riel who put his mouth on the muzzle / and cried for liberty straight / down the barrel' (182), was opposed by

> ... the stolid
> Loyalist wall
>
> John A and the need for
> CANADA
> *a mare* [sic] *usque ad mare*
> railway economics
> irrational steel lines
> denying the natural flow
> North South geese/buffalo &
>
> people who follow
> seasons of flesh (182)

Similarly, in *The Missing Bell of Batoche* (1994), a play by the Métis writer Bob Rock, Riel is the New World David who miraculously achieves a 'small victory over [the Canadian] Goliath' and who passionately advocates not just 'Metis land-entitlement and self-government' but even 'free trade and multiculturalism' (12); whereas the Canadian government is the political body that 'most certainly could have avoided bloodshed and rebellion with a few thousand dollars spent on food supplies and a few weeks explaining the new land survey to the Metis people,' but which deliberately chose to do otherwise (37). Finally, in the unpublished 'Debout mon peuple!' (1992), an interactive play produced at the National Arts Centre in Ottawa, Riel is the focus of a theatrical version of his trial in which the audience-jury invariably judges him innocent. To quote a critique of one of the productions, 'Il est dommage que des jeunes spectateurs contemporains n'aient pas été membres du jury lors des délibérations d'antan car aujourd'hui, Louis Riel n'est presque jamais condamné' (Beddoes 29).

Riel's rehabilitation is thus virtually complete, at least as far as his place in the pantheon of Canadian heroes is concerned. For most contemporary Canadian writers who have dealt with the subject, the apparent Otherness of the Métis leader is simply a non-issue. Riel may have shown considerable reluctance to become part of Canada, even leading two military campaigns against it, yet he seems to have emerged as the ultimate national hero. This newly acquired Canadianism is not unproblematic, however, for it inevitably calls into question the patriotism of the settlers, politicians, and volunteers who opposed him in the name of Canada. As Francis J.P. French, the grandson of a Saskatchewan officer killed at Batoche, reflected when the Trudeau government decided to honour Riel with a stamp in 1969,

> The problem which now arises is this: when a nation rewrites its history, (the USSR has been in the news recently for having done just that) and the old Bad Guys become Good Guys, what then is the status of the old Good Guys who were charged with the responsibility of undoing the old Bad Guys – a responsibility delegated by the legal national government of the day? Does a reciprocal change in status occur, or do the old Good Guys become non-persons? (6)

French notes that as a youngster he was frequently told that 'my grandfather had given his life for his country,' that he had been killed by 'a traitor's bullet ... – they also used terms like "traitor" when I was a schoolboy, and so did my history books.' He is so perplexed by the present 'status' of his forebear since 'I find that it is just as difficult to regard my grandfather as a traitor as it is to accept the idea that he never existed!' As he concludes, 'If the stamp now establishes Riel as a Good Citizen, would not those who were out to get him automatically become posthumous Bad Citizens?' Actually, should his grandfather 'be given a public hanging in effigy, to atone for his misguided actions of 1885?' (6).

Concerns like French's, though, are rare. More reflective of the transformation undergone in contemporary Canadian culture by the main participants in the North-West conflicts is the assertion by Rudy Wiebe that, at least in recent Western Canadian fiction, 'Macdonald (born in Scotland) becomes a conniving bastard ... and Riel a saint' ('In the West'). Wiebe's judgment is not quite correct. While Riel may have become the most popular figure in Canadian history, there are still significant reservations about some aspects of his life and career – as the controversy over the renaming of Highway 11 in Saskatchewan suggests (Racette 46). Particularly among Prairie writers, on both sides of the international border, there has been a growing suspicion the Métis leader is not Western enough; that, despite his Red River birth, he is too intellectual, too Eastern, indeed, too white. This is a trend that begins with Howard's *Strange Empire* in 1952, is reinforced in Woodcock's biography of Dumont two decades later (1975), and culminates in the fictions of E.H. Carefoot (1973), Ken Mitchell (1985), Alfred Silver (1990), and Jordan Zinovich (1999),[7] in which Riel's role is either ignored in favour of Dumont's or openly denigrated. Even Riel's views on the First Nations have begun to be thoroughly scrutinized. In *Loyal till Death: Indians and the North-West Rebellion*, the historians Blair Stonechild and Bill Waiser contend that, instead of being 'a champion of aboriginal peoples,' Riel perceived the First Nations as his own 'foot soldiers – the means by which he would realize his mission and deliver his people' (77).

The aspect of Riel's life and thought about which Canadian writers have been the most divided, however, is his state of mind in general and his religious ideas in particular. For authors like Livesay and Wiebe, Riel is a temperate but misunderstood mystic. He is a modern-day Abel who perishes at the hands of his more sedentary sibling Cain, since 'it is in the very bones of human existence that the literate agrarian always destroys the oral hunter' (Wiebe, 'Louis Riel' 199). Other writers, such as the playwright Michael Hollingsworth, are less charitable, presenting the Métis leader as a megalomaniac with a proclivity to utter such inanities as 'From out of the flock comes the shepherd. And I am he as you are me' (204). Still others are not sure if he is either enlightened or insane, or both at the same time. As Susie Frances Harrison says of her protagonist at the end of 'The Prisoner Dubois' (1886),[8] her thinly disguised fictional portrait of Riel, 'She never quite made up her mind as to whether Pierre had been a lunatic or a fiend, an inspired criminal or a perverted enthusiast. Perhaps he was a mixture of all' (97). Indeed, it might not be unbefitting that Canadian poets, playwrights, and novelists continue to have serious disagreements about Riel's mental state. After all, this was the matter that concerned the Métis leader the most after the fall of Batoche, notably once he became aware of the imminence of his death.

6

The Mystic/Madman
Riel As a Para-rational Individual

> Always beware the leader
> who talks with God
> and leaves you to do the dirty work.
> *Raymond Souster (1958–60)*

Riel's central concern toward the end of his life, along with his efforts to demonstrate that he was a child of the North-West and that he was divinely inspired, was the desire to prove that he was not insane. J.M. Bumsted has written recently that whether the Métis leader's 'visions and revelations were part of his madness is as relevant a question as asking whether Jesus Christ or John the Baptist were sane men' ('Louis Riel' 26). Still, the issue of Riel's mental state seems inevitable in any discussion of the self-declared David of the New World. The matter became especially prominent in Riel's two addresses at the 1885 trial, one before the jury and the other to the judge after he had been found guilty of high treason and sentenced to death. As he began his first address, 'It would be easy for me to-day to play insanity, because the circumstances are such as to excite any man,' and to 'justify me not to appear as usual, but with my mind out of its ordinary conditions' (*Queen* 311). But Riel refused to exploit the legal technicalities and decided to attempt to persuade the court that he possessed a 'sound mind.' Rather than assenting with his own attorneys to plead innocent by reason of insanity, he charged that it was Ottawa that was 'insane and irresponsible.' As he declared, 'I have acted reasonably and in self-defence, while the Government, my accuser, being irresponsible, and consequently insane, cannot but have acted wrong, and if high treason there is it must be on its side and not on my part' (*Queen* 324).

Riel's determination to have the court formally pronounce him mentally competent was not merely a personal whim. He, of course, wished to spare both his family and people the stigma of being associated with a lunatic, stating that it 'would be a great consolation for my mother, for my wife, for my children ..., even for my protectors, for my country-men' that he would 'not be executed as an insane man.' More signifi-cantly, he knew that he had to be judged lucid if he were to have political legitimacy. Throughout the trial, Riel maintained that he had a divine 'mission,' that God had chosen him as 'an instrument to help men in my country' (*Queen* 351, 314). At the same time, he also realized that in order for people to accept he was truly God's earthly agent they had to believe he was mentally capable. Thus, he even appeared to welcome a guilty verdict, for it supposedly proved that he was stable and 'I cannot fulfil my mission as long as I am looked upon as an insane being' (*Queen* 351). As he added, a negative ruling confirmed that 'I am more than ordinary myself.' At least 'to a certain number of people ...,' [it] is a proof that maybe I am a prophet, maybe Riel is a prophet, he suffered enough for it' (*Queen* 351–2).

However, despite Riel's appeals to be cleared of 'the stain of insanity,' most psychiatrists have always judged him to be mentally unbalanced (*Queen* 351; Flanagan, 'Insanity'). Starting in 1876, Dr Henry Howard admitted Riel to the Longue-Pointe Asylum because he considered the patient 'a fool, in virtue of a teratological defect in his psycho-physical organization' (641). At the trial itself, Dr François Roy of the Beauport Asylum stated persistently that Riel suffered from 'megalomania,' and was in no 'condition to be the master of his acts.' As evidence, Roy cited the fact he and his staff 'never could prove' to the would-be prophet that his 'mission never existed' (*Queen* 244, 246, 254). The defence's other psychiatric expert, Dr Daniel Clark of the Toronto Lunatic Asy-lum, agreed, asserting that any individual who held the accused's views and who performed the acts he did 'must certainly be of insane mind.' Clark further contended that Riel's prophetic writings are not similar to those of Joseph Smith and Brigham Young, or Muhammad's, since the latter's books are consistent with 'common sense' (*Queen* 257, 261; D. Clark 50). Writing from Paris a year after the trial, from informa-tion provided to him by a Quebec colleague, Dr Henri Gilson identified the Métis leader as suffering from a 'manie chronique à forme religieuse' and then concluded that had the case been tried 'dans notre pays, un homme comme Riel vivrait encore, interné dans un asile, mais protégé par la loi' (59–60).

Perhaps one could attribute the psychiatric profession's uniformity regarding Riel's mental state to its infancy as a discipline. The first psychiatrists to analyse Riel certainly make some statements that seem to reveal far more about themselves, and their times, than they do about the Métis leader. After explaining that he was the 'medical superintendent' of the Beauport Asylum and that he had studied the mental disease megalomania, Roy said that 'I am not an expert in insanity' (*Queen* 244, 251). Clark, in turn, testified that 'it is all nonsense to talk about a man not knowing what he is doing, simply because he is insane' (*Queen* 257). Finally, in a comment that should be of much comfort to anyone who makes a living by the pen, Gilson stated that the proof of Riel's insanity lay partly in the fact that, like 'tous aliénés ..., il a la manie d'écrire' (56).

The psychiatric consensus about Riel's insanity is not restricted to the nineteenth century, though, but has held well into the present. Toronto's Dr C.K. Clarke, after whom that city's Clarke Institute of Psychiatry is named, claimed in 1905 that the Métis leader's fate was 'sealed' at Regina not for psychiatric reasons but for political ones. In Clarke's words, the 'mass of testimony pointing to Riel's paranoia is so immense that one wonders that there could have been the slightest discussion regarding it' (388, 18). Another Toronto psychiatrist, Dr E.R. Markson, in the mid-1960s, diagnosed Riel as 'a victim of his own prophetic and megalomaniac zeal,' an illness whose most common symptom was 'the unmitigated idealization of both his mother and father' (248, 251). Soon after, Drs Édouard Desjardins and Charles Dumas, the latter a Montreal psychiatrist, pronounced Riel a 'schizophrène paranoïaque.' According to their long, two-part essay, the subject was an 'instable, à tendances dictatoriales,' afflicted by a 'monomanie religieuse,' who would never have been executed except for the 'fanatisme' of his Orange enemies (1656, 1872). Some fifteen years later, on the centenary of the hanging, Dr Camille Laurin classified Riel as psychotic. A psychiatrist and politician best known as the architect of Quebec's French-language charter, Laurin found evidence of Riel's mental instability in the latter's 'incohérent, décousu, [et] répétitif' address to the court after he was condemned to death. Laurin also contended that, unlike the Canadian government's, the Métis leader's strategy at the trial was extremely successful, for 'en niant toute maladie mentale Louis Riel établissait la crédibilité de son personnage et sa cause.' Indeed, rather than being vanquished at Regina, the Métis leader emerged as the 'seul gagnant,' having 'sauvé le sens de sa vie en la sacrifiant et en la perdant' (5, 6).

In contrast to the psychiatrists, the lay and medical people who interacted with Riel in the last days of his life had a considerably more positive view of his mental state. For Captain George Holmes Young, the officer entrusted with escorting Riel from Batoche to Regina and the son of the Methodist clergyman who ministered to Tom Scott at Red River, the prisoner was anything but emotionally unstable. As Young told the court, 'I found that I had a mind against my own, and fully equal to it; better educated and much more clever than I was myself. He would stop and evade answering questions with the best possible advantage' (*Queen* 277–8). General Middleton, the commander of the Canadian forces in 1885, also testified that, far from being unstable, Riel 'was a man of rather acute intellect. He seemed quite able to hold his own upon any argument or topic we happened to touch upon' (*Queen* 281). Likewise, Dr Augustus Jukes, the Mounted Police's senior surgeon, affirmed that 'I have never seen anything during my intercourse with Mr Riel to leave any impression upon my mind that he was insane' (*Queen* 270). In an apparent reply to Daniel Clark, Jukes asserted that the fact Riel believed he was in direct communion with God did not necessarily prove he was insane. As Jukes noted, 'There are men who have held very remarkable views with respect to religion and who have been always declared to be insane until they gathered together great numbers of followers and became leaders of a new sect, then they became great prophets and great men' (*Queen* 272).

Similar conclusions were reached by the three-member medical commission that Prime Minister Macdonald appointed to examine Riel's state of mind after the trial. The commission, comprising Jukes as well as Dr François-Xavier Valade, an Ottawa physician, and Dr Michael Lavell, the warden and surgeon at Ontario's Kingston Penitentiary, had a specific mandate. Its aim was not to establish if the Métis leader was 'sane when his treasons were committed and at the time of the trial' – questions supposedly already answered by the jury – but only whether he was at present 'sufficiently a reasonable and accountable man to know right from wrong' (Macdonald, Letter to Lavell 2; Stanley, *Louis Riel* 7). Jukes again reckoned that Riel was mentally capable, although he stressed to Macdonald that 'I confess I should be well pleased if justice and popular clamour could be satisfied without depriving this man of life' (quoted in Stanley, *Birth* 367). Lavell too reached the conclusion that, while 'holding & expressing foolish & peculiar views as to religion and general government, [Riel] is an accountable being & capable of distinguishing right from wrong' (15). Like his colleagues,

Valade deemed that Riel was mentally competent, but with one critical difference. He believed that the Métis leader could not 'distinguish between right and wrong on politico-religious questions,' and thus was 'not fit to perceive the crime of High Treason of which he had been guilty' (127). But when Valade outlined his position in a telegram to Macdonald, either the prime minister or his staff deleted the line about 'politico-religious questions,' creating the impression the commission was unanimous (Flanagan, 'Riel "Lunacy" Commission' 115–16).

While more than a century has elapsed since Riel's hanging, the matter of his mental state appears no closer to being satisfactorily resolved today than it did at the time of his death. Some authors argue forcefully that he was 'unstable' or 'mad' (Schafer 18; Thomas 48); others, including two of his most recent biographers, insist no less passionately that he was 'not insane' (Siggins 417; Flanagan, 'Insanity' 32, 'Was He Really Crazy?' 18). Sometimes contradictory positions are taken not just by different writers but by the same one. George Woodcock, for example, has made the perceptive observation that 'we have long given up the idea of William Blake as a madman, and yet Riel uttered few things more extravagant than the Prophetic Books' ('Millenarian Riel' 117–18). Yet the same Woodcock grants that 'Riel may have had periods of mental disorder, and even of what is generally considered madness.' In fact, he states that the reason the Métis were doomed when they invited the hero of Red River to Batoche was that they failed to discern 'the veering in Riel's mind away from rationality' ('Millenarian Riel' 118; *Gabriel Dumont* 13). In other words, Riel was not quite mad, but he was not quite sane either.

One of the great ironies about Riel is that it was not his enemies who strove most intensely to show that he was 'crazy / The francophone and the Metis,' but rather his friends and allies (Cuthand; Flanagan, 'Insanity' 35). The Canadian government, as Riel gratefully acknowledged at his trial, undertook 'to prove that I am a reasonable man.' His own lawyers, however, did their utmost to demonstrate that he was 'entirely insane and irresponsible for his acts' (*Queen* 351, 295). Headed by François Lemieux and Charles Fitzpatrick, two brilliant young Quebec City attorneys destined to become respectively Chief Justice of Quebec and Chief Justice of Canada, Riel's counsel was recruited by his Quebec supporters once they realized that he had again become 'the symbol of the French-English quarrel in Canada' (Stanley, *Louis Riel* 342). Riel was convinced that the two jurists would win the case, which he claimed would mark both his personal victory and that of the Conservative party – the party led by his foe Macdonald – over the Liberals (3: 111–12). But, after Lemieux and Fitzpatrick's first interview with their client, the attorneys concluded that their only line of defence was insanity, since Riel was 'un maniaque religieux,' 'un fou ou un sacré hypocrite – peut-être les deux' (quoted in Stanley, *Louis Riel* 420, note 19). In his final address to the jury before sentencing, Fitzpatrick himself provided the court with an extensive list of reasons why Riel was mentally incompetent: from the Métis leader's decision to attack 'the whole power of the Dominion of Canada, with a [sic] power of Britain behind her back' (*Queen* 297); through his 'insane delusion' that he was 'called and vested by God, for the purposes of chastising Canada and of creating a new country and a new kingdom here' (*Queen* 300–1); to his venality in attempting to extract bribes from Ottawa in order 'to rouse up the foreign nations to enable him to come in here and take possession of the country' (*Queen* 302). As Fitzpatrick closed his argument by appealing to the patriotism of the jurors, his fellow 'British subjects,' he knew that they would not send Riel to 'the gallows' and 'hang him high in the face of all the world,' since it was evident to everyone that the defendant was 'a poor confined lunatic; a victim, gentlemen, of oppression or the victim of fanaticism' (*Queen* 311).

Even more critical than the intervention of Riel's legal counsel was the testimony of the Franco-Catholic clergy. Unlike the Quebec lawyers, who as Riel attested were well-meaning but came from 'a far province' and were unacquainted with the local realities (*Queen* 205–7), the priests were quite knowledgeable about the North-West. The Breton-born Father André, for instance, had become almost de-Europeanized. After ministering to the Métis for twenty-five years, on both sides of the border, the missionary sported an 'unkempt beard and greasy cassock' and his manners had become 'abrupt from much contact with the wily redskins. He was the very antithesis to the courtly abbé, of the glowing land of his youth' (Donkin 187). Yet André, like several of his fellow priests, was no less categorical than the lawyers about Riel being mentally unstable. As the director of the Prince Albert Mission testified why he did not like to discuss politics and religion with Riel, 'Upon all other matters, literature and science he was in his ordinary state of mind.' However, 'upon politics and religion he was no longer the same man. It would seem as if there were two men in him, he lost all control of himself upon these questions' (*Queen* 232). Father Vital Fourmond made a similar point. While Riel could be courteous and rational in private conversation, the Saint-Laurent pastor asserted, if contradicted about 'affairs of politics and government ..., he became a different man and would be carried away with his feelings' (*Queen* 240; Frémont, *Secrétaires* 102–9).

Needless to say, the Catholic priests were not disinterested. Hailing chiefly from France, they were acutely aware of being guests in a predominantly English-speaking and Protestant country. The magnitude of their vulnerability is evident when André rationalized the murder of the two 'saints prêtres' at Frog Lake as God's wilful decision to 'exonérer le clergé catholique de toute accusation de complicité avec les insurgés et pour prouver au monde que ce mouvement insurrectionnel a été tramé autant contre la religion que contre le gouvernement' (quoted in Le Chevallier 172). Still, it would be facile to characterize the clergy's contention that Riel was insane as being purely motivated by political expediency. The Métis leader's mother may have believed that her son was practising 'sa religion' and that 'je le prouverai un jour, au ciel' (quoted in Rivard viii). Yet the fact remains there were significant theological conflicts not only between Riel and the priests but also between the politician-mystic and most orthodox Catholics, including some Métis. To quote Louis Schmidt, Riel's schoolmate in Quebec and his former secretary at Red River, Riel had become 'un véritable fanatique' who professed 'ouvertement des idées hérétiques et révolutionaires.' The increasingly influential Riel had diverged so much from the Church, even 'sur les points de doctrine,' that if he were not compelled to leave the Canadian North-West, 'beaucoup de nos métis deviendront infidèles ... Le grand nombre le suivront partout; il se ferait schismatique avec lui' ('Mouvement' 29789, 29808).

For André and Fourmond, as for many of their co-religionists, the confirmation of Riel's mental instability was his open defiance of the Catholic Church. Riel perceived the accusations of madness levelled against him as a mere refusal to accept his religious ideas. In his words to the court, his only lunacy was his Christian ecumenism:

As to my religion, what is my belief? What is my insanity about that? My insanity, your Honors, gentlemen of the jury, is that I wish to leave Rome aside, inasmuch as it is the cause of division between Catholics and Protestants ... If I have any influence in the new world it is to help in that way and even if it takes 200 years to become practical, then after my death that will bring out practical results, and then my children's children will shake hands with the Protestants of the new world in a friendly manner. I do not wish these evils which exist in Europe to be continued, as much as I can influence it, among the half-breeds. I do not wish that repeated in America. (*Queen* 319)

The clergy, however interpreted his views, not as some form of pan-Christianity, but as proof that he was a fanatic, an apostate. By denying the need for sacerdotal mediation between himself and God, Riel rejected both Catholic dogma and the Church's earthly representatives. That is, he became an 'usurper of the priestly function' (Huel 15). As Fourmond stated, Riel 'did not admit the doctrines of the church, of the divine presence,' and threatened that, after reclaiming the North-West, 'he was to go to Italy and overthrow the Pope and then he would choose another Pope of his own making' (*Queen* 240–1). Or, as André claimed, concerning religion, Riel 'was his own judge ... He believed himself infallible' (*Queen* 234).

Although clearly self-serving, the Catholic clergy's response to Riel after his surrender to the Canadian forces was not an uncomplicated one.[1] This was particularly true of André, one of Riel's most vocal critics at Batoche, who later became the Métis leader's most frequent visitor at the Regina prison and 'mon zélé confesseur' (Riel, 4: 429; Donkin 187; Le Chevallier 171–5, 263–71). To the very end, André was adamant that it would be too risky to free the Métis leader, since he was bound to expose 'la paix publique à de grands dangers.' Yet the priest contended that it would be 'un crime impardonnable' to execute Riel, an abomination that would leave 'une tache de sang sur l'histoire du Canada' (quoted in Le Chevallier 264). André gave two main reasons why Riel should not be killed. First, the Canadian government was largely responsible for the events of 1885. As the missionary told the court, federal indifference to Métis petitions and resolutions 'produced a great dissatisfaction in the minds of the people' (*Queen* 229). Or, as he explained elsewhere, despite Ottawa's protestations to the contrary, 'c'est sa négligence coupable qui a attiré Riel dans le pays.' More crucially, André insisted, Riel should not be executed because he was 'réellement et vraiment toqué.' The proof that the Métis leader was mentally unstable lay in the religious ideas to which he had fallen prey. No sooner did Riel retract his 'blasphèmes' than he relapsed again and began claiming that God had anointed him a 'prophète' with 'une mission spéciale à remplir.' In the priest's words, 'Impossible de raisonner avec lui sur ce point; il se rend quand je le menace de le priver de ses sacrements, mais le lendemain les mêmes idées reviennent sur le tapis' (quoted in Le Chevallier 282, 263).

The Catholic clergy's conclusion that Riel's religious heterodoxy proved he was insane, and thus that his execution was a crime, had a tremendous impact in the French-speaking parts of Canada. Even though most nineteenth-century Quebec writers came to accept that the Métis leader's hanging was politically motivated, they were divided about the man and his ideas. Like Schmidt, they tended to believe he was in 'guerre ouverte' with the Church's hierarchy and, 'sans s'en apercevoir sans doute, fait ... l'oeuvre de Satan' ('Mouvement' 29808). But they were suspicious not just of his religious beliefs but also of his political ones. As an editorial in a Montreal newspaper charged at the time, Riel's mission was both 'antichrétienne et antinationale' (quoted in Frémont, Secrétaires 178). Since they disapproved fundamentally of much of what Riel stood for, those writers were forced to concentrate on his political martyrdom and his alleged insanity, an insanity for which they often hold him responsible. As Léandre Bergeron has a priest state in his play L'histoire du Québec en trois régimes (1974), 'Louis Riel est un malade, un rebelle et un fou.' He is 'un apatride, un paria, un proscrit et encore un fois, un fou' (73–4). Or, as Jean Morisset notes, after the fall of Batoche, 'La seule véritable réponse que la Franco-Amérique a toujours proposée par ailleurs est la suivante. Oui, Riel était fou. Et non-seulement l'était-il, mais il était coupable de l'être' ('Postface' 94).

Interestingly, the first significant sympathetic portrayal of Riel as a religious figure does not appear in French but in English, in Anne Mercier and Violet Watt's The Red House by the Rockies: A Tale of Riel's Rebellion (1896?). Published by the Society for Promoting Christian Knowledge, a Church of England missionary organization dedicated 'to convert[ing] the Indian Nations ... and to deale [sic] with them for their soul's good' (Allen and McClure 24), the novel is an overtly pious tract. As the authors describe the Canadian Prairies to the reader, 'the Maker's presence seems very real, and, in the awful yet soothing calm, it is impossible to doubt that there must have been a Mighty Hand at work in the formation of things' (34). The Red House, which is set in the 1880s in what is now southern Alberta, focuses primarily on a group of genteel British settlers. Yet, in depicting the challenges faced by the new arrivals as they attempt to make the country 'our own' (53), it shows them as being surprisingly aware of the fact that they have acquired their new land by dispossessing other peoples, the First Nations and the Métis. As one settler explains to his daughter, the First Nations usually 'keep quiet' on their reserves, 'but we must not suppose they feel friendly to us, who have turned them out of their land, and now keep them like animals in a pen' (41). Or, as the authors themselves contextualize the situation, there have been no real rebellions in Canada, such as Sitting Bull's at Little Bighorn, but only 'the small struggles of a conquered race ..., feeble risings, soon put down.' Nevertheless, the First Nations 'give trouble for a time, and are proof of hatred, hatred deep and inextinguishable, in the Red people against the White race that are crushing them out of life' (49).

Mercier and Watt's sensitivity to the European dispossession of the First Nations is also evident in their characterization of Riel. While a peripheral figure, the Métis leader is portrayed in a rather positive manner. For instance, Riel is presented as 'the son of a brave old fellow, a half-breed himself, a "village Hampden" ... who stood up nobly for his people in his day' (53–4). He is a sort of Cromwell who, even though he knows he is destined to be defeated, 'will have the honour of doing a brave deed before he falls' (55, 57). But, in contrast to both Cromwell and Hampden, the seventeenth-century English firebrand immortalized by Thomas Gray, Riel abhors violence. He is that rarity, a righteous political leader who cannot bear 'the shedding [of] the blood of others' and who undertakes his public career 'only from generosity and a sense of duty' (110–11). Besides, not only is Riel 'a brave man and a patriot' but he is also definitely not mad, the 'pretext of partial insanity' being raised merely 'in order to save his life' (57, 125). As Mercier and Watt portray it, the Métis leader's death is less a miscarriage of justice than a sacrifice, an offering to which they are positive he would joyfully assent:

> Perhaps the execution was a necessity, though a sad and stern one, for peace was restored among the half-breeds, and no further struggle has arisen. Thus one man's death may have saved many lives. And if so, it is what Riel would have chosen; for he took his life in his hand when he followed those who called him from his quiet home to lead them and redress their grievances. Government needs stern measures at times, but we may yet feel a glow of pity and admiration for those who, even in error, arise at the call of their race or land, and give themselves up for others. (125–6)

Or, as the authors conclude, in a note suffused with the Christian piety that pervades their work, 'we may hope that Louis Riel found mercy at the Highest Tribunal of all' (126).

The Red House by the Rockies, however, is an exception among representations of Riel. Instead of continuing to be portrayed as a Christ-like political leader who gives his life for his people, he virtually disappears from the public consciousness for much of the first half of the twentieth century. Furthermore, when Canadian writers finally rediscover him, in the aftermath of the Second World War, they tend to focus almost exclusively on his political role, whether as a victim of Confederation or as a cultural mediator. The few mid-century works that approach the question of Riel's mental state, such as Patrick Anderson's 'Poem on Canada' (1946), usually do so perfunctorily, declaring that Riel is 'not mad. *Pas fou*' (Anderson 39).

A lengthier work that explores Riel's state of mind, although still incidentally, is Edward McCourt's *The Flaming Hour* (1947). Set in the foothills of the Rockies on the eve of the North-West Rebellion, McCourt's novel deals primarily with the trials faced by the white settlers and the Mounted Police. Among those Newcomers there is a most unusual character, an idealistic – or mentally unbalanced – Methodist minister named Steven Conway. Of Irish extraction, as his surname indicates, Conway is a self-declared rebel, like 'all good Irishmen' (33). Even though he has been preaching among the Piegan for fifteen years, and claims to have 'saved the souls of a few of them,' he is extremely ambivalent if not about his faith at least about his fellow Christians and white people in general. As Conway describes the challenges encountered by anyone attempting to convert Aboriginal people to Christianity, 'The Indians think of Christ as the white man's God, and knowing the white man as they do, they're bound to distrust his God. And it would be so easy to save them – if it weren't for the Christians' (43). Or, as he explains why he disapproves of the Mounted Police's edict forbidding the area's First Nations to hold their sacred Sundance, 'We've taken everything else from them' (20).

Conway's views, needless to say, are not widely shared in the larger white community. For example, most settlers and police officers dread the prospect of an uprising by the First Nations and the Métis. As Mrs Scudamore, the wife of a retired British Army major, expresses their moral outrage, 'Think of those wretched Indians fighting against the dear Queen!' Conway, however, welcomes such a confrontation, asserting that if any turmoil does materialize 'we'll have no one but ourselves to blame' (34). He even intimates that a war between Natives and Newcomers is not only probable but inevitable, considering both their divergent political interests and cultural differences. According to

Conway, 'The Indians are poets. That's one reason why we don't understand them' (24). Another reason the two groups fail to communicate is that the First Nations claim title to the land and resources the settlers covet. In his words, 'Everywhere the Indian stands between the white man and the satisfaction of his greed. That's his only crime. But from the white man's point of view there is none greater' (42).

Conway also states that the subjugated First Nations, whom for 'fifteen years now we've been driving ... off the plains, stealing their food ...,, doing our best to destroy them body and soul,' are likely to revolt against the white occupiers if 'Riel returns to lead them' (43). Yet he is not that sanguine about the Métis leader, no doubt because the latter possesses European blood. As he says to Johnny Bradford, the cowhand through whom much of the action is narrated,

> Riel is a strange mixture ... Two-thirds idealist, one-third madman – or is it possible to distinguish between the two? But he's not as bad as people say, although he has done some evil things. And there's a sort of justice on his side that men like Scudamore can't see. After all, he's fighting in the cause of the oppressed ...
>
> ...
>
> In many ways he's mean and petty and stupid. But he's a man with a dream, and it's a good dream. And besides, no man is ignoble who fights in a worthy cause. And the cause of the Metis and Indians is worthy. (42)

Still, Conway's motivation for backing the exile remains perplexing. The minister recognizes that if 'the Indians rise under Riel, there will be bloodshed for sure and some men will die and Riel will be defeated.' But, since he is convinced the First Nations are doomed to wither 'away into extinction,' he feels that it would be more appropriate if they 'disappeared from the earth in one last great, flaming hour of destruction' (43–4). Consequently, in order to precipitate that final conflagration, Conway begins to raid the local cattle ranches so that he can arm the Piegans and the Bloods, and with them help Riel stop the Canadian government and people from 'steal[ing] the land from the Metis' (91).

The one white person who is aware of Conway's direct involvement with Riel, but not of his cattle rustling, is his lover Judith Sumner. The local schoolteacher, Sumner believes that Riel is 'not altogether bad – far from it – but he's got a twisted brain' and also that 'the Indians will rise if the Metis do' (74–5). Thus she attempts, but fails, to have the Mounted Police intercept the Métis leader at the border, hoping to prevent the minister from becoming entangled in any military conflict with the Canadian government. However, when Sumner learns that Conway not only approves of Riel's struggle but, to support it, is robbing his friends and neighbours – even seriously wounding one of them – she realizes that she must stop him. So she follows Conway to the Piegan reserve and, while he addresses a large gathering of armed warriors, 'every able-bodied male of the tribe,' shoots him to death, basically ending any further talk of the Piegan and other members of the Blackfoot Confederacy joining the Métis (157). As Sumner justifies her actions, she kills the man she loves because she was unable to convince him that, even if the First Nations 'rebelled, there would be no quick, clean end – only defeat and greater misery. I could never make him see how useless it would have been, how much more suffering it would have meant' (167).

In *The Flaming Hour*, McCourt clearly conveys mixed political messages. A well-known Saskatchewan novelist and literary scholar, McCourt does not appear unsympathetic to Riel. As he writes in his fictionalized life of the Métis leader, 'Whatever his faults, whatever his crimes – and they were many – his dream was not ignoble ... He believed passionately in the nationhood of his people; and for that belief he died' (*Revolt* 159). Yet for someone who professes to admire the subject, he elects to tell Riel's story, not from his perspective, but from that of a white man. Moreover, this white man, Conway, is not nearly as benevolent as both he and the author seem to believe. Like the other settlers, and much of late-nineteenth-century North American society (Francis, *Imaginary Indian* 23–4), the minister is certain that the First Nations are destined to vanish. His only major disagreement with people like the Scudamores is the length of the process. As Sumner summarizes Conway's views, 'He always felt that way about the Indians ..., always. Better a quick clean end than a slow, lingering death down through the years and generations' (167). But Conway supposedly has such an overwhelming influence over the Aboriginal people to whom he ministers that, the moment he dies, so does all their desire to defend their land and rights. In the words of the daughter of a settler, words with which the minister expresses his agreement before he expires, 'They're quiet now. They'll go back to their homes. They won't fight now' (161).

A no less paradoxical aspect of McCourt's novel is that, at the same time the author describes the opposition to white settlement by the First Nations and the Métis as a noble cause, his work questions the wisdom of any such resistance. As Johnny Bradford tells Conway, '... what's the use of startin' a rebellion ... when the Metis and Indians are licked before they ever fire a shot? They won't go anywhere, and there'll be a lot of bloodshed, and hard feelin's for years afterwards' (42). That is, for McCourt, an uprising ultimately can be nothing more than a romantic gesture. No matter how idealistic Riel and Conway may be, they are both mentally unstable. As the author has Sumner say of her lover, 'He was like Riel – he had a vision – and a twisted brain' (167–8). Or, as she concludes, considering the utter unfeasibility of Conway's political dream, it is salutary that he perished in the struggle, since 'I saved him from the kind of disillusionment that would have been far worse than death' (169).

The portrait of Riel that James McNamee paints in *My Uncle Joe* (1962) is less equivocal than the one sketched by McCourt, but still not unambiguous. Told from the perspective of a boy for whose father the Métis leader worked in the badlands of Montana, the novella traces a journey from the U.S. Great Plains to the Saskatchewan River Valley by the narrator and his uncle, a freighter and 'big, soft-hearted westerner' named Joe Campbell (22). The most notable aspect of both *My Uncle Joe* and the novel into which it was later expanded, *Them Damn Canadians Hanged Louis Riel!* (1971), is their pan-Prairie nationalism – or continentalism. For McNamee, individuals are not good or bad but Western or Eastern, that is, Westerners or Ontarians (Osachoff, 'Louis Riel' 66). As he has Campbell comment, in 'the old days' people 'shared' their food and always charged 'a fair price,' but you 'weren't dealing with Canadians then, you were dealing with westerners' (*Them* 71). Or, as he describes the psychological and moral progress made by a former Easterner, 'Bob Swinton, who came from Ontario but you would never suspect it because he had advanced.' This is no mean achievement since Upper Canadians purportedly excel 'in only three things, in singing Protestant hymns, in burning houses, and in stealing' (*Them* 125, 91).

Not surprisingly, Campbell's East-West Manicheism is not devoid of contradictions. While the Montanan describes himself as 'Scotch,' he, like the Métis leader, is 'one-eighth Chipewyan,' which is the reason he is so sympathetic to the man he invariably calls 'Mr. Riel' (*Them* 1). Yet in order to transform his hero into a purely regional icon, he is forced to deny any other aspect of the latter's identity, including his ethno-racial and cultural heritage. Campbell corrects an Ontario Orangeman who has been sent to Regina by his lodge to witness the hanging by saying that Riel is neither 'a Frenchman' nor 'a half-breed' but 'a westerner.'

As the freighter adds, seemingly oblivious to the irony in his statement, '... he's as white as me' (*Them* 76–7). Campbell's Prairie-centrism is also complicated by the fact that the people on the Canadian side do not share his perspective. With their loyalty to their quaint 'Sovereign Queen,' and perhaps grated by Campbell's frequent threats that if Riel is condemned to death 'President Cleveland will send his bluecoats riding up here,' the Canadians have a dissonant view of the Métis leader. As the narrator complains after he reaches northern Alberta, 'Nearly everybody in Edmonton hated Mr. Riel. I guess they never knew him like my uncle and I did' (*Them* 75, 29). More significantly, even the author appears to have some questions about his hero's mental state, at least in the 1880s. In his short preface to the British edition of *My Uncle Joe*, a note not included in the original version, McNamee explains that the 'Mr. Riel' mentioned in the work is the historical Louis Riel who opposed Canada in Manitoba and who, after his defeat, fled to a life of exile in the United States. Although he remained 'as eloquent as ever' in both French and English when he returned to Canada in 1884, by then 'he was mentally ill' ('Note on Louis Riel,' n.pag.).

A similar level of ambivalence regarding Riel's mental capacity is evident in Giles Lutz's *The Magnificent Failure* (1967). A U.S. historical novelist who has devoted several other works to what his book's jacket calls noble but 'lost causes' in the Great Plains, Lutz is almost elegiac about 'the Bois-Brulés [*sic*], the people of mixed blood.' Instead of attempting to deny that the Métis are the product of miscegenation, or equating racial mixing with degeneration, the author celebrates the phenomenon. As he writes, the Métis' Aboriginal and European ancestors transmitted to their progeny 'the vigor of two races,' producing 'a people singularly adapted to this wild, cruel land.' Unfortunately, destiny conspired against them and 'decreed another fate' (3).

The tragedy for the Métis, according to *The Magnificent Failure*, is that the only political leader who can inspire them to act as one is mentally ill, or at least helplessly quixotic. Early in the narrative, Gabriel Dumont persuades a young Métis hunter named Janvier Ouellette to travel with him to Montana to ask Riel to return to Canada. Ottawa continues to ignore Batoche's grievances, and Dumont feels that only the hero of Red River can 'lead us again,' since he is such a magnetic figure that when he 'says a man can do something, that man does it' (18, 78). Ouellette is sceptical about Riel's inspirational powers, a doubt reinforced when he finally meets the exile. Rather than encountering a spellbinding orator, he faces a man who appears to be so defeated by his dire circumstances that he cannot string 'two coherent words together' (73). Later, after witnessing the warmth and confidence with which the people of Batoche welcome Riel, Ouellette does change his opinion, reasoning that such an impact on the Métis masses must be a sign of 'greatness' and that the newcomer is 'the man who would fashion their deliverance.' But he soon reverts to his earlier position that Riel is less a leader than someone who needs 'directing to make his own way' (138, 73).

Ouellette's conclusion that Riel is not mentally fit to lead the Métis is precipitated by the latter's behaviour at Batoche. No sooner has the visitor arrived in the community than he begins to alienate not only the English-speaking Métis and the white settlers but also the Catholic clergy. Ouellette, who believes that his people's 'fight wasn't against the Church' (191), cannot understand why Riel would clash with the priests until he deduces that his new leader lives in a fantasy world increasingly divorced from the mundane reality around him. Riel's principal objective, Ouellette reasons, is not to defend the welfare of the Métis but to be their supreme political and spiritual leader. So intent is Riel on gaining total control over his people that he is even willing to sacrifice their future, since 'if I cannot lead in all things, my leadership is valueless' (192). Dumont eventually comes to share his young compatriot's view. The veteran buffalo hunter, who bears no little responsibility for the ethno-cultural schisms in the community, concedes that Riel's obsession with spiritual matters is bound to be catastrophic for the Métis. After all, he asks Ouellette, 'Doesn't he realize that if we lose this war there will be no church to attend, nor any men to attend it?' (212).Yet, even though Dumont knows Riel is 'wrong,' he refuses to repudiate Riel because he cannot conceive of any Métis struggle without him, for 'if I accuse him so, what will the people do? If I destroy their belief in him, do I destroy everything?' (213). Or, to phrase it differently, while the Métis' stand at Batoche may be a glorious moment in their history, in light of Riel's troubled leadership, it is one that can only end in defeat. In the words of a friendly white doctor, as well as the book's title, it is a 'magnificent' failure (319).

In contrast to Lutz, Jean-Jules Richard fails to discern much that is magnificent, or even positive, about the Métis leader in his novel *Louis Riel Exovide* (1972).[2] Now largely out of favour with both readers and critics, Richard is one of the true mavericks of Quebec letters, being often considered the first of the province's 'écrivains modernes' and 'le plus ancien' of its 'écrivains socialistes' (Bourassa 216). He is also believed to be one of Quebec's first overt atheists, having 'abjuré officiellement' his Catholicism before the Second World War. Richard's rationale for renouncing the faith into which he was born is that 'la religion catholique m'ennuyait. Je n'étais pas heureux là-dedans' (quoted in R. Martel, 'Jean-Jules Richard' 43–4). Yet he never quite seems to manage to escape its influence, at least in a negative way. So pervasive are the author's anticlericalism and antideism that they completely shape what a critic calls his 'roman historique au titre barbare' (R. Martel, 'Quand').

While Richard castigates religion in general, he is especially caustic toward Catholicism and its byzantine temporal workings. As depicted in his novel, the actions of the clergy at Batoche are less mystical than mystifying. Thus Father André first writes Riel advising him to attend a meeting of the Settlers' Union in Prince Albert but then counsels him to do the opposite. Later, after the Métis leader ignores his second missive and addresses the gathering, the priest declares in church that he wishes 'les Riel soient rois ou empereurs de père en fils afin que leur équité et leur sagesse soient mises d'une façon officielle au service de la nation' (71). Still later, when Riel proclaims that Rome has 'fini de régner' in Saskatchewan and that 'mon église de Batoche est en train de devenir son Vatican,' André and the other clergy denounce him as an apostate (173, 178). But once Riel is condemned to death, it is the Breton missionary who is assigned by the Church to help him 'mourir en paix.' As the narrator cynically evaluates the decision, 'Certes, le Prophète a failli enlever au clergé la direction spirituelle de la nation, mais depuis qu'il est en prison, les Métis reviennent au bercail et il ne faut pas les brusquer' (249).

The author, though, does not restrict his sarcasm to the clergy. He is also quite disdainful of the behaviour of the people of Batoche themselves, especially their propensity for paranormal visions. The most unusual of these apparitions are the ones experienced by Fabienne Golinot. The wife of Charles T'Enfant Colin dit Golinot, a former Manitoba politician and cabinet minister modelled on the reputed double agent Charles Nolin, Fabienne is the 'plus avenante' of all Métis women (24). She was romantically involved with Tom Scott at Red River and, after he dies, begins to receive nightly visitations from him. Feeling responsible for the execution of her 'beau' (35), Fabienne deduces that Scott is haunting her house because of the despicable manner in which Riel and the Métis killed him and then disposed of his body. But it turns out that there is a much simpler explanation for the paranormal phenomena. The Orangeman is not tormenting Fabienne posthumously because he 'erre sans sépulture' in the afterlife and wishes to seek shelter in her home 'pour la saison d'hiver.' Rather, he is being impersonated by a Métis Don Juan, one of Fabienne's many spurned suitors who desires desperately to possess her (88).

Richard's Riel too is prone to visions, but his supposedly originate not with a 'fantôme' but with 'l'esprit de Dieu' (120). The Métis leader's revelations, which seem directly connected to his fasting, at first have a largely political focus. As he describes his earliest communion with the divine, he was meditating on a hill overlooking Washington, when a 'figure ... lumineuse et impressionante' appeared to him and announced: '"Lève-toi, Louis Riel. Pars et va-t-en vers l'Ouest où tu as une mission à remplir"' (88). After Riel and his family relocate to Saskatchewan, he learns that the objectives of his mission are less material than spiritual. Convinced that the Catholic Church has irreparably compromised itself in its relations with the Canadian and imperial governments, becoming 'une faction adverse, hostile, mécréante, [et] injuste,' Riel ascertains that God wishes him to 'me séparer de cette Église qui sert deux papes à la fois, l'un à Rome, l'autre à Londres' (96, 101). He also discovers that God has bestowed upon him the title of Exovide, or 'celui qui voit l'avenir et qui sauvera son peuple,' and wants him to establish a 'gouvernement théocratique de l'Exovide' called the Exovidate [Exovidat, in French], an ostensibly independent council whose first motion is to recognize 'Louis Riel comme un Prophète au service de Jésus-Christ' (166, 171).

Interestingly, Riel becomes conscious of the import of his visions only after William Henry Jackson joins his entourage. A historical personage, the Ontario-born Jackson was the secretary of the Prince Albert–based Settlers' Union. He was also a member of a devout Protestant family, both of his grandfathers having been Wesleyan Methodist ministers (D.B. Smith, 'Honoré Joseph Jaxon' 83–4), and a 'natural egalitarian' who believed that the 'oppression of the aboriginal has been the crying sin of the white race in America' (quoted in D.B. Smith, 'Ordered to Winnipeg' 7). Yet, in Richard's novel – which in this instance does not diverge radically from the historical record – Will Jackson is the first person to call Riel 'maître.' Along with Bishop Bourget, he is also the individual most responsible for persuading the 'Prophète' that his voices are genuine, since 'jouir de l'extase' is 'la caractéristique des saints de ton Église qui n'ont pas été des martyrs' (87). Or, as he argues with the Catholic clergy, the evidence that his 'chef est prédestiné' is that he has been 'élu non seulement par la majorité de la population, mais aussi par Dieu' (110). Such is Jackson's attachment to 'l'élu de Dieu' that he changes his name to Jaxon and converts to Catholicism (115, 174). Even after Riel has Jackson arrested as a spy (217) – ostensibly to protect him from the Métis community – he never loses his faith in the man who declares him 'mon plus fidèle ami' (129).

Jackson plays another pivotal role in Riel's life, a uniquely Richardian one, by introducing his sister to the Prophet History, when it acknowledges her at all, records that Jackson had one sister named either Cicely or Cecily (Beal and Macleod 128; Siggins 347). A schoolteacher in Prince Albert, she is not reported to have been involved in the events of 1884–5. However, in *Louis Riel Exovide*, this hitherto unknown heroine becomes so central to Riel's mission that she overshadows her controversial brother. Now christened Cécile, she is the Métis leader's own Maid of Batoche, his kilted Joan of Arc. Their first meeting is an inauspicious one, as Riel mistakes pepper for poison and falsely accuses the young woman of trying to kill him. But he soon discovers that, rather than wishing him ill, Cécile is attempting to help him realize his vision. Moreover, she is not just a divine instrument but a most attractive one at that, a living apparition along whose inviting 'hanches' he can freely run his hands (129).

Richard is not utterly insensitive to the fate of Riel and the Métis. Still, when he does show concern with their plight, it is usually not because of who they are, or what they have done, but because of what has been done to them. For example, he describes the Canadian forces at Batoche as a debased 'bande de vagabonds et de fiers-à-bras, de tueurs à gages' (179). Motivated by an 'esprit racial' and 'anglais jusqu'à la haine,' the police and volunteers are more interested in raiding the defenceless Métis women in the surrounding area during their customary 'skin drive,' than in confronting the men defending the village (180, 179). Curiously, he accuses 'un Canadien français, sir Georges-Etienne Cartier,' in complicity with Bishop Taché, of being responsible for Riel's 'défaite, son bannissement, [et] ses quinze années d'errance' (44). As Richard has Riel charge,

... les Canadiens français veulent me faire passer pour un fou. Eh bien! J'ai vu des leurs venir me combattre et on peut faire dire aux Canadiens français que je décline l'honneur de passer pour leur égal, que je leur rends l'honneur de passer pour fou. Ils sont trop ignorants pour comprendre le mysticisme et les choses scientifiques et spirituelles. Ils préfèrent le sport qui leur tient la tête vide. Et je ne serais pas surpris que leur clergé soit au fond de toute l'affaire. Imaginez, j'ai osé résister à son pouvoir temporel et commercial. J'ai osé dire la vérité en faisant connaître que leur Église n'était pas si bonne que ça. (227)

Yet, despite Richard's awareness of Riel's dual victimization by English-speaking Canada and Quebec, he ultimately does not trust the Métis leader, especially his mysticism. The author seems embarrassed by his protagonist's dependence on religion, an intellectual failing he attributes to Riel's pathological fear of death and to his heterogeneous heritage, which is 'indienne, française, irlandaise, scandinave et pourquoi pas ultra-terrestre?' In Richard's words, 'Seul un héritier de ceux-ci peut être divin en ce bas monde. Et la religion n'est-elle pas avant tout un grand désir de retour dans les galaxies?' (213). That is, for Richard, Riel is mentally unbalanced. He is a political leader who believes 'Dieu arrangera les affaires des Métis comme des experts en compatibilité,' someone who 'prend ses rêves pour des prophéties claires et nettes' (198, 164).

If anything, in *Tales from a Prairie Drifter* (1973), Rod Langley is even more unforgiving than Richard in his treatment of Riel. First staged at Regina's Globe Theatre, Langley's two-act play could best be described as a political farce, or even a cartoon. Subtlety is definitely not its forte, as is evident when the governor general opens the work by declaring that Macdonald's government has only one objective:

[E]xpansion. National expansion, continental expansion. To the glory of God, Empire and the Queen. The North West Territories shall soon ring to the axe of English men. The flag of civilization and freedom shall unfold on every flagstaff north of the 49th Parallel [sic] – from Atlantic to Pacific. A railroad, already begun, shall be completed, linking the great Prairie empire – already white for the harvest – forever to other jewels in the imperial crown. O God, save the Queen – God save her. May Britannia's righteous rule illuminate with Christian light every dark corner of our great West. Destiny – God – Queen. (1–2)

Similarly, almost from the moment that General Middleton enters the scene, one has little doubt as to his imperialism and snobbery. As the British commander of the Canadian forces appeals to the prime minister, 'If these raw colonial troops are not replaced by regulars, I cannot be responsible for their actions.' Or, as Middleton later confides to one of his officers, 'I have no confidence in these damned Sunday soldiers. If only I had British regulars' (41–2).

An Australian-born writer best known for his play about another Canadian iconoclast, Norman Bethune, Langley does not always indulge in broad caricature. In a brilliant sketch, which owes much to Joseph Kinsey Howard's *Strange Empire*, he is able to convey the complex personality of Lieutenant Arthur Howard. The enigmatic Connecticut Yankee voluntarily joins the Canadian military, even though he bears no personal animosity toward the Métis. His motivation is simply technological, his need to test his state-of-the-art Gatling gun in a real war, 'to kill men, not to drill spruce planks.' As Howard explains to the minister of the interior, 'I am not the least bit interested in brutality or the mass murder of your enemies – whoever they are. My mission is purely scientific. Your rebellion is merely my laboratory' (29). Langley also provides a unique view of Macdonald. Like Frederick Walsh and other recent writers and scholars on Riel, the playwright alleges that the prime minister orchestrates the North-West Rebellion for political reasons, 'to finish the railroad' (15, 25–6). However, Langley introduces a novel element into the discussion. For Macdonald, the transcontinental rail line that would unite the country is not just a mammoth construction project but 'a great cathedral from Atlantic to Pacific,' a national temple for which fate itself has chosen him 'high priest, chief builder.' Since people have always had 'to bleed and suffer' in order to erect great monuments, the prime minister is philosophical about the fact the same situation will happen in Canada. After all, he confides to his mistress, a giant whisky bottle, 'small things of beauty must be destroyed so the greater beauty can take its place. Blood and pain – the only way. Come. Comfort me' (19).

What is most conspicuous about *Tales from a Prairie Drifter*, though, is its contempt for Riel, a scorn bordering on hatred. Langley considers that the only genuine leader of the Métis is Dumont. Unluckily for the playwright, the polyglot but formally uneducated Prince of the Prairies feels that he is incapable of understanding 'the white man' and 'his language – or what goes on in his head. To me they are mad men.' So the buffalo hunter readily yields the political guidance of his people to the one-time divinity student who claims that he understands not only 'the ways of the whites, the Indians, and the Métis – for I am a Métis – but even greater I understand the ways of God' (22). Unable to fathom why Dumont would defer to an obviously lesser being like Riel, Langley proceeds to demonize the latter, ridiculing him as a destructive if banal leader. To begin with, the self-proclaimed 'David' of the New World is an arch hypocrite. As Langley has Riel describe the Exovidate that will control his theocratic New Empire of Saskatchewan, 'I will not even be on this council, I won't even have a vote. Mind you. The first thing I want the Exovidat [sic] to do is to officially vote me in as a prophet.' Riel also has a propensity for making fatuous theological pronouncements, such as 'Hell is no longer eternal. It exists but only for a certain Duration [sic] – thanks to the mercy of God.' Or 'Christ is real in my visions – but it is pagan nonsense to think He is present in the Host' (35–6). Worst of all, Riel is a political leader willing to sacrifice his people for his private vision. Convinced that Providence will ensure a Métis victory, since he is 'God's annointed [sic],' he systematically opposes Dumont's plans to defend the community, thus provoking the military debacle at Batoche. Indeed, Langley suggests that there may be method to Riel's madness, for it is only through the crushing of his people that the 'cardboard prophet' is able to realize his overriding ambition in life – martyrdom (42, 45).

The focus on Riel as a religious mystic continues in Claude Dorge's *Le roitelet* (1976), but in a much more positive vein. First produced by Saint Boniface's renowned Cercle Molière, the oldest French-language theatre in Western Canada, Dorge's two-act play is one of the most original works inspired by the Métis leader. Although heavily influenced by Riel's own writings, *Le roitelet* is less a historical play than an expressionist one. It is a formally innovative work that interrogates not only the subject's 'mission and martyrdom' but also 'the concept of the mimetic representation of historical reality' (Joubert, 'Current Trends' 125; 'Mythe' 100). The action is set at Quebec's Longue-Pointe Asylum, but it takes place entirely in the head of the central character. With the exception of Riel, the unidentified nun who runs the mental hospital, and the psychiatrist Henry Howard, all the characters are not real figures but projections in the protagonist's mind.

While the Riel of *Le roitelet* is very much an interior Riel, he is one troubled by all sorts of demons, not the least of which is his purported incestuous relationship with his sister Sara. As portrayed by Dorge, the two siblings are unnaturally close to each other and even express the hope to one day 's'épouser' (47, 34–5). Sara, however, frustrates their conjugal plans when she resolves to sublimate her carnal desires for her brother in order to dedicate herself wholly to God and become a nun. As she declares, 'Dieu mérite tout notre amour. Oui, mon frère, aimons-le. Servons-le. Ah! Louis, l'éternité nous dédommagera de nos sacrifices, de nos travaux. Le ciel! C'est Dieu! C'est l'engloutissement de notre néant, dans Dieu!' (63). Riel attempts to persuade Sara to become 'homme et femme,' but his sister is firm if diplomatic. She tactfully reminds him that she has given 'mon coeur, mon corps et mon âme' not to any mere mortal but to God, the divine force the historical Sara calls 'mon Divin Epoux, fidèle et puissant entre tous les Epoux' (78; S. Riel 169).

Riel is also deeply affected by the relationships with the other women in his life, notably his overly protective mother, who expects him to return from his Montreal studies 'en soutane,' and Marie-Julie Guernon, the young Quebecker whose father categorically rejects him as a prospective son-in-law because he does not wish that 'ma fille épouse un sang-mêlé. Un Métis' (32, 42). However, at the heart of Le roitelet is not the bond between Riel and any woman but between him and another man, Tom Scott. Dorge's Scott remains an Orangeman, but he is not one consumed by hatred of all things Catholic and French. On the contrary, he is Riel's closest supporter and ally, the steadfast friend who shelters the Métis leader from his 'idées noires' and who convinces him that 'tu seras le soldat du Seigneur et son roi, car ton combat est juste' (24, 26). Scott is a combination of John the Baptist and Judas to Riel, the faithful disciple who both announces Riel and sacrifices himself for his master by betraying him. As the Ontarian describes their relationship, 'Je suis ton précurseur. Le nouveau Baptiste. Et toi, tu es le nouveau Christ. Tu es le nouveau Christ!' (85). Although Scott's foremost role is to enable Riel to become leader of the Métis people, he still opposes Riel politically, since it is by precipitating Riel's execution that he makes possible the latter's death and triumphant martyrdom. In Scott's words to the man who calls him 'ma force, mon réconfort, mon ami,' 'Je dois mourir pour que tu meures' (64, 116).

Dorge's characterization of the Riel-Scott relationship is clearly ahistorical. As we saw in chapter 1, there is no evidence that Riel was ever distressed by the execution of the Orangeman, to say nothing of Scott perceiving himself as the Métis leader's political and spiritual forerunner. The fact that a literary work is not true to the historical record, of course, does not necessarily mean it fails as literature. Still, Dorge's distinctive treatment of the relationship between the two adversaries is problematic because it reflects his tendency to transform negative situations into positive ones, a tendency that at times makes his play surprisingly undramatic. For instance, Dr Henry Howard relates how when he first met Riel at Longue-Pointe and addressed him as 'Mr. David,' the surname under which the latter had been institutionalized, Riel promptly corrected him. To prove his real identity, he then took out 'a small prayer-book, and opening it at the fly-leaf, handed it to me, saying, "Look at my name there, Louis D. Riel, written by my dear sister."' But no sooner had Riel shown the missal to the psychiatrist than 'the Sister that was present snatched the book from our hands and tore out the fly-leaf, which she tore into pieces, saying, "You are only known here, sir, as Mr. David."' Howard adds that Riel was so incensed by the nun's action that 'I believe if the guardians and I were not there, and she had not cleared out of the room, he would have torn her in pieces. For a few moments I certainly never saw a man more angry' (645). In *Le roitelet*, by contrast, when the nun tells Riel that the best way to ensure he has an enjoyable stay at the hospital is to respect its rules, he responds meekly: 'Pardonnez moi, ma soeur, je ne voulais pas faire le rebelle, mais mon nom ... ' When she then tears out the page, saying imperiously, 'Ici, monsieur, votre nom est David,' he does not react at all (21). That is, in an apparent attempt to portray Riel as a Christ-like martyr, Dorge turns him into an uncharacteristically passive figure, someone to whom things happen as opposed to someone who makes things happen.

This trend to accentuate Riel's positive qualities reaches its apogee in the work of Rudy Wiebe. A native of northern Saskatchewan, Wiebe has been fascinated by the politician-mystic for most of his writing career. While the author does not include Riel as a character in his award-winning novel *The Temptations of Big Bear* (1973), he does have Dumont describing his compatriot as the only possible pan-Aboriginal leader in the North-West, since he is the 'one Person [*sic*] who talks white' (108). In 'Riel: A Possible Film Treatment' (1975), a sketch for a CBC TV documentary, Wiebe outlines his plans for a fictionalized life of the Métis leader. He particularly stresses Riel's 'veneration' of both the sacred and the secular word, his desire to give his people 'a permanent voice' through 'the *written* word which speaks though the speaker be dead' (159). In the short story 'Games for Queen Victoria' (1976), Wiebe probes a historical encounter between Riel and William F. Butler to convey the insidiousness of European cultural chauvinism, a jingoism so pervasive that it prevents even someone like the celebrated British adventurer from accepting that the 'New World Genghis Khan' is not a bloodthirsty despot but a soft-spoken pacifist. To quote Wiebe's Butler, 'A leather-clad Indian on the prairie grass has presence, has dignity, but to suppose that this half-caste could ever play the part of the greatest man on earth since Alexander, dressed in the garb of a priest and the footwear of a savage, was simply absurd. Absurd' (59–60; Butler 135–6).[3] In the novel *My Lovely Enemy* (1983), Wiebe has his historian-protagonist not only discuss the nature of historical truth but even charge that Riel was hanged purely for political reasons, 'to give Macdonald his political coup in the East' (7).

It is in *The Scorched-Wood People* (1977), however, that Wiebe most thoroughly explores the many permutations of the Riel story. Narrated mainly by Pierre Falcon, like Roux's *Bois-Brûlés*, the novel portrays the Métis leader as both a spiritual and a political figure, a religious visionary as well as his people's 'singer-king' (129).[4] Early in his student days in distant Montreal, Riel becomes aware that he has entered a foreign world that not only 'would never be his' but would not even acknowledge his collective reality. As Falcon has the adult protagonist recollect his impressions when he first went East, the Métis were 'mere pemmican-eaters, not a word about them necessary anywhere in the libraries of the world, while their words crowded upwards in him until he felt his head would burst!' (80). The narrator even states, without developing the idea, that Riel's initial Quebec sojourn inculcates in him a 'life-long sense of inadequacy in the face of white custom,' an inferiority complex that ultimately results in his agreeing to be defended by the Eastern lawyers at Regina, since 'the mysteries of a treason trial were suddenly all overwhelming white mysteries to him' (322). Yet, it is also as a consequence of his Quebec experience that Riel ascertains that, if his people's reality is to be inscribed in the consciousness of the outside world, he '*must* write their words down, the persistent sound of their words rising, vanishing with the grass, the fading buffalo'. As he asks rhetorically, '... who would hear them if he did not speak, did not write, write?' (80). In short, Riel's first Eastern journey induces him to sacrifice himself for his nation, to become a writer, not to express his private fears and aspirations, but 'to give my people a voice' (159).

Wiebe's Riel is, above all, a mystic, a 'giant' who if 'God had willed it ..., could have ruled the world' (36). Juxtaposed throughout the novel to the more 'primitive' Dumont, who incongruously plays a pivotal role both at Batoche and at Red River, Riel is a socially conscious prophet bent on transforming the North-West into an earthly paradise. In his words to his military commander, 'If I can think of a heaven to come where the good God allows no death, then I can think of such a heaven having been once, too ... perhaps it is right now, but we aren't in it' (52). Or, as Wiebe has Falcon describe Riel's mission, echoing the author's own views elsewhere, the Métis leader's vision is nothing less than to 'build a Christian nation' in the Saskatchewan Valley, to create 'God's perfect kingdom' (138, 245; 'Louis Riel' 204, 215). For Riel, as for Falcon, the proof that the protagonist is his people's political and spiritual saviour is that God has granted him special prophetic powers. He is the Lord's chosen and, as such, discerns that private revelation enables the individual believer to attain a deeper 'comprehension of God' than the Catholic clergy, whose perception is 'bound by the Church, by the necessity of formula' (329). More specifically, Riel learns that God has entrusted him with 'a mission to complete for which all mankind will call you blessed' (139). This is a rather political crusade that appears to consist chiefly of his taking a 'heavy hammer in your right hand and hurl[ing] it against Ottawa' and convincing the Métis that if they hope to liberate themselves intellectually, they must 'change their thinking not only about politics but also about their religious faith' (164, 284).

Not surprisingly, neither the Catholic Church nor the Canadian government embraces the notion that Riel is divinely inspired, much less that he is 'the most saintly man in the North-West' (331). Whether clerical or lay, Wiebe writes, Catholics reject the transcendence of unmediated revelation, since 'only the Pope can declare divine truth.' The Church's hierarchy, in particular, resents Riel's claim that 'Rome ha[s] fallen' and his vows to transfer the Holy See to Saint Boniface (166, 326). The central Canadian–dominated political establishment, too, is openly antagonistic toward the Métis leader. 'Eastern' politicians like Macdonald and Cartier, 'Canada's greatest statesmen and her greatest rogues,' fear that his plans to divide the North-West among 'the landless believers of the world' are bound to jeopardize their dream of a transcontinental country (88, 325). Feeling threatened by the 'prodigy who had so unbelievably created Manitoba,' the priests and politicians together declare war on Riel under the false pretext that he is mentally unbalanced. Yet, even though they eventually succeed in killing their antagonist, they are unable to vanquish his spirit, since Riel's 'body on the end of that rope would prove forever how Canada destroyed us' (125, 351).

As one can sense from the above description, The Scorched-Wood People is not exactly a 'neutral text' (Duffy, 'Wiebe' 210; van Toorn 140). But it is contentious in ways that the author does not seem to have anticipated, for it situates him in a tradition that he often disparages. Wiebe has charged Edmund Collins with beginning a Canadian school of writing that obliterates 'any distinction between historical fact and hackneyed invention,' resulting in the glorification of certain figures and the demonization of others based solely on their political orientation or geographic origin. At the same time, while he idolizes the very individuals Collins vilifies, and vice versa, Wiebe does not seem any more respectful of what he terms 'cold – or warmed over – facts' than does the Newfoundlander ('Albert Johnson' 239, 226). Thus, in order to portray Riel as a Canadian patriot, in *The Scorched-Wood People* Wiebe conveniently fails to draw attention to his protagonist's pro-U.S. sympathies. Quite the opposite, he has the Métis leader praying to God to spare his people 'the misfortune of having to join the United States! ... May the United States help us, according to the disposition of your Providence, but never through union, never through our agreement' (276–7; Riel, 3: 187, 307). To justify Riel's sanctioning of the execution of Scott, Wiebe also depicts the Orangeman, not just as a contemptible imperialist and 'blasphemer,' but as the murderer of a mentally handicapped Métis (326, 47). Finally, again like the author of *The Story of Louis Riel* and *Annette, the Metis Spy,* Wiebe is not above using the mystique of historical fiction to invest his novel with truthfulness, even attempting to naturalize his narrative by relating it through a historical Métis figure.

The most common criticism of Wiebe's choice of Falcon as narrator is the Métis bard's temporal implausibility. Since Falcon died in 1876, almost a decade before the events at Batoche, 'the idea of his continuing as a spectral narrator strains one's credence to the wrenching point' (G. Woodcock, 'Riel and Dumont' 99; Duffy, 'Wiebe' 205). Falcon himself seems aware of his chronological displacement. One moment he is very much grounded in space and time, a beloved minstrel who christens his people 'Bois-brûlés' and whom even someone like Riel reverentially addresses as 'Grandfather' (25, 35). The next, though, he is a ghostly Methuselah who, while describing Will Jackson's baptism as 'a son of the New Nation,' casually notes that 'sixty-seven years later Jaxon would die a pauper on the sidewalk in front of the New York hotel that had expelled him' (225). However, far more problematic than Falcon's lack of verisimilitude is his inconsistency. Wiebe's narrator often appears confused, uncertain whether 'he is omniscient or intimately involved' (Lecker 132), an intellectual turmoil that likely arises from his being not so much an independent character as an authorial device for reading Riel.

Wiebe opens the first edition of *The Scorched-Wood People* with a most curious epigraph:

And who has made this song?
Who else but good Pierre Falcon.
He made the song, and it was sung
To mark the victory we had won;
He made this song that very day,
So sing the glory of the *Bois-brûlés*. (1977, n.pag.)

The epigraph, which is not identified, is a translation of the last stanza of 'La Bataille des Sept Chênes,' Falcon's poetic celebration of the Métis victory over the Selkirk Settlers at Red River in 1816 (Falcon 9).[5] Moreover, in subsequent interviews about *The Scorched-Wood People*, Wiebe explains that one of the reasons for having Pierre Falcon narrate the novel is that he is 'the community singer ..., the oral recorder of the history of the community telling it to us.' He is 'the voice of the people' (quoted in Juneja 10; Struthers 26). That is, the novel is not just written by the most acclaimed of Métis bards but by the Métis people themselves. Yet, since the epigraph is excised from the more widely circulated paperback edition, one is led to deduce that the author – or, perhaps more correctly, the transcriber – does not quite trust his own reading of Riel. Considering the uncanny tendency of this nineteenth-century collective Franco-Catholic Métis voice to sound like a late-twentieth-century white Western Canadian Protestant, one also cannot help but suspect that the narrator is really a thinly disguised spokesperson for Wiebe.

The extent to which Wiebe manipulates Falcon to serve the author's 'own rhetorical and polemical purposes' (van Toorn 143) is evident in his depiction of Riel as a Western protest leader and as a crusading Anabaptist. For Wiebe's narrator, the two North-West conflicts are not manifestations of the archetypal American clash over territory between Natives and Newcomers, a reflection of the fact that settler societies in the New World are built on what Bruce Cockburn calls 'stolen land' (n.pag.). Rather, they are a regional confrontation between a pioneering multicultural West and a pseudo-civilized East of land speculators. But since there is little evidence that the benign West is any more tolerant of Riel's Catholicism and Frenchness than the predatory East – as Dick Harrison has noted, the Métis leader was considered 'a villain' in the region 'for generations' ('Cultural Insanity' 293) – Wiebe is forced to have his narrator minimize those aspects of his protagonist's life. Instead of being profoundly aware of his religious and linguistic heritage, as befits someone who fights passionately 'for the extension of French-language and Roman Catholic rights to Western Canada,' the Riel imagined by Wiebe's Falcon embraces the contemporary Prairie view that his struggle is 'a western revolt against unfair living conditions' imposed on the region by an uncaring Ottawa (Rocan 94, 122). Then again, Falcon's pan-Westernism has so estranged him from the land of his paternal ancestors that he conflates Franco-Catholic Quebec and Anglo-Protestant Ontario as the Métis people's obdurate 'Eastern' enemy. As Falcon toasts the raising of the Métis flag at Red River, it will 'cinch the North-West light against Ontario and Quebec, forever. What piddling difference does it make – strangers all laughing and fixed upon our potential' (44).

No less unlikely than Falcon's pan-Westernism is his attitude toward Catholicism. While describing the narrator as 'a pious man,' who loves 'to contemplate the divine mystery of the mass which I attend every day' (39), Wiebe suggests that Falcon shares his own opinion that the Catholic Church does not support Riel mainly because, in contrast to Protestantism, it has degenerated into a formulaic faith incapable of helping its adherents to experience 'the infinity of God' (329). A devout Mennonite, Wiebe has claimed that there are numerous affinities between Riel's religious views and Anabaptist theology, which is 'totally anti-Catholic.' As he asserts, the Métis leader 'hits the Catholic Church on exactly the same point that the Anabaptists did: that is, the Church putting form and structure over and above justice to the poor – the kind of human justice that everyone should expect' (quoted in Bergman 167). But if Anabaptism is in essence individualistic, if it insists 'that each individual must decide the Bible message for himself,' then Riel makes an unlikely Anabaptist. For, in religion, as in politics, the Métis leader brooks no dissension. Instead of granting the 'greatest degree of liberty' to 'the individual conscience in spiritual matters,' he is the only person who can interpret doctrine, branding as traitor anyone who disagrees with him (C. Smith 21; Wiebe, *Scorched-Wood* 227). In other words, Riel does not reject mainstream Catholicism in favour of some text-centred faith like that of the Anabaptists, whose devotion to the individual reading of the Scriptures has led to their being called '*Biblicists*' (C. Smith 21). Rather, he parts with Rome in order to embrace an even more autocratic Catholicism, a highly personal religion in which he is the Pope, the Church, and perhaps even Christ (Riel, 2: 73; 3: 374).

What renders Wiebe's characterization of Riel as an Anabaptist especially paradoxical is that it derives its authenticity from an unexpected source, Bishop Bourget. For the author, as for the historical Riel, the proof that the Métis leader's revelations are genuine is to be found in the 1875 letter in which the ultramontane cleric informs his protégé that God 'has given you a mission which you must fulfil in every respect' (Wiebe, *Scorched-Wood* 138–9; Bourget 437). Or, as Wiebe has Riel state, the fateful letter, which 'has strengthened me in my sad hour,' demonstrates that the 'Spirit of God fell upon the sainted Bourget of Montreal, blesséd be his name, who knew us and knew our prayers, who told me my grand commission for our people of the North-West' (157, 223). Wiebe's reliance on Bourget's letter for the validation of Riel's mysticism is peculiar for a series of reasons. First, the letter does not seem to support that conclusion, as Bourget himself stresses (quoted in Riel, 3: 320). Second, it is debatable whether even a high-ranking member of the Church Militant could ever adequately prove the veracity of divine revelation. Third, and most significant, Wiebe's conclusion runs counter to the whole tenor of the novel. After repeatedly asserting that individuals do not need the Catholic Church as a mediator between themselves and God, the author turns to an ultra-orthodox Catholic bishop like Bourget to prove the truthfulness of unmediated divine revelation. That is, he appeals to the authority of the Church he has discredited to demonstrate it has no authority.

A radically different portrait of Riel emerges in George Woodcock's *Six Dry Cakes for the Hunted* (1977). In may ways, Woodcock's play is a direct response to *The Scorched-Wood People*. The founding editor of the journal *Canadian Literature*, and a Dumont biographer known for castigating Canadians for their preference of the frenzied martyr over the heroic man of action, Woodcock was extremely critical of Wiebe's depiction of the Prince of the Prairies as a crude and violent figure, 'a bloody hunter, killer' (*Gabriel Dumont* 10; Wiebe, *Scorched-Wood* 337). So, in his play, he attempts to redress this perceived imbalance by focusing primarily on Dumont. Although Riel is still given a prominent position, the action does not revolve around him but around his military commander, the fearless warrior who Woodcock feels has been reduced by Canadian writers to playing 'Sancho Panza to the Canadian Don Quixote' (*Gabriel Dumont* 8).

Six Dry Cakes, which comprises sixteen relatively brief scenes, unfolds in flashback. Only two weeks after the fall of Batoche, along with Michel Dumas, Dumont is captured at the U.S. border as he tries to flee south. There Riel's lieutenant relates to the post's commander why he is on 'the safe side of the border' when his leader awaits trial in Regina and why 'the rebellion of the Métis against the Canadian government has gone the way of all lost causes' (63, 59). One of Dumont's explanations is that, unlike at Red River, the Catholic priests oppose the Métis struggle, first refusing the fighters 'the sacrament' and then tempting them 'with whispers of surrender' (93, 105).[6] Even more important, he contends, Riel repeatedly undermines his commander's military strategy. Since Riel is convinced that theirs is 'God's fight' and that their victory is ultimately assured, he refuses to grant Dumont permission to ambush the advancing Canadian forces until 'God has ... given the sign' (84, 103). The divine sign, of course, never materializes, and the Métis debacle becomes not only inevitable but, for Riel, desirable. Like several other recent writers, Woodcock suggests that the Métis leader is not disappointed with his people's defeat, since his main objective is less to vanquish the Canadians than to publicize his cause. As the playwright has Riel tell Dumont why he will not flee with him to the United States, 'If they want to hang me, they have to try me. That is the law of the English. And they have to try me in public. I shall make the court my platform. I shall expose our sorrows to the final sigh, and so I shall fulfill my mission' (107).

While still not the central figure, Riel is presented in a considerably more positive light in Ken Mitchell's *Davin: The Politician* (1978). As its title indicates, the Saskatchewan author's two-act play centres mainly on the life of Nicholas Flood Davin, both his professional career and his romantic relationship with the early suffragist and writer Kate Simpson Hayes. An Irish-born journalist and politician, Davin was the founder of the Regina *Leader*, the first newspaper in southern Saskatchewan. In his capacity as a reporter, he disguised himself as a priest in order to interview Riel at the Regina prison and convey the latter's 'last message to the world' (Davin, 'Interview' 52; Doyle 16–26). Like his historical model, who wrote a poem lauding the volunteers who raised their 'patriot's sword' to bring peace to 'where first Riel kindled strife' (Davin, 'Forward!'), Mitchell's Davin is not completely enamoured of the Métis leader. As he rationalizes his refusal to help Riel escape from jail, 'You preached armed rebellion. The penalty is death. It's harsh, but it's the law – and without law, there can be no civilization' (35). Still, Davin does not camouflage his immense respect for the man who dreams of creating a new nation on the Prairies in which 'Indians and whites will meet and become one – the Pacific and the Atlantic – Europe and Asia! Right here – eh? A new breed of men. Plainsmen' (39). Indeed, he feels that Riel deserves the 'admiration' and 'sympathy' of all Westerners, not only because he has shown that 'no one can suppress true Western interest without a fight' but also because of his intellectual acuity (36, 94). In Davin's words to Hayes – who, as Mary Markwell, also bemoans the day when 'o'er this lovely prairie land there fell / The blight of a proud's heart unrest, Riel!' (Hayes 42) – the Métis leader 'died with calm courage. He was a triumph of rationality over the mob of brutes who shouted so lewdly over his death – or the atheists who thought it a further sign of insanity that he gave himself to prayer in his last moment' (41).

Interestingly, Mitchell's view of Riel's mental state undergoes a major metamorphosis in *The Plainsman* (1985). Like *Six Dry Cakes*, Mitchell's full-length play examines the North-West Rebellion largely from Dumont's perspective. The whole cast consists of the adjutant-general, his wife, Madeleine, Dumas, and Nolin. Although there are numerous references to Riel, he himself does not appear as a character, for reasons that soon become apparent. Early in the action, after she learns the Métis are considering inviting the hero of Red River to return from Montana, Madeleine informs Dumont that she has just had a dream or prophecy in which 'Riel appeared to me.' As she explains, she was down by the river when a pelican told her to 'listen to this dream. A false messiah will talk to you. And there is a Judas – who will be unknown till the final hour. Then Riel appeared, coming up the river on a York Boat [*sic*] – borne on a tide of blood' (9). Needless to say, Riel and Nolin are respectively the 'false messiah' and the 'Judas,' the cursed pair whose thoughts and actions will have disastrous consequences for the Métis nation, in general, and for the Dumonts, in particular.

Madeleine, though, is not merely a mouthpiece for her husband. Thus, she claims that the decision by the Red River Métis not to seek the assistance of their more nomadic Saskatchewan compatriots in 1869–70 was motivated by class, saying that 'Gabriel had five hundred horsemen! He could've saved your precious government. But we weren't civilized enough for the citizens of Fort Garry!' (22). She also questions Dumont's conclusion that if only he had not deferred to Riel in 1885, 'we could've cut [the Canadian forces] down like cattle on the plains. But we waited for them to reach Batoche and shell our families! We should've smashed Middleton's troops before he left Qu'Appelle!' In her words, any Métis victory over the Canadians would only postpone the inevitable, since the 'battle was lost before it began' (39–40). Yet there is no mistaking who is the leader who Madeleine considers has the power to inspire the Métis people. It is not the pragmatic Nolin, the turncoat she attempts to kill in order to prevent the Saskatchewan

Valley from 'drown[ing] in Metis blood.' It is also not Riel, the self-styled 'Prince of Manitoba,' whose empty rhetoric earns him nothing but a 'shack in Montana – rotting in exile'; the would-be leader who 'wanted to play Christ, but ... couldn't be a peacemaker. Only the martyr' (24, 40). Instead, it is Dumont, the fearless warrior whose gun is his 'Holy Book!' As Madeleine tells her husband, articulating what seems to be the play's central message, 'You are the hope, Gabriel. You who can keep the spirit alive. You'll be the model for the future. For those grandchildren. It will be your courage they talk about. Not my visions. Or Louis Riel's. It will be you they look to, Gabriel. People need live heroes. Not dead martyrs' (14, 40).

In *Beyond Batoche* (1985), Rex Deverell provides a more sympathetic but still not unequivocal portrait of Riel. An Ontario-born and -raised Baptist minister who spent several years as the playwright-in-residence at Regina's Globe Theatre, Deverell has acquired a reputation as a creator of documentary drama. He has written on a tremendous variety of social issues, from medicare, to labour strife, poverty, religion, and football. Curiously, *Beyond Batoche* is not so much an examination of Riel's life as it is a reflexive exploration of the myriad ways in which Canadians have come to terms with the Métis leader. As the playwright stated while writing the two-act play, 'I'm finding that the real drama for the stage will be how a person like me deals with the material' (quoted in Berzensky, 'In Place' 49).

Beyond Batoche is a play-within-a-play, or rather a screenplay-within-a-play.[7] Beginning in an author's study, it dramatizes the personality and political conflicts among a screenwriter, an actor, and a producer as they collectively attempt to concoct a film about Riel. For the writer, the Métis leader is essentially a mystic, someone who calls 'down the wrath of God against his enemies.' The actor, for his part, perceives him as a revolutionary, 'the first Canadian Socialist political leader.' The producer, in turn, is not overly concerned with what Riel is as long as he can interest some television network in the concept. As he tells his partners, 'I'm going to sell Riel and somebody's going to buy him ... but first you gotta give me ten minutes of what they most want to see' (78–9). Since the matter of what sort of Riel people wish to see is not a simple one, the inevitable complications ensue. Once the actor becomes more familiar with Métis history, he starts to suggest that 'I should play Dumont' instead. After all, the buffalo hunter is a brilliant military strategist, and 'I'd make a better guerilla fighter than a politician' (106). The producer, who is obviously unacquainted with the work of

Gutteridge, Wiebe, or Rosenstock and Adair, ponders what sorts of 'adjustments' the 'three piece suits in Ontari-ario' will demand, because 'you can't criticize John A. Macdonald' (90, 98–9). Most unexpectedly, the writer begins to entertain serious doubts about the peaceable nature of his subject. He remains convinced that Riel is a 'mystic who wanted to better the lot of his people,' a religious visionary who 'dreamed the voice of God and acted on it.' Yet he finds it increasingly difficult to reconcile that 'such a good man could become involved in so much bloodshed' (94–5). In the words of another character, the writer becomes so disenchanted with the Métis leader's seemingly insane behaviour that he ultimately discovers that 'he always saw himself as Louis Riel, but when the chips were down he found out he was John A. Macdonald' (134).

Another pivotal lesson the writer learns while writing the screenplay is that the story's structural confusion may be connected to the ethno-racial homogeneity of its creators. As he tells the group, 'We were really arrogant S.O.B.s thinking we could do a program about Riel without working hand in hand with the Métis people' (127). Largely through the influence of his wife and research assistant, the writer comes to the conclusion that the project is not viable without a 'native consultant,' someone who will be able to convey the fact that 'the Métis people weren't obliterated at Batoche ... that there's an ongoing reality here' (102–3). To that end, the writer and his associates hire a 'real' Métis. But this 'authority' on Riel and his people does not seem very knowledgeable about or interested in Christianity. She also does not understand Riel's native language, failing to identify one of his poems when it is recited to her (118–19). Thus, the consequence of Deverell's conscious effort 'not to claim proprietorship' of Riel's story is that he ends up 'focusing more on the dilemma of the white playwright attempting to write the story than on the story itself or its significance' (Knowles 57). Despite or perhaps because of the author's political sensitivity, *Beyond Batoche* falls very much in the tradition of the representations of Riel that largely exclude their ostensible protagonist (Braz, 'Absent Protagonist'). As Deverell noted afterwards, once he was finished, 'I realized I had written a play not about Riel but about us. And about me.' Indeed, 'I could have called the play "The Selling of Louis Riel"' ('Beyond Batoche' 40).

The question of voice appropriation, or even appropriateness, is not so central to Michael Hollingsworth's *Confederation and Riel* (1988). First staged at the Calgary Olympic Arts Festival, the two-act play is part of the Ontario playwright's multi-volume dramatic history of Canada, *The History of the Village of Small Huts*. Along with the other works in the series, *Confederation and Riel* comprises what Hollingsworth calls a 'Canadian nationalist project,' but a most irreverent one. His scenes, short and vertiginously fast-paced, are more like those of a film or television show than a stage play, since the playwright believes that 'you have to keep the wheels of history rolling. Never let it sit. Never give the audience time to assess what they're watching. Being raised in a 60-miles-an-hour culture, I go for 60 scenes an hour' (quoted in Bettis 41, 38). While Hollingsworth claims his main wish is that 'the place would learn to have a sense of itself,' he privileges dramatic intensity over the raising of national consciousness and invariably depicts Canadian history and historical figures through a heady mixture of burlesque and satire (quoted in Bettis 40–1, 38).

Confederation and Riel has been described as a mixture of 'Victorian melodrama' and 'Gilbert and Sullivan operetta' (M. White 52), but it could also be characterized as a universal debunking project. Hollingsworth does not seem to have much sympathy for any political figure, regardless of party affiliation. For instance, his Riel is a mentally undeveloped soul who is never able to overcome the effects of his pious upbringing. Almost from the moment he is born, his mother starts pleading with him to make her 'heart sing. Become a religious.' Bishop Taché, too, reminds the young man he is 'the future' of his people, that he has been chosen to study in Montreal, and, when he returns, he will be 'Louis Riel, Métis priest. The first. The Church's dream come true' (169). Considering his awareness of 'the great expectations' that his community has for him, Riel begins to believe he is destined to accomplish great deeds, for 'I am a man of some importance' (169, 187). Unluckily for him, his political and religious utterances tend to suggest that he is not divinely inspired but mentally disturbed. As Riel asserts his claim to Fort Garry, 'The fort is ours. The flag is proof that we are a nation' (183). Or, as he attempts to convince Evelina Barnabé that he is the new David, 'I hear voices'; 'I am a prophet'; 'I have a mission'; 'Gaganagagaga' (197).

Hollingsworth, however, is no less scathing in his portrayal of Riel's enemies, especially the tragicomic Macdonald. For the playwright, the country's founding prime minister is less the architect of Confederation than the ultimate colonial, a politician whose greatest ambition is not to be the leader of an independent country but of 'a self-governing colony within the British Empire' (179). The 'corruptionist himself,' as a rival politician calls him, Macdonald is more than willing to 'buy ... off' both friend and foe in order to expand Canada's territorial base (181, 180). He is also not averse to sacrificing anyone who opposes his dream of a transcontinental nation, such as Riel, asserting such individuals 'should be destroyed for the good of others' (212). Yet he does so for essentially colonial reasons. As Hollingsworth has Macdonald close the play, with what is the prime minister's most celebrated saying, 'A British subject I was born, a British subject I will die' (213; Macdonald, 'Sir John Macdonald's Last Address' 777).

In her collection *Batoche* (1989), Kim Morrissey is not nearly as cynical as Hollingsworth. The Saskatchewan poet's work explores the North-West Rebellion through a variety of voices, from Dumont and the volunteers to a Miss Kurtz from Prince Albert, who exclaims in relief: 'God's in His heaven, Riel hung today' (62). Most significant, though, Morrissey devotes several poems to the plight of Marguerite Riel, particularly following her husband's defeat.[8] Pregnant with a baby that she will miscarry, Marguerite becomes ensnared in a tragic web which is hardly of her design:

> she of all people
> cannot move, run away
> she of all people
> cannot deny   melt
> change her name
> or the children of a traitor (49)

Yet, despite the negative impact of Riel's actions on his wife or the people of Batoche, Morrissey makes little attempt to mask her support of the Métis leader. As she writes in a poem entitled 'October Crisis,' now that Canada has had 'guns in our streets' and 'prime ministers who listen with guns,' if at all, 'crazy louie / crazy louie riel' is 'looking saner every day' (68). Actually, for the poet, Riel is not only ':pas fou' but also ':not guilty / :not dead' (69).

Morrissey's suggestion that Riel's vindication is generally accepted is not quite true, as Alfred Silver's *Lord of the Plains* (1990) attests. While it could be argued that Hollingsworth is very democratic in the way he showers his sarcasm on virtually every political figure who crosses his path, the Saskatchewan-born author saves his vitriol almost exclusively for Riel. The middle volume of his 1400-page Red River Trilogy, Silver's historical novel is an unadulterated paean to Gabriel and Madeleine

Dumont. Riel not only occupies a marginal place in the narrative, but, when he does surface, it is to be savaged by the buffalo hunter and his wife. The literate Madeleine, or Madelaine as her name is spelled, is especially vicious toward her husband's one-time spiritual and political leader. Having read Riel's writings, she is incapable of grasping why Dumont is so submissive to a leader who is not only impractical but also mentally unbalanced. As she confronts him, 'Goddammit, Gabriel, I am trying to tell you that the man you're allowing to tell you what to do is insane!' (227). Her only explanation for her husband's subservience to a deranged mystic who entertains visions about 'celestial milk' is that 'Riel had him hypnotized' (227, 345), an assessment that Dumont comes to accept. In his words, 'It was a sad mistake from the beginning. My mistake more'n anybody else's; Riel never wanted to fight. I can't but feel bad for those that couldn't escape like I did' (393).

Silver, whose unproduced play *The Dancing Bear* has been described by Chris Johnson as 'one of the best, most complex, and fascinating plays about Riel, and about our attempts to mythologize and give meaning to the events of the Northwest Rebellion' (204),[9] obviously shares the Dumonts' hostility toward Riel. As he writes in a long epilogue to *Lord of the Plains*, which echoes Madelaine's feelings about her husband being overshadowed by the Exovede, 'I've never been able to understand the prevailing Canadian fascination with Riel – other than the fact that the people with a vested interest in the official version also happen to be the people teaching Canadian history' (419). Silver so disapproves of Riel that he joins forces with Madelaine to administer what is unquestionably the most pernicious attack on him, the accusation that the defeat at Batoche is the result of his deliberate strategy; that it is not so much a tragedy as a crime. As the narrator interprets Madelaine's state of mind near the end of the novel, 'She was definitely past caring about Louis Riel. After all the blood had soaked into the ground and all the smoke and ashes had blown away on the wind, the only person who'd got what he wanted was Louis David Riel. "You don't get to be a saint without getting martyred"' (399).

In contrast to Silver's, the Riel of David Day is nothing less than a saint. Day's adulatory view of the Métis leader is already evident in *The Scarlet Coat Serial* (1981), his poetic history of the North West Mounted Police. The collection presents the fabled Riders of the Plains, not as a hallowed national icon, but as murderers, the armed trailblazers who make possible 'the holocaust that ... emptied the land.' The force, which is plagued by desertions, is so dissolute that missionaries accuse its members of actively engaging in prostitution and 'spreading venereal disease at a terrible rate among the Indians throughout the country' (3, 31). It is such a context that Riel emerges and is eventually defeated or, perhaps better, sacrificed. As Day suggests when he writes Riel's full name in the shape of a cross, the Métis leader is not just a politician or mystic but the very embodiment of Christ (90).

Day's apotheosis of Riel is again unmistakable in a more recent work, *The Visions and Revelations of St. Louis the Métis* (1997). A hybrid text, in which excerpts from the subject's journals are juxtaposed with English translations by Day, the collection is a conscious effort to redeem not just Riel the historical figure but also Riel the writer. The author states that he has not 'altered Riel's language or changed or dropped words from his sentences.' All that Day does is 'lift Riel's words out of their flat prose context and give them shape through poetic phrasing, so that they convey some of the force Louis Riel might have given them had he recited them himself' (12). Yet, in the process of transmuting the protagonist's prose into poetry, Day also strives to establish his indisputable holiness. As the work's title indicates, Riel does not merely implore Saint Louis the Métis to be an 'advocate' for the mixed-race people of the North-West, he is Saint Louis the Métis (85).

Judging by the disparate responses of writers over the years, the matter of Riel's mental state remains a polemical one. For some, notably Silver, Hollingsworth, Langley, and nineteenth-century Quebec authors, the Métis leader is indisputably deranged. Others, such as Mercier and Watt, Wiebe, Morrissey, and Day, are no less adamant that not only is Riel not mad but that the question itself is poorly framed, agreeing with Emily Dickinson that

> Much Madness is divinest Sense –
> To a discerning Eye –
> Much Sense – the starkest Madness –
> 'Tis the Majority
> In this, as All, prevail –
> Assent – and you are sane –
> Demur – you're straightway dangerous –
> And handled with a Chain – (209)

As Wiebe's Falcon asserts, echoing Dr Jukes's testimony at Regina, 'we are too likely to call men whose understanding of life goes counter to our usual opinion, insane. Sanity becomes then a mere matter of majority opinion, not a test of the wisdom of what is spoken' (*Scorched-Wood People* 330). Or, as Gael Turnbull asks in the poem 'Riel' (1983), 'Is the truth / insanity?' (91).

Without denying the possible existence of a political element in any definition of insanity, it seems somewhat disingenuous to suggest that Riel has been perceived as insane simply because the 'majority' has arbitrarily decided so, that there is no connection between his reputation and his behaviour. Even Woodcock's otherwise incisive comparison of the Métis leader to Blake is ultimately inadequate, since the two men's circumstances are not analogous. Ideas that may be perfectly legitimate as a private aesthetic fantasy or vision, may not be so if someone intends to use them as a blueprint for collective action, potentially imperilling a whole people. Or, to phrase it differently, Riel was not just a writer. He was also a political and spiritual leader and, as such, must be judged. Granted, the lucidity he exhibited both during the Regina trial and in his later writings makes it extremely difficult to dismiss him as a madman. Yet those same writings also reveal another dimension of his personality. First, he not only initiated an armed conflict he knew he could not win but even prevented his military commander from preparing the community for the coming onslaught. Later, while in prison, instead of formulating his defence, he concerned himself with renaming geographical sites, the days of the week, and the signs of the Zodiac. Indeed, while agreeing that Riel was not insane, one cannot help but conclude that he was not quite rational either.

Conclusion

Riel: Canadian Patriot in spite of Himself

Riel, je te ressuscite d'entre les morts, même si je ne suis pas dieu [*sic*], car j'ai besoin de toi.

Paul Savoie (1984)

As one reflects on the aesthetic representations of Riel in Canadian culture since the mid-1800s, one cannot help but be struck by two interconnected yet distinct features: the sheer volume of those representations and their enormous disparity. Despite the publication of all known writings by the Métis leader, which one might think would have grounded him in some sort of historical reality, he continues to be portrayed in rather conflicting ways. To mention only the most prominent roles attributed to him, Riel is simultaneously a sage and a madman; a Catholic mystic and an Anabaptist visionary; an Aboriginal leader and a puppet of white forces; a cultural mediator and a promoter of racial warfare; a Prairie maverick and a pan-Canadian patriot. As well, while those representations are supposedly about the same individual, most of them do not have much in common, suggesting that perhaps there is not one Riel but a series of Riels. Most significantly, they bear little resemblance to their ostensible model, underscoring not only the fluidity of the Métis leader's image but also his continuing elusiveness even more than a century after his death.

The intangibility of historical figures, of course, is not restricted to Riel. Actually, few writers have better captured the phenomenon than does the nineteenth-century New Zealand author Alan Clyde in his poem about the Maori politician-mystic Te Kooti Arikirangi Te Turuki. As Clyde traces the evolution of the story as depicted in the popular press, first he reads: '"Te Kooti's knocked upon the head, / It's pretty certain now he's dead.'" Later, after being informed that the Maori leader has '"killed and eaten"' an enemy officer, the author learns that the government forces have '"captured all Te Kooti's squaws, / We've hanged himself and burnt his pahs [fortified settlements]!"' Still later, the 'rebel host' and his '"fiends once more appear, / And all the land is full of fear."' Yet, when confronted by the New Zealand forces, Te Kooti flees, but not before losing '"his nose"' in a skirmish with a soldier (5–7):

> Then, overjoyed, once more I read,
> 'Te Kooti certainly is dead,
> They've brought to camp the traitor's head.'
>
> This paragraph went on to say,
> 'The Government intend to pay
> One thousand pounds reward to-day!'
>
> Such tidings who on earth could doubt,
> Te Kooti's pipe at last put out!
> I called my friends and made them shout!
>
> But then, a week or so at most,
> Appeared Te Kooti or his ghost,
> And with the nose which he had lost! (6)

As Clyde concludes, the media's account of Te Kooti's confrontation with the government forces changes '"from day to day," / Thus doth he eat whom he doth slay, / Yet still gets licked in every fray!' (7).

The slipperiness of historical figures, Clyde intimates with a humour seldom encountered in works about Riel, reflects the multifarious versions of an individual's life or career. The matter, though, is compounded by that person's subsequent cultural reception, the fact that he or she can disappear from the consciousness of a society for decades only to be re-adopted with a fervour that completely masks the earlier neglect. For instance, after having been virtually forgotten since the end of the nineteenth century, Riel was rediscovered by historians in the 1930s and then by fiction writers in the aftermath of the Second World War. But this was only a gradual, and partial, embrace.[1] As late as 1963, the Quebec author Jean-Robert Rémillard entitles a poem about Riel 'Pour un pendu oublié' and vows to christen him 'en sa canonisation / Saint-Louis-de-batoche[sic]-Riel-sur-Oubliance' (55). That same year,

Margaret Laurence writes to Adele Wiseman that she has 'always felt so drawn to that strange man' and wonders 'why his story [has] not been done, in dramatic terms, I mean, over and over again, instead of mainly being done in history books, etc.' (Letter 153). Even more recently, in her influential 1972 manual on Canadian literature, *Survival*, Margaret Atwood declares that 'Riel is the perfect all-Canadian failed hero – he's French, Indian, Catholic, revolutionary and possibly insane, and he was hanged by the Establishment.'[2] In her words, 'Riel's defeat is absolute, and unlike [Jean de] Brébeuf he doesn't even get to be a tourist attraction' (167–8).

Atwood's assessment of Riel, 'the small David battling the Goliath of Ottawa,' has less to do with the Métis leader than it does with the structure of Canadian history, which she claims victimizes the marginal and the powerless. This is supposedly in contrast to the Bible, in which 'God helps, miracles happen, David wins' (*Survival* 168). However, judging by the portrayals of the Métis leader in Canadian culture since the Centennial year, perhaps miracles happen even in Canada. As we have seen throughout this study, Riel's transformation into a Canadian hero is evident in a multitude of literary works. But it is never more conspicuous than in the saga of three statues that have graced the grounds of the Saskatchewan and Manitoba provincial legislatures.

Produced by the Saskatchewan modernist sculptor John Nugent, and unveiled in Regina by Prime Minister Pierre Trudeau in 1968, the first monument had a controversial history from the beginning. It was the 'pet' project of Ross Thatcher, the illiberal, Liberal premier at the time (Kaye 112). Thatcher would seem to be an unlikely champion of Riel, except perhaps for the fact that he too believed he had been entrusted with a divine mission. A former member of Parliament for the socialist Cooperative Commonwealth Federation, the forerunner of the New Democratic party, Thatcher abandoned his comrades and became convinced that 'I've been chosen by God to get rid of these socialists.' Although not above evoking Riel's 'sense of justice' during federal-provincial negotiations, Thatcher appears not to have thought any more highly of the Métis leader than he did of his former associates (quoted in Eisler 129, 219). As one critic charges, the Saskatchewan premier 'despised' Riel and commissioned a statue of him for purely political reasons, 'in order to gain the votes of a group of newly enfranchised Indians' (Kaye 112). Or, as Nugent is reported to have suggested afterwards, 'Thatcher would have hanged Riel again had he had the chance' (quoted in Kaye 110).

Furthermore, Thatcher possessed not only a conservative political sensibility but also an aesthetic one. He envisaged a realistic statue of Riel 'dressed in a mackinaw,' Riel basically 'as the bourgeois, Europeanized, assimilated man' (Kaye 112, 114). Nugent, however, strongly resisted Thatcher's conception of the Métis leader. A devout left-wing Catholic, whose faith is reflected in his production of numerous 'liturgical pieces – tabernacles, chalices, monstrances, ciboria' – the artist had a more spiritual vision of the man who believed himself to be the Prophet of the New World (Pincus-Witten 15). He thus attempted to persuade Thatcher to allow him to create an abstract steel statue of a 'soaring' Riel, but the premier was utterly opposed to what he termed 'the modernistic proposal' (quoted in Kaye 119). Realizing that Thatcher would never approve a non-representational structure, Nugent finally compromised and agreed to produce a more traditional work, even acquiescing to 'a makeshift garment for the leader of the Métis Rebellion though he thought nakedness more proper to the noble yet abjectly reduced condition of the defeated rebels' (Pincus-Witten 22). Yet his statue remains less realistic than classical, portraying Riel naked except for a cloak and seemingly as defiant as ever (pl. 8).

For Nugent, his Riel is 'a figure of "ultimate humiliation."' While almost bereft of clothes, the Métis leader is 'still standing in opposition to government policy, his right hand toward the sky, his head tilted back as if he were seeking divine guidance – or, ominously, as if his neck had been snapped by the hangman's noose' (Kaye 119–20). Unfortunately for the artist, not too many people have shared his enthusiasm for the work. Thatcher never liked it. The Saskatchewan Métis community, too, was severe in its appraisal of the statue, particularly resenting the fact Riel's genitals were visible under his cloak. Indeed, the community's leadership soon started demanding the removal of the monument, arguing that it was both 'historically inaccurate' and 'demoralizing for Metis people' (quoted in Kaye 127). Perhaps more surprisingly, even some prominent Saskatchewan artists openly dissociated themselves from Nugent's work. As the well-known representational sculptor Joe Fafard charges, 'It's an awkward piece that is completely melodramatic and it seems to me it does not speak the language of sculpture. I agree with its removal. I think it should have never been accepted' (quoted in Kaye 123).[3] So unrelenting was the criticism of Nugent's Riel that twenty-four years later, in 1991, the Saskatchewan government finally acceded to take it out of public view. Citing the Métis community's discomfort with the work's 'semi-nudity,' the government consented that the statue 'be removed from its present site' and then donated it to the nearby MacKenzie Art Gallery, which now keeps it safely stored in its vault (quoted in Kaye 122).

The second statue (pl. 9), unveiled at the back of the Manitoba Legislature in 1971, would suffer an equally ignominious fate. Created by the Manitoban sculptor Marcien Lemay and the architect Étienne Gaboury, it shows a naked and angst-ridden Riel enclosed within two round concrete towers (Lemay is responsible for the figure; Gaboury, for the cylindrical shells). Given the subject's overwhelming sense of personal and collective oppression, the conception of the monument would seem to be a legitimate one, with Riel's nakedness and tortured expression symbolizing his endemic poverty and the two cylinders representing the mental institutions in which he was confined against his will (Wells). As Glen Campbell writes, the Lemay/Gaboury statue 'reflects the tormented soul of the Metis leader,' revealing 'the anguish of a man caught up in his destiny, a man who has been unable to reconcile his utopian idealism with the surrounding hostile reality' ('Tormented Soul' 364). But, like Nugent's work, it has elicited a singularly negative response, an aesthetic and moral condemnation best encapsulated in Tom Wayman's 'Canadian Culture: Another Riel Poem' (1988). According to the British Columbia poet, when Euro-Canadians at last decided to honour Riel, they created an oversized statue of the Métis leader, but 'then stripped him, lashed his wrists / behind his back,' and placed the work 'behind' the Manitoba Legislature:

> To further mark the shame
> of his failure to defeat the government of Canada
> they erected two high cement semicircles
> to conceal the representation of him.
> Around the base of these
> they placed in English and French
> Riel's quote: 'I consider myself to be
> the founder of Manitoba.'
> They carefully didn't say he *was*
> the founder, just that he considered himself such,
> thus leaving the issue open-ended,
> dependent on your point of view
> – in other words, unresolved, confused
> or what they insist is
> *Canadian*. (30)

Wayman, who evidently is unaware that the tentativeness in the quotation does not originate with Lemay but simply reflects the subject's own discourse (*Queen* 314, 322), adds that by the time he saw the statue of Riel, in 1987, someone had 'smashed off his genitals / and gouged a hole in one bent knee.' Since the authorities had not done anything about the vandalism, he concludes that they must approve of this image of the Métis leader: 'bound helpless, / struck at and spat upon / by those he meant to aid' (30–1).

The Manitoba Métis political establishment was no less irate than Wayman about Lemay's piece. Even though the statue was commissioned by the Métis provincial politician Jean Allard, the Manitoba Métis Federation mounted a concerted campaign against what its one-time president Angus Spence called the 'incongruous monstrosity.' In the words of another of the Federation's later presidents, Billyjo Delaronde, Riel 'was a good, young and vibrant leader of the Metis people. Without him, there might not have been a Canadian West to speak of.' He deserved to be represented in a 'more proper, statesmanlike' manner (quoted in 'Riel Statue'). Therefore, claiming that Riel's 'naked likeness was undignified,' the Manitoba Métis leadership lobbied federal and provincial politicians to contribute to a new monument, both levels of government eventually dispensing 'more than $150,000' (D. Roberts). Lemay and Allard protested vehemently against any attempt to remove the statue, Allard at one point even chaining himself to it. But their objections were to no avail and, early one morning in 1994, the work was unceremoniously carted away and relocated across the Red River to a hidden corner of the Collège universitaire de Saint-Boniface ('Riel Statue').

Approximately two years later, in 1996, the Lemay/Gaboury monument was replaced on the Legislature's grounds by a 'less volatile' one obviously intended to accentuate Riel's contribution to Canadian history (Bower 31). The work of the Manitoba sculptor Miguel Joyal, the new piece could perhaps best be described as a specimen of Canadian Populist Realism. Presenting Riel in an overcoat, bow tie, and moccasins, it celebrates the Métis leader in a way that Lemay's introspective piece never could (pl. 10). As a local critic had anticipated, the Manitoba Métis Federation had finally succeeded in having a statue of Riel that made 'him look just as boring and constipated as the other statues that dot the grounds' (Doug Smith). In any case, whether Joyal's Riel is 'statesmanlike' or merely 'constipated,' there is little doubt that he is meant to be perceived as a patriarchal figure. With the officious parchment held triumphantly in his hand, he is the founder of Manitoba, or perhaps rather its Great Red Father. In an ironic touch that its promoters may not have calculated, Riel dominates the Assiniboine River side of the Legislature, while on the opposite end, facing downtown Winnipeg, stands the province's Great White Mother, Queen Victoria.

Frances Kaye, who has written a comprehensive study of the controversy over the Nugent and Lemay/Gaboury statues, contends that the quarrel is first an 'aesthetic' one. It is a clash about 'the legitimate manner to represent' the Métis leader between 'highbrow' white artists, who are deeply immersed in Western art traditions, and 'lowbrow' Métis for whom those traditions are not only alien but spiritually anathema (107). Kaye stresses another reason why the Métis may have reacted in such a negative way to the two works. With their nudity, or partial nudity, the Nugent and Lemay statues not only conjure up 'the iconographic tradition of the naked "savage"' but, more crucially, raise 'the question of Riel and insanity' (109, 124). Ultimately, though, she argues, the dispute is really about the power and ethics of representation, about who has the right to claim the Métis leader as their own. As she asserts, 'Part of the problem with the Riel monuments is in making the hero of one group serve as the representative of another larger group which he in some measure opposed' (109).

The removal of the Nugent and Lemay/Gaboury statues, and the latter's replacement by Joyal's, are clearly political acts, establishing as they do the beginning of the official rehabilitation of Riel by different levels of government. As Prime Minister Trudeau stated at the unveiling of the first work, it symbolizes the 'reversal of official and public opinion' about Riel (109; D. Roberts). No less important, the imbroglios also mark some of the rare instances in which the Métis have directly affected the image of their leader. While it may be true that contemporary Métis dominate the 'campaign' to turn Riel into a Father of Confederation, as Desmond Morton asserts ('Riel Revisionists'), they have had conspicuously little influence over his aesthetic image. Despite Riel's fervent Métis nationalism, and his scepticism if not antagonism toward Confederation, he has become basically a Euro-Canadian hero. As bp Nichol writes in 'The Long Weekend of Louis Riel' (1978), white Canadians 'killed louis riel & by monday they were feeling guilty' (n.pag.). To assuage their consciences, they soon began writing about the dead man and have yet to stop, a development that has caused no one more discomfort than to their victim/champion:

outside in the rain louis was dying
its always these damn white boys writing my story these
same stupid fuckers that put me down try to make a myth out of
me   they sit at counters scribbling their plays on napkins
their poems on their sleeves & never see me

                              hell said george
its the perfect image the perfect metaphor   he's a symbol
said johnny   but he's dead thot billie but didn't say it out
loud   theyre crazy these white boys said louis riel (n.pag.)

As Nichol adds, 'louis rolled over in his grave & sighed / its not enough they take your life away with a gun they / have to take it away with their pens' (n.pag.).

To be more precise, Riel has been transformed not just into a white Canadian hero but, increasingly, into an English-speaking one. The only genre in which French-speaking Canadians have been dominant in the treatment of the Métis leader is the cartoon biography, a modest category that begins with Robert Freynet's *Louis Riel en bande dessinée* (1990) and ends with Christian Quesnel's *Le crépuscule des Bois-brûlés* (1995) and Zoran and Toufik's *Louis Riel: le père du Manitoba* (1996).[4] Although at times entertaining, these works are not substantial enough either quantitatively or qualitatively to prevent Riel from becoming an almost exclusively English-Canadian icon. The one significant contribution they have made is the suggestion that the Guernons rejected the young Métis as a prospective family member less for ethno-racial than for class reasons. As the situation is interpreted by Freynet – the creator of what is incontestably the most compelling of the works – a 'daylabourer' like Joseph Guernon (Siggins 61) not only sports a frock, cane, and top hat but, in order to prevent his daughter from marrying 'UN MÉTIS, UN VA-NU-PIEDS, UN VAURIEN!' such as Riel, he sends her overseas (16).

Ironically, very few English-speaking writers have explored the inherent contradictions in transforming into a national hero an individual who so unequivocally resists becoming part of the Canadian political family; someone who, in Nichol's words, spends 'his time planning freedom the triumph / of the metis over the whiteman' (n.pag.). One notable exception is the team of Wayne Schmalz and Rex Deverell in *The Riel Commission: An Inquiry into the Survival of a People* (1985). A five-part radio series, only the first segment of which has been published, *The Riel Commission* is the brainchild of Schmalz, a CBC-Radio Saskatchewan producer who determined to investigate 'how the "myth," the story of Riel and the Métis, had changed from 1885 to the present' (Schmalz 151). Schmalz says that he had been struck by the dramatic change in the perception of Riel in Canadian popular culture, the way journalists and writers, who supposedly 'subscribed to the principle of journalistic objectively [*sic*]', barely concealed their support for the Métis and wished that the Canadian forces that battled them had been crushed. Those writers tended to be middle-class whites, 'related at least racially to the eastern Canadian militiamen who had been brought out to quell the disturbance, yet here they were urging Riel and Dumont to rout the whites. How could this happen?' Schmalz's answer to his own question is that anyone 'writing or speaking about Riel and the Métis in the [nineteen-]eighties was also operating within a myth' (Schmalz 151). Consequently, working in conjunction with playwright Deverell, he decided 'to find out what the myth was and what it told us about ourselves' by producing a documentary radio play in the form of a commission of inquiry, that 'typically Canadian way of getting at the root of a matter and finding solutions to problems' (151, 153). Schmalz organized a 'public forum' to which Métis from all walks of life were invited, and Deverell then 'create[d] the commissioner after all the material had been assembled.' In an attempt to reach a higher level of truth about Riel, they consciously fashioned a hybrid work combining a fictional structure with 'real people speaking their own thoughts' (153).

The Riel Commission was extremely successful, with both the public and the critics. It was broadcast nationally on the CBC program *Ideas* and garnered a major U.S. radio award for its '"creative use of the medium."' It also starred Donald Sutherland as the commissioner, with the veteran Hollywood actor telling the audience that he was honoured to play the role, since 'Louis Riel had been sitting on my back for ten years. He and Norman Bethune had both been my heroes and the guides to my Canadian spirit' (Deverell and Schmalz 62, 64). Yet, in the end, the play is not radically different from the other works on Riel against which its creators juxtapose it. As Schmalz realized after a number of 'natives ... refused to participate in the series,' regardless of its formal innovations, *The Riel Commission* still channels the 'natives' opinions through the character of a white, middle-class commissioner ... Instead of being progressive, I had in fact simply found a new way to keep an old attitude and an outmoded approach entrenched' (Schmalz 153). Thus, while the story may be about Riel and the Métis, it is still controlled by whites. As Schmalz phrases it, in more crudely economic terms, 'Here, as always before, whites received the money, the air time, the glory, while natives remained the subjects, the specimens, searching futilely for a forum in which to express their realities on their own terms' (Schmalz 154).

The control of Riel's image by white, English-speaking Canadians was perhaps inevitable considering the country's demographics. Nevertheless, the situation has been exacerbated by the extraordinary lack of interest that most Métis writers have shown in the subject. For instance, in her ground-breaking memoir *Halfbreed* (1973), Maria Campbell writes passionately about the Red River mystic, with one of her more rebellious characters styling himself as the 'new Riel.' Yet in a narrative whose central concern is the need to disprove the belief allegedly held by white Canadians that because 'they killed Riel ... they have killed us too,' the historical Métis leader is virtually absent (74, 11). Similarly, in Beatrice Culleton's *In Search of April Raintree* (1983), the author has one of her two sister-protagonists give the other a book about Riel in order to instil in her pride in 'our heritage.' But again, although April Raintree comes to discern that she must persevere, for 'MY PEOPLE, OUR PEOPLE,' there is no indication that Riel plays much of a role in her discovery of her collective identity (45, 228). Laure Bouvier's *Une histoire de Métisses* (1995), which traces a Métis woman's pilgrimage from Montreal to her 'géographie originelle' in her native Manitoba, also has little place for Riel (11). Set in 1992, the five-hundredth anniversary of Columbus's arrival in the New World, the novel culminates in an epiphany by the protagonist before Riel's grave in Saint Boniface, in which she realizes not only that the Métis leader's hanging at Regina was 'un meurtre en réalité' but also that he has been denationalized. As she notes, the memorial to the 'père du Manitoba' bears no 'mention de sa pendaison, ni qu'il est Métis' (100, 102). But by the time the narrative unravels, the protagonist is back in her adoptive hometown of Montreal, 'au milieu des Blancs,' and seemingly no closer to Riel and her Métis ancestors than she was when she began her journey (186). The situation is somewhat more positive in Gregory Scofield's *Thunder through My Veins: Memories of a Métis Childhood* (1999), where a journey to Batoche provides the young author with the sense of being 'home at last' thanks to his discovery of Riel and Dumont, 'the half-breed soldiers who had given their lives for *our* homeland, freedom and independence' (166). Still, even in *Thunder through My Veins*, Riel's presence is sporadic. Certainly, none of the above works creates the impression that Riel continues to live in the present the way Carol Bolt does in her play *Gabe* (1973), in which a contemporary Métis repeatedly models himself on the leader of 'the old North-West Rebellion of 1885' (85).

There are several explanations for the ambivalence that Métis writers exhibit toward Riel. To begin with, there is the fear that he has come to represent the totality of Métis life. As Emma LaRocque remonstrates, 'Riel overshadows his own people' (quoted in Enright 45). There has also been a considerable alienation by contemporary Métis from his linguistic and cultural heritage, especially his all-pervasive and conservative Catholicism, his 'religious zeal' (Racette 45). Finally, since most contemporary Métis hail from Western Canada, they tend to feel uncomfortable with his Eastern-acquired education; indeed, with his intellectualism. In LaRocque's words, Riel eclipses the Métis not only because of the European 'hero-oriented treatment of history in which the people are forgotten' but also because 'Riel was different from the people. He really believed in civilization.' Thus, while those writers may consider Riel 'a symbolic figure of who the Métis wanted to be' and the personification of 'the grave injustice that the Métis people went through,' they usually find him and his 'peaceful way' wanting. This is particularly true when they compare him with an instinctive leader like Dumont (LaRocque quoted in Enright 45; M. Campbell 4–5).

So widely accepted has Dumont become as the quintessential Métis hero that he figures prominently even in works that purport to celebrate Riel, such as Upisasik Theatre's collective creation *Gabrielle* (1985). First staged in Ile-à-la-Crosse, the northern Saskatchewan Cree-Métis community in which Riel's sister Sara died and is buried, the play is a modern recreation of the North-West Rebellion. It contemplates not only 'what might happen if the 1885 "rebellion" were to occur in 1985' but also if it 'were to occur in Ile-à-la-Crosse instead of Batoche' and if it 'were to be led by a woman – Gabrielle – who is visited by visions of Riel, just as Riel had been visited by visions of God' (Borgerson 49). The protagonist is a law student who, when a multinational oil company discovers oil near Ile-à-la-Crosse, is approached by the community's leading citizens to draft 'a Bill of Rights and take it to the Minister in Regina' (46). After being repeatedly snubbed by the Minister, Gabrielle persuades those same individuals to 'form our own provisional government, just like Riel did' and later takes the politician hostage in order to establish her government as 'the only lawful authority now in existence in this area' (61, 64). However, the symbolically named 'Mr. Scott' has 'a heart attack or something' and dies while trying to escape from the well-stocked cabin in which he is being held (67). With the Minister dead, all the Métis promptly abandon the heroine, calling her crazy for insisting that 'I have been seeing' and 'speaking to Louis Riel' (68). The exception is Riel, who, to the very end, assures her, 'If I could have lived I could have continued fighting for the Metis. I knew it in 1885 and I know it now' (71). Tellingly, in a play whose central character is reputedly inspired by Riel to become the voice of her people, her first name is not Louise but Gabrielle. That is, she is not named after her hero but after his commander.

Dumont clearly poses the most formidable threat to Riel's reputation. Particularly for Westerners, both Métis and non-Métis, the famed buffalo hunter appears to be a much more palatable hero than the brilliant but 'unstable ... Moses' whose 'hysterical vacillation ... tied Dumont's hands' and spelled the end of 'the *métis* as a cultural and political possibility' (Stegner 62, 61, 60). Riel is also vulnerable from an Aboriginal perspective.[5] While Blair Stonechild and Bill Waiser seriously undermine their critique of the Métis leader by evaluating his words out of context, they have amply demonstrated how difficult it will be to continue to portray him as an unproblematic promoter of the First Nations (77, 115, 197). Yet, it might be premature to prophesy that Riel will soon vanish from the consciousness of Canadians. As the Métis poet Marilyn Dumont notes in 'Letter to Sir John A. Macdonald' (1996), 'Riel is dead / but he just keeps coming back' (52). Or, as the British Columbia poet Lyle Neff writes in 'Riel's Last Letter from Vancouver' (1997), 'whenever I die, / I get new ideas' (17). The reason Riel is likely to keep inspiring Canadian writers and other artists, however, is not that, 'after all that shuffling us around to suit the settlers, / we're still here and Metis,' as Marilyn Dumont suggests (52). Rather, it is because he has been embraced as a forebear by the descendants of those very settlers, people who, like Paul Savoie, need him in order to realize themselves both as citizens and as artists (*À la façon* 109). This is especially true of English-speaking Canadians, for many of whom Riel has come to represent the single most important link to the nation's pre-European past.

Riel's apparent emergence as the only feasible Anglo-Canadian hero is not easy to fathom. Ian Dowbiggin, who sees Canada as 'the world's first postwar paranoid nation,' claims that the Métis leader is simply 'the paradigmatic historical icon for delusional times, a role model for a paranoid citizenry' (169, 172). George Woodcock offers a somewhat different explanation. The West Coast critic contends that Riel appeals to white Canadians because – unlike the author's hero, Dumont – 'he belongs to a world like our own, more conscious of twilight than of dawn.' As Woodcock elaborates, Riel 'seems the personification of a besieged minority, and most Canadians see themselves as members of besieged minorities. He is a victim, and most modern men (not Canadians only, by any means) gain satisfaction from seeing themselves as victims' (*Gabriel Dumont* 14). Doug Fetherling tends to agree with Woodcock's assessment, although he stresses that the reason 'we admire Riel' is that he is 'so close to us materially and culturally,' with one foot in the 'the buffalo hunts of another age' and the other 'in our own' (28). Indeed, much of Riel's attraction to Euro-Canadians, in general, and Anglo-Canadians, in particular, probably lies less in his foreignness than in his similitude.[6] With his considerable European genetic and cultural heritage – as well as his occasional ecumenism and multiculturalism – Riel can legitimately be assimilated into the white Canadian world in a way that very few other pre-twentieth-century Métis or Aboriginal political figures ever could. He thus becomes the ideal human bridge between Euro-Canadians and not just the First Nations but Canada itself.

Anglo-Canadians, like their francophone compatriots and the non-Aboriginal citizens of other settler societies in the Americas and elsewhere, necessarily have a complicated relationship with their land and its first inhabitants, a schizophrenia that reflects their despairing fear of being perpetual foreigners in their native landscape. As Terry Goldie captures the dilemma, 'The white Canadian looks at the Indian. The Indian is Other and therefore alien. But the Indian is indigenous and therefore cannot be alien. So the Canadian must be alien. But how can the Canadian be alien within Canada?' The solution for some writers has been to attempt to efface 'the alien within' by embarking on a nativist genealogical quest (Goldie 12–13). In John Newlove's often-quoted words in 'The Pride,' white Canadians may not be biologically related to the First Nations but are in the process of being indigenized

> ... until at
> last we become them
>
> in our desires, our desires,
> mirages, mirrors, that are theirs, hard-
> riding desires, and they
> become our true forebears, moulded
> by the same wind or rain,
> and in this land we
> are their people, come
> back to life. (111)

Of course, the complication with the 'desperate longing' by white people to claim kinship with the First Nations is that they 'may not particularly *want* to be our ancestors' and might even find such filiation immoral (Atwood, *Strange Things* 60), a calculated attempt 'to appropriate the American Indian imagination in the same way the colonists appropriate the land and resources of the New World' (Cook-Lynn 39).

Perhaps one ought to rejoice that so many Euro-Canadian writers and artists have come to embrace Riel as an ancestor, the quintessential Canadian. There seems to be nothing intrinsically negative about their using the Métis leader to indigenize themselves. However, one is led to contain one's euphoria since there is such a palpable sense of unreality about most representations of the David of the New World, as is evident in the fact he is often missing from narratives ostensibly about him – this is true even of postmodern works in which he magically triumphs over the Canadian forces yet somehow is overshadowed by none other than the founder of the Boy Scouts, Robert Baden-Powell (Murphy). Considering Riel's scepticism about Confederation, his British–United States citizenship, as well as his Métisness, Riel could have been an enemy of Canada but almost certainly not a 'traitor,' false or otherwise. As Jan Truss has the Métis leader state in her juvenile novel *A Very Small Rebellion* (1977), 'My people are my country. I have never been a traitor to my people' (77). But, for those very same reasons, he can be transformed into a Canadian patriot only if one denies his own story, his specificity, and his alterity. Needless to say, this is what has happened in most of the works about Riel, not only in the more overtly xenophobic nineteenth century but right up to the present. In fact, it could be argued that the most common trait of the literature on Riel from Edmund Collins, through Elzéar Paquin, to Rudy Wiebe is that it is less about its purported subject than it is about Euro-Canadian society. The Afro-American writer James Baldwin once asserted that segregation had been so successful in the U.S. South that it had 'allowed white people, with scarcely any pangs of conscience whatever, to *create*, in every generation, only the Negro they wished to see' (65). Arguably, this is also the most significant aspect of the representations of Riel. They are important not so much because of what they tell us about Riel but because of what they reveal about Euro-Canada, the dominant sector of Canadian society that for over a century has been able to create essentially the Riel it wishes – or needs – to see.

Notes

Introduction – Louis Riel: A Central Voice from the Margins

1 Unless otherwise specified, all references to Riel are to *The Collected Writings / Les écrits complets*, under the general editorship of George F.G. Stanley. Although Riel's spelling and grammar can be rather idiosyncratic, all quotations from his writings are reproduced as printed by Stanley et al.
2 I do not wish to imply that the Métis have vanished, but they certainly no longer exist as a separate polity with a territory of their own.
3 Reaney made his comments in 'Scapegoats Who Fought Back: The Donnellys,' a lecture he presented at the Peterborough (Ontario) Public Library, in October 1999. I would like to express my gratitude to him for providing me with a transcript of his talk.
4 At least outside Brazil, Euclides da Cunha's *Rebellion in the Backlands* seems to have been supplanted as the dominant work on Conselheiro by Mario Vargas Llosa's *The War of the End of the World*. However, the latter work's perspective remains a cosmopolitan one. Indeed, one of the central figures in Vargas Llosa's novel is a 'nearsighted' journalist who bears more than a few resemblances to Cunha himself (8).
5 For a much more representative view, see the response to Goldring by the Edmonton Liberal MP David Kilgour.

1: The Red River Patriot: Riel in His Biographical and Social Context

1 Riel, who was always partial to Ireland, also claims he had some Irish blood (2: 72). His nephew-in-law Auguste Vermette goes further and states that the very name 'Riel venait de O'Rielly [O'Reilly?]. C'est un nom irlandais. À Saint-Vital, ils disaient toujours "Riel dit l'Irlande"' (quoted in Ferland 80).

In his 'novel history' *Gabriel Dumont in Paris,* Jordan Zinovich has the Métis Albert Monkman assert that one of the reasons Riel wanted him hanged for treason at Batoche was that Monkman 'made a joke about Riel being a Fenian, not Reilly a Frenchman at all' (145).

2 Riel's colonial subservience to Quebec is considerably downplayed, if not effaced, in Paul Savoie's translation of the poem. Savoie renders 'Mère Colonie' as 'our motherland'; 'Province chérie' as 'beloved home'; and 'le berceau de tes enfants chéris' as 'your descendants' place of birth.' He completely expunges the line 'O Québec! Malgré toi, jamais notre pays!' (Riel, *Selected Poetry* 47).

3 Alfred Rousseau, for example, contends that it was the Hudson's Bay Company, not Riel, that paid to wrap Scott's body with chains and throw it into the Red River (34–5). Manie Tobie, however, maintains that Scott was secretly buried by four Riel supporters, including her paternal grandfather, Elzéar Goulet (66). Manie Tobie's version of events is corroborated by Auguste Vermette, whose father told him that, after the Métis disinterred Scott's body, they re-buried the coffin with 'un chien dedans' (quoted in Ferland 108). Sam Steele writes that when Wolseley's officers opened Scott's grave, 'the box was empty.' He adds that the troops believed the victim's remains had been 'weighed down with chains and forced through a hole in the ice of the Red River,' but he does not mention any dog (35).

4 Alexandre Taché was named (the first) Archbishop of Saint Boniface in 1871. Thus, a text may refer to him as either Bishop or Archbishop Taché, depending on whether it focuses on the first or the second North-West conflict.

5 Some remnants of this hostility, at least on a folkloric level, seem to have lingered until recently. Yvonne Johnson, Big Bear's great-great-granddaughter, says that the 'standing joke' at the Blood Reserve near Lethbridge in the late 1970s was that 'Blackfoot kill Crees,' and that her local boyfriend 'initiated my drinking with stories about Bloods who slit the throat of every Cree they meet' (Wiebe and Johnson 153).

6 Even Riel's cultural oneness with the Franco-Catholic Métis is complicated by his not sharing his community's dominant Aboriginal ancestry. While most *métis* were descended from the Algonkian Cree and Saulteaux, Riel's paternal grandmother was Chipewyan, a branch of the Athapaskan-speaking Dene Nation (Champagne 151).

2: The Traitor: Riel As an Enemy of Confederation

1 I owe much of the information on the Scottish history of 'Johnnie Cope' to John Baird, to whom I would like to express my thanks.

2 The first part of Collins's name has been written variously as J.E., Joseph, or Edmund. However, J. Edmund seems to be the proper form.

3 As J.M. Bumsted has pointed out, the Orangeman's overwhelmingly negative image is not surprising, since 'what we know about Thomas Scott comes mainly from those who executed him.' Indeed, Bumsted quotes the unpublished diary of one A.W. Graham, who spent four weeks in jail with Scott and writes that 'I found him quiet, civil and always gentlemanly' ('Thomas Scott' 146, 154). Similarly, Sam Steele describes Scott as a pious individual. In the legendary Mountie's words, 'On the way to his execution Scott prayed fervently and continued to do so until he was unconscious, and he said, as he was led down the steps, "This is a cold-blooded murder"' (11).

4 By 1893, there were some dissenting voices. E.W. Thomson describes the vast majority of poems on the 1885 conflict as 'mawkish, mawkish,' and adds that 'all the songs of that time ought to be for the poor devils// of Metis – harried and debauched by the brutal crew sent to the Northwest – the pathos of the sacrifice of the volunteers was that they have been the instruments of a hideous, vulgarized, filthy collection of tyrannical scrip-jobbers, landsharks, boodling inept politicians' (83). I owe this reference to Tracy Ware, to whom I would like to express my thanks.

5 Both General Frederick Middleton and Elizabeth McLean, one of the white people taken captive at Fort Pitt, also allege that Riel used his prior knowledge of an eclipse in order to manipulate his followers (Middleton 7; McLean 273). The Métis buffalo hunter Norbert Welsh, who clashed with Riel, identifies the eclipse as having taken place on 'the 16th of March, 1885' (quoted in Weekes 151).

6 All references to *D'un océan à l'autre* are to the first or Paris edition (1924).

7 The script of *North West Mounted Police* has not been published. Therefore, all references are to the film (DeMille), and no page number is provided.

8 However, the are some exceptions. In a recent dispute with the Métis leader's biographer Maggie Siggins, D'Arcy Jenish contends that 'Riel committed treason' (D 19). Ian Dowbiggin also writes that Riel was 'a rebel against duly constituted political authority' (171).

3: The Martyr (I): Riel As an Ethnic and Religious Victim of Confederation

1 In *La légende*, Fréchette divides *Le dernier des martyrs* into three parts: 'Le gibet de Riel' (279–81); 'Le dernier martyr' (283–92); and 'L'orangisme' (293–5). As well, he excises the envoy to the readers of *La presse*, which reads in its totality:

Frères, d'un nouvel an voici l'aube sublime;
Du plus saints des devoirs c'est le commencement;
L'an qui vient de finir s'est appelé le Crime;
Que l'an qui va s'ouvrir s'appele Châtiment! (*Le dernier* 8)

2 The poem has been published by Denis Vaugeois and Jacques Lacoursière, but their version comprises only the first three stanzas (441).

3 The translations from Carvalho's Portuguese are mine. The reader may wish to contrast my version with Morisset's French one, which faces the original. Although there are numerous typographical errors in Carvalho's poem – such as 'condemnal-a' (13), 'emtanto' (26), and 'ohlar' (52) – all quotations are reproduced as printed by Morisset since I have not been able to consult Carvalho's original. For a more comprehensive analysis of Carvalho's portrait of Canada, see Braz, 'Promised Land.'

4 This is a view shared by Carvalho's translator, Jean Morisset, who contends that Anglo-Canadians should not be called Canadians but 'Britamians' or British North Americans, since they have usurped the names 'Canada' and 'Canadians' ('*Canadiens*') from their lawful owners, the descendants of the French pioneers who first settled the country (*Identité usurpée* 9, 55; 'Conquête' 281).

5 Riel is included in a slightly different American pantheon, a purely Aboriginal one, in Carl Beam's etching *The Proper Way to Ride a Horse*. In his 1990 work, the Anishnabe painter juxtaposes a satirical representation of the nineteenth-century anthropologist Frank Hamilton Cushing with reverential portraits of Big Bear, Geronimo, Sitting Bull, and Riel. The etching is reproduced in Ryan (150).

6 Crowfoot's role in 1885 may not have been as unproblematic as is sometimes suggested. According to Sam Steele, 'Crowfoot tried to induce Red Crow, the Blood chief, to rebel, but that chief, the best in the Blackfeet Nation, was loyal throughout' (185).

4: The Go-Between: Riel As a Cultural Mediator

1 In *The Practice of the Wild*, Gary Snyder quotes a Crow elder who makes a similar point: 'You know, I think if people stay somewhere long enough – even white people – the spirits will begin to speak to them. It's the power of the spirits coming up from the land' (39).

2 While there was an Aboriginal figure at Red River named L'Ours or Bear, he was not a Cree chief but the main medicine man of Henry Prince's Saulteaux band (Butler 131), and there appears to be no connection between him and Roquebrune's character.

3 This is basically the gist of Elizabeth Cook-Lynn's critique of the idea that the Métis form 'a buffer race.' She contends that the Métis can hardly be called 'neutral' since they are '*already converts* to the hostile and intruding culture simply through their marriage into it' (35).

4 The historical Riel's recantation was directed by Father Vital Fourmond (Riel, 3: 164–72).

5 Lakefield is a village outside Peterborough. It was Laurence's home late in her life and, indeed, where she died.

5: The Martyr (II): Riel As a Sociopolitical Victim of Confederation

1 The historical Riel also appears to have been quite chivalrous, reportedly telling Annie Bannatyne and another woman, '"Ladies have always the first consideration, in war as in love!"' (Healy 229).

2 While Stanley is still widely respected by contemporary Riel scholars, there are dissenting voices. The most vocal of these is Howard Adams, who describes Stanley as 'a colonizer academic' and *The Birth of Western Canada* as a 'pseudo-Bible ..., one of the more racist and mythical histories of Aboriginal people in Canada' (*Tortured People* 95).

3 Unless otherwise specified, all references to Howard's book are to the Canadian edition, *Strange Empire: Louis Riel and the Métis People* (1974).

4 In Jim Williamson's television film *From Sea to Sea*, an episode of *Canada: A People's History*, McDougall still travels in regal fashion, with his own piano and custom toilet seat (n.pag.).

5 I would like to express my gratitude to Peter Baxter not only for bringing this essay to my attention but also for presenting me with an issue of the magazine in which it appears.

6 Most Red River historians maintain that Agnes (not Elizabeth) Campbell Farquharson was 'a Roman Catholic' who married Schultz 'according to Catholic rite' in the Saint Boniface Cathedral (Bumsted and Owen 164–5). However, the idea that Schultz's wife had a romantic relationship with Scott has a certain currency. Auguste Vermette, for instance, states that the reason Scott did not return to Ontario after he escaped from jail the first time was because of his involvement with Agnes Schultz, who was his mistress or '"girl friend" ... Il était bon ami avec Madame Schultz' (quoted in Ferland 99).

7 Of the writers who have focused on Dumont, over Riel, Zinovich is an exception in that he celebrates the master buffalo hunter without disparaging the Prophet of the New World as a bumbling mystic.

8 I owe the reference to Harrison's story to Jennifer Chambers, to whom I would like to express my thanks.

6: The Mystic/Madman: Riel As a Para-rational Individual

1 For a fascinating exploration of the conflict between the Catholic clergy and the Métis in 1885, see Laurier Gareau's one-act play, *La trahison / The Betrayal.*
2 The proper title of Richard's novel is somewhat unclear. While the cover bears the words *Louis Riel Exovide,* the title page reads *Exovide Louis Riel.*
3 The portrayal of Riel drawn by the historical Butler, from whom Wiebe borrows freely, is much more complex than Wiebe implies. This is obvious when one compares Wiebe's text to Butler's *The Great Lone Land,* especially chapters 1, 3, 9, and 10. For a detailed analysis of Wiebe's unacknowledged reliance on Butler, see Braz, 'Omnipresent Voice.'
4 Unless otherwise specified, all references to *The Scorched-Wood People* are to the 1984 paperback (New Canadian Library) edition.
5 As Marie Vautier has noted, Wiebe's epigraph 'closely resembles' the translation of Falcon's poem printed in N. Brian Davis's *The Poetry of the Canadian People* (Vautier 63; Falcon, 'Battle' 247). For a different rendition of 'La Bataille,' see James Reaney's translation in Margaret Arnett MacLeod's *Songs of Old Manitoba* (9).
6 In 'Mme. Tourond,' the second section of its collective play *The West Show* (1975), Theatre Passe Muraille also has Dumont accuse the priests of informing the Canadian forces 'that we had not enough food or ammunition – and that made the difference' (37). Similarly, in his novel *Gabriel Dumont in Paris,* Jordan Zinovich has the title character charge that 'the priests were openly ranged against us ... I think they were just like the Government: they lied to us from the beginning' (153).
7 One of the structural problems in Deverell's *Beyond Batoche* is that one can never quite believe that the writer is working on a screenplay, as opposed to a stage play. The scenes are simply too long. But more significantly, the production of a film does not usually revolve around an actor, much less a writer, but a director – the one figure missing from Deverell's entourage.
8 Another artist who deals extensively with Marguerite Riel is the British / New Zealand painter Patrick Hayman, especially in *Louis Riel with Wife and Child.* For reproductions of his works, see Parke-Taylor 69, 73–4.
9 Although an excerpt of *The Dancing Bear* has been published, it is too short to enable one to discern much about the play, except for its overt antagonism toward Riel. See Alfred Silver, *The Dancing Bear.*

Conclusion – Riel: Canadian Patriot in spite of Himself

1 So dim was the public memory of Riel well into the late 1940s that, in his poem 'Farewell to Winnipeg' (1948), Roy Daniells felt the need to add a note

on how to pronounce the Métis leader's name: '"Riel," (pronounced as two syllables with the stress inclining toward the latter)' (75, note 64).

2 Jean Morisset contends that those are the very reasons the Métis leader 'fut pendu par le système ... En fait, Riel avait une identité dans un pays qui n'en avait pas. C'était là une faute impardonable et c'est pourquoi il devra être supprimé' ('Miroir indogène' 307).

3 Ironically, Fafard has recently undergone an experience similar to Nugent's. His outdoor sculpture for the city of Regina, *Oskana-ka-asatcki* or *The Place of the Pile of Burned Bones*, has been criticized by members of the Saskatchewan First Nations – including the painter Edward Poitras – for being both historically inaccurate and culturally insensitive (Beatty).

4 Even the control of this one genre by French-speaking artists may be threatened, as the cartoonist Chester Brown has begun a multi-volume biography of Riel (Brown).

5 This ambivalence toward Riel is particularly evident in the work of Gerald McMaster. In 1985, McMaster marked the centenary of the North-West Rebellion with an exhibition of his drawings entitled *Riel Remembered*. However, his portrayal of the Métis leader is so irreverent that the show's curator suggests that while McMaster is 'sympathetic towards Riel's efforts, [he] is poking fun at the "prophet" Louis Riel' (Podedworny n.pag.).

6 As scholars like Sherry Farrell Racette have noted, the asymmetrical responses by white Canadians to the fates of the different combatants in 1885 suggest that 'Riel's European ancestry, his intelligence (which he expressed in culturally appropriate ways), and his devout Christianity affronted the collective Canadian conscience in the ways that the mass execution of seven Cree men did not' (48).

Bibliography

Adams, Howard. *Prison of Grass: Canada from a Native Point of View*. Rev. ed. Saskatoon: Fifth House, 1989.
– *A Tortured People: The Politics of Colonization*. Penticton, BC: Theytus, 1995.
Adams, John Coldwell. 'Roberts, Lampman, and Edmund Collins.' *The Sir Charles G.D. Roberts Symposium*. Ed. Glenn Clever. Ottawa: University of Ottawa Press, 1984. 5–13.
Allen, W.O.B., and Edmund McClure. *Two Hundred Years: The History of the Society for Promoting Christian Knowledge, 1698–1898*. 1898. New York: Burt Franklin, 1970.
Amabile, George, and Kim Dales [Morrissey], eds. *No Feather, No Ink*. Saskatoon: Thistledown, 1985.
Anderson, Patrick. 'Poem on Canada.' *The White Centre*. Toronto: Ryerson, 1946. 29–45.
André, Alexis. 'Dénonciation du Rev. Père André.' Grandin et al., 5–8.
Anonymous 1. 'The Ballad of Monsieur Riel.' *Grip*, 25 Oct. 1873, n.pag.
Anonymous 2. 'The Man with the Gatling Gun.' Mulvaney, *History*, 246–7.
Anonymous 3. *À la mémoire de Louis Riel: La Marseillaise canadienne*. N.p.: Carmel, 1885?
Arnold, Abraham. 'If Louis Riel Had Spoken in Parliament or, Louis Riel's Social Vision.' *Prairie Fire* 6.4 (1985): 75–83.
Atwood, Margaret. *Strange Things: The Malevolent North in Canadian Literature*. Oxford: Clarendon, 1995.
– *Survival: A Thematic Guide to Canadian Literature*. Toronto: Anansi, 1972.
Baldwin, James. 'The Hard Kind of Courage.' *Harper's*, Oct. 1958, 61–6.
Banks, Eleanor. *Wandersong*. Caldwell, ID: Caxton, 1950.
Bayer, Charles, and E. Parage. *Riel*. 1886. Saint Boniface, MB: Éditions des Plaines, 1984.

Beal, Bob, and Rod Macleod. *Prairie Fire: The 1885 North-West Rebellion.* Edmonton: Hurtig, 1984.

Beatty, Greg. 'The Skeletons in Regina's Cultural Closet.' *Globe and Mail,* 16 May 1998, E4.

Beauregard, Georges. *Le 9me bataillon au Nord-Ouest (journal d'un militaire).* Quebec City: Imprimerie de J.-G. Gingras, 1886.

Beddoes, Joël. 'Tourisme scolaire: Louis Riel suscite encore la controverse.' *Liaison* 82 (1995): 28–9.

Begg, Alexander. *'Dot It Down': A Story of Life in the North-West.* 1871. Toronto: University of Toronto Press, 1973.

– *The Red River Journal of Alexander Begg.* 1869–70. W. Morton, 149–394.

Bégin, Luc A. *L'abitibien-outan. L'abitibien-outan, suivi de L'Ariane.* Montreal: Éditions miniatures, 1966. 11–70.

Beissel, Henry. 'Introduction.' Lacey, *Magic,* 5–16.

Bélanger, Reine. *'Riel,* tragédie de Elzéar Paquin.' Lemire, 1: 661–2.

Belkin, Roslyn. 'The Consciousness of a Jewish Artist: An Interview with Adele Wiseman.' *Journal of Canadian Fiction* 31.2 (1981): 148–76.

Bengough, J.W. 'The Charge at Batoche.' 1885. *Motley: Verses Grave and Gay.* Toronto: William Briggs, 1895. 69–71.

Bercuson, David, and Barry Cooper. 'Riel: Fanatic or Father of Confederation?' *Globe and Mail,* 23 May 1998, D2.

Bergeron, Léandre. *L'histoire du Québec en trois régimes.* Montreal: L'aurore, 1974.

Bergman, Brian. 'Rudy Wiebe: Storymaker of the Prairies.' Keith, 163–9.

Berton, Pierre. *Hollywood's Canada: The Americanization of Our National Image.* Toronto: McClelland and Stewart, 1975.

Berzensky, Steven Michael [Mick Burrs]. 'In Place: Spiritual Explorations of a Rooted Playwright.' *Canadian Theatre Review* 42 (1985): 41–9.

– 'Introduction.' *Towards a New Past II: Found Poems of the Metis People.* Ed. Steven Michael Berzensky. Interviewer Carol Pearlstone. Regina: Saskatchewan Department of Culture and Youth, 1975. iii–iv.

– *Moving In from Paradise.* Moose Jaw: Coteau, 1976.

Bessai, Diane, and David Jackel, eds. *Figures in a Ground: Canadian Essays on Modern Literature Collected in Honor of Sheila Watson.* Saskatoon: Western Producer Prairie Books, 1978.

Bettis, Paul. 'Making History: Michael Hollingsworth.' *Canadian Theatre Review* 52 (1987): 36–44.

Blais, Jacques. *'Coups d'aile et Coups de bec,* poésies et chansons de Rémi Tremblay.' Lemire, 1: 158–9.

– *'A la mémoire de Louis Riel,* chant anonyme.' Lemire, 1: 8–9.

Bloomfield, George, dir. *Riel*. Screenplay by Roy Moore. Green River Pictures, 1979.

Bolívar, Símon. 'Contestacion de un americano meridional a un caballero de esta isla [Jamaica].' *Cuarto cartas y una memoria (1804–1815)*. Ed. Charles V. Aubrun. Paris: Centre de Recherches de l'Institut d'études hispaniques, 1969. 42–58.

Bolt, Carol. *Gabe*. 1973. *Buffalo Jump, Gabe, Red Emma*. Toronto: Playwrights Co-op, 1976. 81–127.

Borgerson, Lon. 'Ile-à-la Crosse: Upisasik Theatres in Our Schools.' *Canadian Theatre Review* 65 (1990): 48–51.

Botkin, Alex. 'The John Brown of the Metis.' *Rocky Mountain Magazine* 1.1 (1900): 18–22.

Bourassa, André-G. *Surréalisme et littérature québécoise*. Montreal: Éditions l'Étincelle, 1977.

Bourget, Ignace. Letter to Louis Riel, 14 July 1875. 'Correspondance Louis Riel-Mgr Bourget.' Ed. Léon Pouliot. *Revue d'histoire de l'Amérique française* 15.3 (1961): 437.

Bouvier, Laure. *Une histoire de Métisses*. Montreal: Leméac, 1995.

Bower, Shannon. '"Practical Results": The Riel Statue Controversy at the Manitoba Legislative Building.' *Manitoba History* 42 (2001–2): 30–8.

Bowering, George. 'A Great Northward Darkness: The Attack on History in Recent Canadian Fiction.' *Imaginary Hand*. Edmonton: NeWest, 1988. 1–21.

– *Shoot!* Toronto: Key Porter, 1994.

– *A Short Sad Book*. Vancouver: Talonbooks, 1977.

Braz, Albert. 'The Absent Protagonist: Louis Riel in Nineteenth-Century Canadian Literature.' *Canadian Literature* 167 (2000): 45–61.

– 'The Omnipresent Voice: Authorial Intrusion in Rudy Wiebe's "Games for Queen Victoria."' *Studies in Canadian Literature* 26.2 (2001): 91–106.

– 'Promised Land / Cursed Land: The Peculiar Canada of Mathias Carvalho.' *Interfaces Brasil/Canadá* 1.1 (2001): 119–28.

– 'The Vengeful Prophet: Revenge in Louis Riel's Writings.' *Dalhousie French Studies* 35 (1996): 19–32.

– 'Wither the White Man: Charles Mair's Lament for the Bison.' *Canadian Poetry: Studies, Documents, Reviews* 49 (2001): 40–55.

Brewster, Elizabeth. 'At Batoche.' *The Way Home*. Ottawa: Oberon, 1982. 50–2.

Broughall, George. *The 90th on Active Service; or, Campaigning in the North West*. 1885. Winnipeg: George Bishop, 1886.

Brown, Chester. *Louis Riel*. Montreal: Drawn and Quarterly Publications, 1999–.

Bumsted, J.M. 'Crisis at Red River: 125 Years Ago Riel Defied Canada.' *Beaver* 75.3 (1995): 23–34.
– 'Louis Riel and the United States.' *American Review of Canadian Studies* 29.1 (1999): 17–41.
– 'The "Mahdi" of Western Canada? Louis Riel and His Papers.' *Beaver* 67.4 (1987): 47–54.
– 'Thomas Scott and the Daughter of Time.' *Prairie Forum* 23.2 (1998): 145–69.
– 'Thomas Scott's Body.' Bumsted, *Thomas Scott's Body*, 3–10.
– *Thomas Scott's Body and Other Essays on Early Manitoba History.* Winnipeg: University of Manitoba Press, 2000.
– 'Why Shoot Thomas Scott? A Study in Historical Evidence.' Bumsted, *Thomas Scott's Body*, 197–209.
Bumsted, J.M., and Wendy Owen. 'John Christian Schultz and the Founding of Manitoba.' Bumsted, *Thomas Scott's Body*, 163–77.
Butler, William F. *The Great Lone Land: A Narrative of Travel and Adventure in the North-West of America.* 1872. Edmonton: Hurtig, 1968.
Cameron, William Bleasdell. *Blood Red the Sun.* 1950. S. Hughes, 5–158. [Cameron's book has also been published under the title *The War Trail of Big Bear*.]
Campbell, Glen. 'Dithyramb and Diatribe: The Polysemic Perception of the Métis in Louis Riel's Poetry.' *Canadian Ethnic Studies* 17.2 (1985): 31–43.
– 'Notes.' Louis Riel, *Selected Poetry*, 127–50.
– 'The Tormented Soul: Riel's Poetic Image of Himself.' Hathorn and Holland, 353–64.
Campbell, Maria. *Halfbreed.* 1973. Halifax: Goodread Biographies, 1983.
Campbell, William Wilfred. 'In the North-West.' *Songs of the Great Dominion: Voices from the Forests and Waters, the Settlements and Cities of Canada.* Ed. William Douw Lighthall. London: Walter Scott, 1889. 267–8.
Carefoot, E.H. *Gabriel Dumont at Batoche.* Saskatoon: n.p., 1973.
Carvalho, Mathias. *Poemas americanos I: Riel.* 1886. *Louis Riel, poèmes amériquains.* Ed. and trans. Jean Morisset. Trois Pistoles, QC: Éditions Trois Pistoles, 1997. 15–57.
Chadbourne, Richard. 'Robert de Roquebrune, romancier québécois méconnu.' *French Review* 54.3 (1981): 436–47.
Chamberlin, J. Edward. *The Harrowing of Eden: White Attitudes toward Native Americans.* New York: Seabury, 1975.
Champagne, Antoine. 'La famille de Louis Riel: notes généalogiques et historiques.' *Mémoires de la Société généalogique canadienne-française* 20.3 (1969): 142–57.
Chartrand, Luc. 'L'affaire Roux: les confessions d'un lieutenant-gouverneur.' *L'actualité*, 16 Nov. 1996, 17–28.

Clark, Daniel. 'A Psycho-Medical History of Louis Riel.' *American Journal of Insanity* 44 (1887): 33–51

Clark, Joe. *A Nation Too Good to Lose: Renewing the Purpose of Canada.* Toronto: Key Porter, 1994.

Clarke, C.K. 'A Critical Study of the Case of Louis Riel.' *Queen's Quarterly* 12.4 and 13.1 (1905): 379–88, 14–26.

Clarkson, Adrienne. 'Speech on the Occasion of the National Celebration to Mark Louis Riel Day.' Ottawa, 16 Nov. 1999.

Cleomati. 'To One of the Absent.' *Two Months in the Camp of Big Bear: The Life and Adventures of Theresa Gowanlock and Theresa Delaney.* By Theresa Gowanlock and Theresa Delaney. Parkdale, ON: Times, 1885. 63–4.

Clyde, Alan. 'Te Kooti.' *'Te Kooti' and Other Poems.* Dunedin, New Zealand: Mills, Dick, 1872. 5–7. ['Te Kooti' is reprinted in *Redemption Songs: Te Kooti Arikirangi Te Turuki,* by Judith Binney (Auckland: Auckland University Press, 1995), 535–7.]

Cobban, William, dir. and writer. *Taking the West.* Episode 10 of *Canada: A People's History.* CBC, 2000–1.

Cockburn, Bruce. 'Stolen Land.' *Waiting for a Miracle.* Toronto: True North Productions, 1987.

Cohen, Nathan. 'Drama.' *The Critic* [Toronto] 1.2 (1950): 4–6.

Cohn, Dorrit. *The Distinction of Fiction.* Baltimore: Johns Hopkins University Press, 1999.

Collet, Paulette. Rev. of *Riel,* by Charles Bayer and E. Parage. *Theatre History in Canada* 7.2 (1986): 247–9.

Collins, J. Edmund. *Annette, the Metis Spy: A Heroine of the N.W. Rebellion.* Toronto: Rose, 1886.

– *Life and Times of the Right Honourable Sir John A. Macdonald … Premier of the Dominion of Canada.* Toronto: Rose, 1883.

– *The Story of Louis Riel the Rebel Chief.* Toronto: Rose, 1885.

Colmer, J.G. 'Introduction.' Steele, v–vii.

Colombo, John Robert. 'The Last Words of Louis Riel.' *Abracadabra.* Toronto: McClelland and Stewart, 1967. 112–18.

Comité historique de l'Union métisse de Saint-Joseph du Manitoba. 'Appendice.' *Histoire de la nation métisse dans l'Ouest canadien.* By Auguste-Henri de Trémaudan. Montreal: Albert Lévesque, 1935. 403–48.

Complin, Margaret. 'Pierre Falcon's "Chanson de la Grenoulière."'*Transactions of the Royal Society of Canada* 33.2 (1939): 49–58.

Connor, Ralph. *The Patrol of the Sun Dance Trail.* Toronto: Westminster, 1914.

Constantin-Weyer, Maurice. *La bourrasque.* Paris: Rieder, 1925.

– *The Half-Breed.* New York: Macaulay, 1930.

– *Manitoba*. Paris: Rieder, 1924.
– *A Martyr's Folly*. Toronto: Macmillan, 1930.
– *Vers l'Ouest*. Paris: Renaissance du livre, 1921.
Cook-Lynn, Elizabeth. 'Why I Can't Read Wallace Stegner.' *Why I Can't Read Wallace Stegner and Other Essays: A Tribal Voice*. Madison: University of Wisconsin Press, 1996. 29–40.
Coulter, John. 'The Canadian Theatre and the Irish Exemplar.' *Theatre Arts Monthly* 22.7 (1938): 503–9.
– *The Crime of Louis Riel*. 1966. Toronto: Playwrights Co-op, 1976.
– *In My Day*. Toronto: Hounslow, 1980.
– Letter to Dora Mavor Moore, 11 Aug. 1949. New Play Society Papers, MS 228, Box 18. Thomas Fisher Rare Book Library, University of Toronto.
– *Riel*. 1950. Hamilton, ON: Cromlech, 1972.
– *The Trial of Louis Riel*. 1967. Ottawa: Oberon, 1968.
Coutts-Smith, Kenneth. 'CBC's "Riel."' *Centerfold* 3.5 (1979): 228–36.
Crawford, Isabella Valancy. 'The Rose of a Nation's Thanks' and 'Songs for the Soldiers.' 1885. *The Collected Poems of Isabella Valancy Crawford*. Ed. J.W. Garvin: Toronto: William Briggs, 1905. 45–7, 70–4.
Culleton, Beatrice. *In Search of April Raintree*. 1983. Winnipeg: Peguis, 1992.
Cumming, Carman. *Sketches from a Young Country: The Images of 'Grip' Magazine*. Toronto: University of Toronto Press, 1997.
Cunha, Euclides da. *Rebellion in the Backlands*. Trans. Samuel Putnam. Chicago: University of Chicago Press, 1944.
Cuthand, Beth. 'The Anglais, They Say.' *Gatherings* 2 (1991): 70.
Daniells, Roy. 'Farewell to Winnipeg.' *Deeper into the Woods*. Toronto: McClelland and Stewart, 1948. 61–6.
Daniels, Greg, and Robert Winslow. *Crossings (The Bell of Batoche)*. 4th Line Theatre. Millbrook, ON, 5 Aug.–3 Sept. 2000.
Daniels, Harry W. Letter to A.W. Johnson [president of the CBC], 26 April 1979. Reprinted in Coutts-Smith, 231.
Dassylva, Martial. 'Jean-Louis Roux: si la saga des Métis m'était contée.' *Un théâtre en effervescence: critiques et chroniques 1965–1972*. Montreal: La presse, 1975. 134–6.
Davey, Frank. *The Clallam or Old Glory in Juan de Fuca*. Vancouver: Talonbooks, 1973.
– 'Riel.' *The Louis Riel Organ and Piano Company*. Winnipeg: Turnstone, 1985. 47–57.
Davin, Nicholas Flood. 'Forward!' *Grip*, 30 May 1885, n.pag.
– 'Interview with Riel: His Parting Message to Mankind.' 1885. *A Century of Reporting: The National Press Club Anthology / Un siècle de reportage: anthologie*

du Cercle national des journalistes. Ed. Lucien Brault et al. Toronto: Clarke, Irwin, 1967. 51–3.

Day, David. *The Scarlet Coat Serial*. Victoria: Porcépic, 1981.

– *The Visions and Revelations of St. Louis the Métis*. Saskatoon: Thistledown, 1997.

DeGuise, Charles. 'Vive le bataillon!' *Le neuvième bataillon au Nord-Ouest (journal d'un militaire)*. By Georges Beauregard. Quebec City: J.-C. Gingras: 1886. 16–17.

DeMille, Cecil B., dir. *North West Mounted Police*. Screenplay by Alan LeMay, Jesse Lasky, Jr, and C. Gardner Sullivan. Paramount, 1940.

Dempsey, Hugh A. *Big Bear: The End of Freedom*. Vancouver: Greystone, 1984.

– *Crowfoot: Chief of the Blackfeet*. 1972. Edmonton: Hurtig, 1976.

Desaulniers, Gonzalve L. *L'absolution avant la bataille (dédié aux braves de la Butte-aux- Français)*. Montreal: L'étendard, 1886.

Desjardins, Édouard, and Charles Dumas. 'Le complexe médicale de Louis Riel.' *L'union médicale du Canada* 99.9 and 99.10 (1970): 1656–61, 1870–8.

Deverell, Rex. *Beyond Batoche*. 1985. *Deverell of the Globe: Selected Plays by Rex Deverell*. Ed. Don Perkins. Edmonton: NeWest, 1989. 73–134.

– 'Beyond Batoche.' *Prairie Fire* 7.1 (1986): 40–51.

Deverell, Rex, and Wayne Schmalz. *The Riel Commission: An Inquiry into the Survival of a People. Studio One: Stories Made for Radio*. Ed. Wayne Schmalz. Regina: Coteau, 1990. 61–79.

DeVoto, Bernard. 'Joseph Kinsey Howard.' *Strange Empire: A Narrative of the Northwest*. By Joseph Kinsey Howard. New York: William Morrow, 1952. 3–10.

Dickinson, Emily. Poem 435. *The Complete Poems of Emily Dickinson*. Ed. Thomas J. Johnson. Boston: Little, Brown, 1961. 209.

Dixon, L. *Halifax to the Saskachewan: 'Our Boys' in the Riel Rebellion*. Halifax: Holloway Bruce, 1886.

Doctorow, E.L. 'False Documents.' *Essays and Conversations*. Ed. Richard Trenner. Princeton: Ontario Review, 1983. 16–27.

Doležel, Lubomír. 'Possible Worlds of Fiction and History.' *New Literary History* 29.4 (1998): 785–809.

Donkin, John G. *Trooper and Redskin in the Far North-West: Recollections of Life in the North-West Mounted Police, Canada, 1844–1885*. London: Sampson Low, 1889.

Dorge, Claude. *Le roitelet*. 1976. Saint Boniface, MB: Éditions du blé, 1980.

Doucette, L.E. 'Louis Riel sur scène: l'état de la dramaturgie québécoise en 1886.' *Theatre History in Canada* 6.2 (1985): 123–32.

Dowbiggin, Ian. *Suspicious Minds: The Triumph of Paranoia in Everyday Life*. Toronto: Macfarlane Walter and Ross, 1999.

Doyle, David G. *From the Gallows: The Lost Testimony of Louis Riel*. Summerland, BC: Ethnic Enterprises, 2000.

Dragland, Stan. *Floating Voice: Duncan Campbell Scott and the Literature of Treaty 9*. Toronto: Anansi, 1994.

Duffy, Dennis. *Gardens, Covenants, Exiles: Loyalism in the Literature of Upper Canada / Ontario*. Toronto: University of Toronto Press, 1982.

– 'Wiebe's Real Riel? *The Scorched-Wood People* and Its Audience.' *Rough Justice: Essays on Crime in Literature*. Ed. M.L. Friedland. Toronto: University of Toronto Press, 1991. 200–13.

Dugas, Georges. *La première Canadienne du Nord-Ouest*. Montreal: Cadieux and Derome, 1883.

Dumas, Georges. *Histoire véridique des faits qui on préparé le mouvement des métis à la Rivière-Rouge en 1869*. Montreal: Beauchemin, 1905.

Dumont, Gabriel. 'Récit sur les événements de 1885.' *La vérité sur la question métisse au Nord-Ouest*. By Adolphe Ouimet and B.A.T. de Montigny. Montreal: n.p., 1889. 120–42.

Dumont, Marilyn. 'Letter to Sir John A. Macdonald.' *A Really Good Brown Girl*. London, ON: Brick, 1996. 52.

Dunn, Willie. 'Louis Riel.' *Singin' about Us*. Ed. Bob Davis. Comp. Bruce Burron. Toronto: James Lorimer, 1976. 48–9.

Edgar, Pelham. 'Introduction.' Constantin-Weyer, *A Martyr's Folly*, v–vii.

Eisler, Dale. *Rumours of Glory: Saskatchewan and the Thatcher Years*. Edmonton: Hurtig, 1987.

Enright, Robert. 'Standing-in-Between: A Conversation with Métis Writer Emma LaRoque [LaRocque].' *Arts Manitoba* 4.3 (1983): 45–6.

Ens, Gerhard J. 'Prologue to the Red River Resistance: Pre-liminal Politics and the Triumph of Riel.' *Journal of the Canadian Historical Association* 5.5 (1994): 111–23.

Everson, R.G. 'The Métis.' *The Dark Is Not So Dark*. Montreal: Delta, 1969. 20.

Falcon, Pierre. 'La Bataille des Sept Chênes.' 1816. MacLeod, 5–7. [James Reaney's translation of the poem, entitled 'The Battle of Seven Oaks,' follows on pages 7–9.]

– 'The Battle of Seven Oaks.' *The Poetry of the Canadian People, 1720–1920: Two Hundred Years of Hard Work*. Ed. N. Brian Davis. Toronto: NC, 1976. 246–7.

Ferguson, Will. *Bastards and Boneheads: Canada's Glorious Leaders Past and Present*. Vancouver: Douglas and McIntyre, 1999.

Ferland, Marcien. *Au temps de la Prairie: l'histoire des Métis de l'Ouest Canadien, racontée par Auguste Vermette, neveu de Louis Riel*. Saint Boniface, MB: Éditions du blé, 2000.

Fetherling, Doug. 'George Woodcock Past and Present.' *The Blue Notebook: Reports on Canadian Culture.* Oakville, ON: Mosaic, 1985. 21–32.

Filewod, Alan. *Collective Encounters: Documentary Theatre in English Canada.* Toronto: University of Toronto Press, 1987.

Flanagan, Thomas. *Louis 'David' Riel: 'Prophet of the New World.'* Rev. ed. Toronto: University of Toronto Press, 1996.

– 'Louis Riel: Icon of the Left.' *Transactions of the Royal Society of Canada,* series 5.1 (1986): 219–28.

– 'Louis Riel: Insanity and Prophecy.' Palmer, 15–36.

– 'Louis Riel: Was He Really Crazy?' *Humanities Association of Canada Newsletter* 13.2 (1985): 7–27.

– 'Louis Riel's Name "David."' *Riel and the Métis: Riel Mini Conference Papers.* Ed. Antoine Lussier. Winnipeg: Manitoba Métis Federation, 1979. 48–65.

– 'The Riel "Lunacy" Commission: The Report of Dr. Valade.' *Revue de l'Université d'Ottawa* 45.1 (1976): 118–27.

Foucault, Michel. *Discipline and Punish: The Birth of the Prison.* Trans. Alan Sheridan. New York: Vintage, 1979.

– *The History of Sexuality.* Volume 1. *An Introduction.* Trans. Robert Hurley. New York: Vintage, 1990.

– *Power/Knowledge: Selected Interviews and Other Writings 1972–1977.* Ed. Colin Gordon. New York: Pantheon, 1980.

Fourmond, Jean-Vital. 'Dénonciation du Rev. P. Fourmond.' Grandin et al., 14–15.

Francis, Daniel. *The Imaginary Indian: The Image of the Indian in Canadian Culture.* Vancouver: Arsenal Pulp, 1992.

– *National Dreams: Myth, Memory, and Canadian History.* Vancouver: Arsenal Pulp, 1997.

Fréchette, Louis-Honoré. *Le dernier des martyrs.* N.p., 1885–6.

– 'Le gibet de Riel,' 'Le dernier martyr,' and 'L'orangisme.' *La légende d'un peuple.* Paris: Librairie illustrée, 1889. 279–81, 283–92, 293–5.

– 'Pamphile Le May.' *L'opinion publique,* 17 April 1873, 181.

Frémont, Donatien. *Les secrétaires de Louis Riel: Louis Schmidt, Henry Jackson, Philippe Garnot.* Montreal: Éditions Chantecler, 1953.

– *Sur le ranch de Constantin-Weyer.* Winnipeg: La liberté, 1932.

French, Francis J.P. Letter ('Louis Riel'). *Globe and Mail,* 3 Nov. 1969, 6.

French, Orland. 'Pope Louie I.' *File 23: The Shocking Truth about Canada.* Toronto: Methuen, 1985, 103–14.

Freynet, Robert. *Louis Riel en bande dessinée.* Saint Boniface, MB: Éditions des Plaines, 1990.

222   Bibliography

Frye, Northrop. 'Dean of Critics.' *Canadian Forum* 28.11 (1948): 169–70.
– *Fables of Identity: Studies in Poetic Mythology.* San Diego: Harcourt, 1963.
Garay, Kathleen. 'John Coulter's *Riel*: The Shaping of "a Myth for Canada."'
    Hathorn and Holland, 277–310.
Gareau, Laurier. *La trahison / The Betrayal.* Regina: Éditions de la nouvelle
    plume, 1998.
Gilson, Henri. 'Étude sur l'état mental de Louis Riel.' *L'encéphale* (1886): 51–60.
Goldie, Terry. *Fear and Temptation: The Image of the Indigene in Canadian, Austral-
    ian, and New Zealand Literatures.* Kingston and Montreal: McGill-Queen's
    University Press, 1989.
Goldring, Peter. 'Louis Riel Fought the Fathers of Confederation.' Oct. 2000.
    <http://www.petergoldring.ca/articles/artva024.htm>.
– 'Riel: An Anomaly, Not a Hero.' Sept. 1999. <http://www.petergoldring.ca/
    articles/artva022.htm>.
Grandin, Vital, et al. *Le véritable Riel.* Montreal: Imprimerie générale, 1887.
Gratton, Denis. 'Louis Riel: la réhabilitation d'un patriote.' *Le droit,* 17 April
    1999. <http:www.vigile.net/hist/biographie/grattonriel.html>.
Greffard, Madeleine. '*Bois-Brûlés,* drame de Jean-Louis Roux.' Lemire, 4:
    106–8.
Groulx, Lionel. *Louis Riel et les évenements de la Rivière-Rouge en 1869–70.*
    Montreal: L'action nationale, 1944.
– *Mes mémoires 1.* Montreal: Fides, 1970.
Gutteridge, Don. *Riel: A Poem for Voices.* Fredericton: Fiddlehead, 1968.
– 'Riel: Historical Man or Literary Symbol?' *Humanities Association Bulletin*
    21.3 (1970): 3–15.
Harrison, Dick. 'Cultural Insanity and Prairie Fiction.' Bessai and Jackel,
    278–94.
– *Unnamed Country: The Struggle for Prairie Fiction.* Edmonton: University of
    Alberta Press, 1977.
Harrison, Susie Frances [Seranus]. 'The Prisoner Dubois.' *Crowded Out! and
    Other Sketches.* Ottawa: Evening Journal, 1886. 90–7.
Harron, Don. *Charlie Farquharson's Histry of Canada.* Toronto: McGraw-Hill
    Ryerson, 1972.
Harron, Martha. *Don Harron: A Parent Contradiction.* Toronto: Collins, 1988.
Hart, Jonathan. 'Translating and Resisting Empire: Cultural Appropriation
    and Postcolonial Studies.' *Borrowed Power: Essays on Cultural Appropriation.*
    Ed. Bruce Ziff and Pratima Rao. New Brunswick, NJ: Rutgers University
    Press, 1997. 137–68.
Hathorn, Ramon, and Patrick Holland, eds. *Images of Louis Riel in Canadian
    Culture.* Lewiston, NY: Edwin Mellen, 1992.

Hayes, Kate Simpson [Mary Markwell]. 'Riel.' *Prairie Pot-pourri*. Winnipeg: Stovel, 1895. 42.

Hayne, David-M. '*Le dernier des martyrs*, poème de Louis Fréchette.' Lemire, 1: 173.

Healy, W.J. *Women of Red River: Being a Book Written from the Recollections of Women Surviving from the Red River Era*. 1923. Winnipeg: Peguis, 1967.

Heath, Martin. 'Louis Riel.' Music by Susan MacKay. *New Frontiers* 1.2 (1952): 9.

Henham, Ernest G. *Menotah: A Tale of the Riel Rebellion*. London: Hutchison, 1897,

'Highway 11 Named Louis Riel Trail.' <http://www.gov.sk.ca/newsrel/2001/06/20-470.html>.

Hollingsworth, Michael. *Confederation and Riel*. 1988. *The History of the Village of the Small Huts, I–VIII*. Winnipeg: Blizzard, 1994. 167–213.

Hood, Hugh. 'Moral Imagination: Canadian Thing.' Kilbourn, 29–35.

Hope, Adrian. 'An Ode to the Metis.' Preface to *The New Nation – Christ's Chosen People*. By Mary Madeline (Bobby) Lee. N.p., 1987. iv–vii.

Howard, Henry. 'Medical History of Louis David Riel during His Detention in Longue Pointe Asylum.' *Canada Medical and Surgical Journal* 14 (1886): 641–9.

Howard, Joseph Kinsey. *Strange Empire: Louis Riel and the Métis People*. Toronto: James Lewis and Samuel, 1974.

– *Strange Empire: A Narrative of the Northwest*. New York: William Morrow, 1952.

Huel, Raymond. 'The Oblates, the Métis, and 1885: The Breakdown of Traditional Relationships.' *Historical Studies* 56 (1989): 9–29.

Hughes, Katherine. *Father Lacombe: The Black-Robe Voyageur*. Toronto: McClelland and Stewart, 1920.

Hughes, Stuart, ed. *The Frog Lake 'Massacre': Personal Perspectives on Ethnic Conflict*. Toronto: McClelland and Stewart, 1976.

Hutcheon, Linda. *The Canadian Postmodern: A Study of Contemporary English-Canadian Fiction*. Toronto: Oxford University Press, 1988.

Hutcheon, Linda, and Michael Hutcheon. 'Otherhood Issues: Post-national Operatic Narratives.' *Narrative* 3.1 (1995): 1–17.

Idriess, Ion L. *Outlaws of the Leopolds*. Sydney: Angus and Robertson, 1952.

Imrie, John. *Welcome Home, Brave Volunteers*. Music by F.H. Torrington. Toronto: Imrie and Graham, 1885.

Jenish, D'Arcy. 'Did "Riel Apologist" Get Her Bigots Wrong?' *Globe and Mail*, 19 Feb. 2000, D19.

Johnson, Chris. 'Riel in Canadian Drama, 1885–1985.' Hathorn and Holland, 175–210.

Johnson, E. Pauline (Tekahionwake). 'A Cry from an Indian Wife.' *The Week*,

18 June 1885, 457. [The poem is reprinted, with minor variations, in *Flint and Feather: The Complete Poems of E. Pauline Johnson (Tekahionwake)* (Toronto: PaperJacks, 1972), 15–17.]

Jonasson, Jonas A. 'The Riel Rebellions.' Ph.D. diss., Stanford University, 1933.

Joubert, Ingrid. 'Askik, le Riel anonyme dans *Tchipayuk ou le chemin du loup* de Ronald Lavallée.' *Cahiers franco-canadiens de l'Ouest* 1.2 (1989): 175–9.

– 'Current Trends in Franco-Manitoban Theatre.' Trans. Jean Sourisseau. *Prairie Fire* 11.1 (1990): 118–28.

– 'Mythe et recherche identitaire dans le théâtre de l'Ouest canadien.' *Mythes dans la littérature contemporaine d'expression française*. Ed. Metka Zupančič. Ottawa: Nordir, 1988. 94–102.

Juneja, Om P., M.F. Salat, and Chandra Mohan. '"Looking at Our Particular World": An Interview with Rudy Wiebe.' *World Literature Written in English* 31.2 (1991): 1–18.

Kaldor, Connie. 'Maria's Place / Batoche.' Amabile and Dales, 178–9.

Kaye, Frances W. 'Any Important Form: Louis Riel in Sculpture.' *Prairie Forum* 22.1 (1997): 103–33.

Keith, W.J., ed. *A Voice in the Land: Essays by and about Rudy Wiebe*. Edmonton: NeWest, 1981.

Keller, Betty. *Pauline: A Biography of Pauline Johnson*. Halifax: Goodread Biographies, 1987.

Kilbourn, William, ed. *A Guide to the Peaceable Kingdom*. Toronto: Macmillan, 1970.

Kilgour, David. 'Riel Did What Was Right.' *Ottawa Citizen*, 14 May 1999. <http://www.david-kilgour.com/speeches/riel.htm>.

Klassen, William. 'Two Wise Men from the West: Canadian Identity and Religion.' *Religion and Culture in Canada / Religion et culture au Canada*. Ed. Peter Slater. Waterloo, ON: Canadian Corporation for the Study of Religion, 1977. 271–89.

Klooss, Wolfgang. 'Louis Riel and the West: Literary Images of a Canadian Myth.' *Zeitschrift der Gesellschaft für Kanada-Studien* 2.2 (1982): 19–36.

Knowles, Ric. '"Marlon Brandon, Pocahontas, and Me."' *Essays on Canadian Writing* 71 (Fall 2000): 48–60.

Knutson, Simone. 'Constantin-Weyer's *La bourrasque*: A Process of Mythification.' Hathorn and Holland, 257–77.

Kogawa, Joy. *Obasan*. Toronto: Lester and Orpen Dennys, 1981.

Kroetsch, Robert. 'Canada Is a Poem.' *Open Letter*, 5th series, no. 4 (1983): 33–5.

– *The Lovely Treachery of Words: Essays Selected and New*. Toronto: Oxford University Press, 1989.

– 'On Being an Alberta Writer.' *Open Letter*, 5th series, no. 4 (1983): 69–80.

Lacey, Edward A. *A Magic Prison: Letters from Edward Lacey.* Ed. David Helwig. Ottawa: Oberon, 1995.
- 'Poetry Chronicle IV.' *Edge* 9 (1969): 127–39 [130–5].
- 'Saudade.' *Path of Snow: Poems 1951–1973.* Scarborough, ON: Ahasuerus, 1974. 59–61.
Lamb, R.E. *Thunder in the North: Conflict over the Riel Risings 1870, 1885.* New York: Pageant, 1957.
Lampman, Archibald. 'At the Mermaid Inn, 19 March 1892.' *At the Mermaid Inn: Wilfred Campbell, Archibald Lampman, Duncan Campbell Scott in the Globe 1892–93.* Ed. Barrie Davis. Toronto: University of Toronto Press, 1979. 39–40.
Langley, Rod. *Tales from a Prairie Drifter.* 1973. Toronto: Playwrights Co-op, 1974.
Laurence, Margaret. 'Best Wishes to Journal.' *Pemmican Journal* 1.2 (1981): 1.
- *The Diviners.* Toronto: McClelland and Stewart, 1974.
- 'In the Air.' *Winnipeg Citizen*, 22 March 1948. Partially reproduced in Donez Xiques, 'Early Influences: Laurence's Newspaper Career.' *Challenging Territory: The Writing of Margaret Laurence.* Ed. Christian Riegel. Edmonton: University of Alberta Press, 1997. 187–210 [205–6].
- 'Letter from Lakefield.' Lennox and Panofsky, 357–62.
- Letter to Adele Wiseman, 2 Jan. 1963. Lennox and Panofsky, 153–6.
- 'Man of Our People.'1965. *Heart of a Stranger.* Toronto: Seal, 1980. 227–36.
Laurin, Camille. 'Louis Riel (1885–1985).' Photocopy of a paper presented at the annual meeting of the Canadian Psychiatric Association. Quebec City, 1985. Regina, Saskatchewan Archives Board.
Lavallée, Ronald. *Tchipayuk ou le chemin du loup.* Paris: Albin Michel, 1987.
Lavell, Michael. 'The Lavell Report.' *Douglas Library Notes* 12.2 (1963): 10–15.
Le Chevallier, Jules. *Batoche: les missionaires du Nord-Ouest pendant les Troubles de 1885.* Montreal: L'œuvre de presse dominicaine, 1941.
Le May, Pamphile. 'À ceux qui demandent la tête de Riel. Crucifiez-le! Crucifiez-le!' *Les guêpes canadiennes 2.* Ed. Augustin Laperrière. Ottawa: A. Bureau, 1882. 207–9.
Lecker, Robert. 'Wiebe and Riel.' Rev. of *The Scorched-Wood People*, by Rudy Wiebe. *Essays on Canadian Writing* 10 (1978): 129–33.
Lemay, Georges. 'Chant du Métis.' 1886. *Anthologie de la poésie franco-manitobaine.* Ed. J.R. Léveillé. Saint Boniface, MB: Éditions du blé, 1990. 566–7.
- 'Épisodes d'une insurrection au Nord-Ouest.' *Petites fantaisies littéraires.* Quebec City: P-G. Délisle, 1884. 151–71.
Lemire, Maurice, gen. ed. *Dictionnaire des œuvres littéraires du Québec.* 5 vols. Montreal: Fides, 1978–87.

Lennox, John, and Ruth Panofsky, eds. *Selected Letters of Margaret Laurence and Adele Wiseman*. Toronto: University of Toronto Press, 1997.

Lipking, Lawrence. 'The Genius of the Shore: Lycidas, Adamastor, and the Poetics of Nationalism.' *PMLA* 111.2 (1996): 203–21.

Livesay, Dorothy. 'The Documentary Poem: A Canadian Genre.' *Contexts of Canadian Criticism*. Ed. Eli Mandel. Chicago: University of Chicago Press, 1971. 267–81.

– 'The Native People in Our Canadian Literature.' *English Quarterly* 4.1 (1971): 21–32.

– 'Prophet of the New World: A Poem for Voices.' *Collected Poems: The Two Seasons*. Toronto: McGraw-Hill Ryerson, 1972. 148–56.

Logan, John Edward [Barry Dane]. 'Metis, 1885' and 'A Cry from the Saskatchewan, March 1885.' *Verses*. Montreal: Pen and Pencil Club, 1916. 93, 118–29.

Lusty, Terrance. *Louis Riel Humanitarian*. Calgary: Northwest Printing, 1973.

Lutz, Giles A. *The Magnificent Failure*. Garden City, NY: Doubleday, 1967.

Macdonald, Sir John A. Letters to William McDougall (1869) and 'Sir John Macdonald's Last Address to the People of Canada'(1891). Pope, 407–14, 772–7.

– Letter to Dr Michael Lavell, 31 Oct. 1885. *Douglas Library Notes* 9.3 (1960): 1–2.

Machar, Agnes Maule. 'Quebec to Ontario, a Plea for the Life of Riel, September, 1885.' *Lays of the'True North' and Other Canadian Poems*. London: Elliot Stock; Toronto: Copp Clark, 1899. 36–7.

Mackie, John. *The Rising of the Red Man: A Romance of the Louis Riel Rebellion*. London: Jarrold, 1902.

MacLeod, Margaret Arnett, ed. *Songs of Old Manitoba: With Airs, French and English Words, and Introductions*. Toronto: Ryerson, 1960.

Mair, Charles. 'The American Bison.' *Transactions of the Royal Society of Canada* 8.2 (1890): 93–108.

– Letter to Holmes Mair, 19 Nov. 1868. Reprinted in W. Morton, 395–9.

Major, J.C. *The Red River Expedition*. Winnipeg: n.p., 1870.

Manzoni, Alessandro. *On the Historical Novel*. 1850. Trans. Sandra Bermann. Lincoln: University of Nebraska Press, 1984.

Margolin, Uri. 'Text Worlds, Fictional Worlds, Narrative Fiction.' *Canadian Review of Comparative Literature* 27.1–2 (2000): 256–73.

Markson, E.R. 'The Life and Death of Louis Riel, a Study in Forensic Psychiatry: Part 1 – a Psychoanalytic Commentary.' *Canadian Psychiatric Association Journal* 10.4 (1965): 246–52.

Martel, Gilles. 'Les Indiens dans la pensée messianique de Louis Riel.' *Recherches amérindiennes au Québec* 8.2 (1978): 123–37.

– 'Louis Riel à la télé.' *Relations* 448 (1979): 154–5.
– *Le messianisme de Louis Riel.* Waterloo, ON: Wilfrid Laurier University Press, 1984.
Martel, Réginald. 'Jean-Jules Richard au présent.' *Liberté* 14.1 (1972): 40–52.
– 'Quand les héros sont ambigus.' Rev. of *Louis Riel Exovide*, by Jean-Jules Richard. *La presse,* 23 Sept. 1972, E3.
Martin, Sandra. 'Atwood Interactive.' *Globe and Mail,* 26 Aug. 2000, R1, R4.
Mattes, Catherine. 'Rielisms.' *Rielisms,* 12–22.
– 'Whose Hero? Images of Louis Riel in Contemporary Art and Métis Nation hood.' M.A. thesis, Concordia University, 1998.
McCourt, Edward A. *The Canadian West in Fiction.* Toronto: Ryerson, 1949.
– *The Flaming Hour.* Toronto: Ryerson, 1947.
– *Revolt in the West: The Story of the Riel Rebellion.* Toronto: Macmillan, 1958.
McLean, Elizabeth M. 'The Siege of Fort Pitt,' 'Prisoners of the Indians,' and 'Our Captivity Ended.' S. Hughes, 272–95.
McNamee, James. *My Uncle Joe.* Toronto: Macmillan, 1962.
– 'A Note on Louis Riel.' *My Uncle Joe.* London: Macmillan, 1963. N.pag.
– *Them Damn Canadians Hanged Louis Riel!* Toronto: Macmillan, 1971.
McWilliams, Charles A. 'L'abbé McWilliams et Riel.' Grandin et al., 52–3.
Mercier, Anne, and Violet Watt. *The Red House by the Rockies: A Tale of Riel's Rebellion.* [London: Society for Promoting Christian Knowledge, 1896.] Toronto: Musson, 1896?
Mercier, Honoré. 'Discours prononcé sur le Champs de Mars, le 22 novembre 1885.' *Biographie, discours, conférences, etc. de l'hon. Honoré Mercier.* Ed. J.O. Pelland. Montreal: n.p., 1890. 328–33.
Middleton, Frederick. *Suppression of the Rebellion in the North West Territories of Canada, 1885.* Ed. G.H. Needler. Toronto: University of Toronto Press, 1948.
Miller, Joaquin. 'Riel, the Rebel.' *The Poetical Works of Joaquin Miller.* Ed. Stuart P. Sherman. New York: G.P. Putnam's Sons, 1923. 413.
Mitchell, Ken. *Davin: The Politician.* 1978. Edmonton: NeWest, 1979.
– *The Plainsman.* 1985. Regina: Coteau, 1992.
Mitchell, W.O. *According to Jake and the Kid.* Toronto: McClelland and Stewart, 1990.
Monkman, Leslie. *A Native Heritage: Images of the Indian in English-Canadian Literature.* Toronto: University of Toronto Press, 1981.
Mooney, James. *The Ghost-Dance Religion and the Sioux Outbreak of 1890.* 1965. Ed. Anthony F.C. Wallace. Chicago: University of Chicago Press, 1976.
Moore, Mavor. 'Canadians Need Heroes, and Riel Fits the Bill.' *Globe and Mail,* 23 Nov. 1985, D3.
– 'Haunted by Riel.' Hathorn and Holland, 411–16.

– *Reinventing Myself.* Toronto: Stoddart, 1994.

Moore, Mavor, and Jacques Languirand. *Louis Riel.* 1967. Comp. Harry Somers. Toronto: Canadian Opera Company, n.d.

Morisset, Jean. 'Cent ans après sa mort, c'est la nationalisation de Louis Riel.' *Le devoir*, 30 Nov. 1985, 11.

– 'La conquête du Nord-Ouest, 1885–1985: The Imperial Quest of British North America.' *As Long as the Sun Shines and Water Flows: A Reader in Canadian Native Studies.* Ed. Ian A.L. Getty and Antoine S. Lussier. Vancouver: University of British Columbia Press, 1983. 280–7.

– *L'identité usurpée 1: l'Amérique écartée.* Montreal: Nouvelle optique, 1985.

– 'Louis Riel: écrivain des Amériques.' *Nuit blanche* 28 (1987): 59–63.

– 'Miroir indogène / reflet eurogène: essai sur l'américanité et la fabrication de l'identité canadienne.' *Recherches amérindiennes au Québec* 9.4 (1980): 285–312.

– 'Postface: Louis Riel, écrivain des Amériques.' Carvalho, 61–112.

Morrissey [Dales], Kim. 'The Art of Rebellion: Batoche and the Lyric Poem.' *Prairie Fire* 6.4 (1985): 6–15.

– *Batoche.* Regina: Coteau, 1989.

Morton, A.S. *A History of the Canadian West to 1870–71.* Toronto: University of Toronto Press, 1931.

Morton, Desmond. 'Des canadiens errants: French Canadian Troops in the North-West Campaign of 1885.' *Journal of Canadian Studies* 5.3 (1970): 28–39.

– 'Reflections on the Image of Louis Riel a Century Later.' Hathorn and Holland, 47–62.

– 'Riel Revisionists Can't Alter History.' *Toronto Star*, 15 Jan. 1998, A18.

Morton, W.L., 'Introduction.' *Alexander Begg's Red River Journal and Other Papers Relative to the Red River Resistance of 1869–1870.* Ed. W.L. Morton. Toronto: Champlain Society, 1956. 1–148.

Mosdell, D. 'Theatre.' *Canadian Forum* 30.1 (1950): 15.

Motut, Roger. *Maurice Constantin-Weyer: écrivain de l'Ouest et du Grand Nord.* Saint Boniface, MB: Éditions des Plaines, 1982.

Mouré, Erin. 'Riel: In the Season of His Birth.' *Empire, York Street.* Toronto: Anansi, 1979. 62–8.

Mousseau, J.O. *Une page d'histoire.* Montreal: W.F. Daniel, 1886.

Mulvaney, Charles Pelham. 'Our Boys in the North-West Away.' *The History of the North-West Rebellion of 1885.* Toronto: A.H. Hovey, 1886. 73–4.

Murphy, Derryl. 'Cold Ground.' *Arrowdreams: An Anthology of Alternative Canadas.* Ed. Mark Shainblum and John Dupuis. Winnipeg: Nuage, 1997. 73–84.

Murray, Alexander Hunter. 'Capture of Fort Garry, or Riel's Retreat' and 'The Marching Song.' 1870. MacLeod, 58–9, 50.

Murray, Laura J. 'The Aesthetic of Dispossession: Washington Irving and Ideologies of (De)Colonization in the Early Republic.' *American Literary History* 8.2 (1996): 205–31.

Needler, G.H. *The Battleford Column: Versified Memories of a Queen's Own Corporal in the Northwest Rebellion 1885.* 1947. Montreal: Provincial, n.d.

– *Louis Riel: The Rebellion of 1885.* Toronto: Burns and MacEachern, 1957.

Neff, Lyle. 'Riel's Last Letter from Vancouver.' *Ivanhoe Station.* Vancouver: Anvil, 1997. 16–17.

New Play Society. Program. *Heartbreak House,* by G.B. Shaw, 3–11 Feb. 1950. New Play Society Papers, MS 228, Box 18. Thomas Fisher Rare Book Library, University of Toronto.

Newlove, John. 'The Pride.' *Black Night Window.* Toronto: McClelland and Stewart, 1968. 105–11.

Nichol, bp. 'The Long Weekend of Louis Riel.' *Craft Dinner: Stories and Texts 1966–1976.* Toronto: Aya, 1978. N.pag.

Nicol, Eric. *Dickens of the Mounted. The Astounding Long-lost Letters of Inspector F. Dickens NWMP 1874–1886.* 1989. Toronto: McClelland and Stewart, 1990.

– *An Uninhibited History of Canada.* Toronto: Musson, 1965.

Niven, Frederick. *The Flying Years.* 1942. Toronto: McClelland and Stewart, 1974.

Nora, Pierre. 'Présentation.' *Les lieux de mémoire 1: la République.* Ed. Pierre Nora. Paris: Gallimard, 1984. vi–xii.

Nutting, Stéphanie. 'Le *pharmakos* dans *Bois-Brûlés* de Jean-Louis Roux.' *Littérature québécoise: la recherche en émergence.* Ed. François Dumont and France Fortier. Quebec City: Nuit blanche, 1991. 187–95.

O Broin, Padraig. Rev. of *Riel,* by John Coulter. *Canadian Forum* 42.5 (1962): 137–8.

Osachoff, Margaret Gail. 'Louis Riel in Canadian Literature: Myth and Reality.' *Canadian Story and History 1885–1985.* Ed. Colin Nicholson and Peter Easingwood. Edinburgh: Edinburgh University Centre of Canadian Studies, 1985. 61–9.

– 'Riel on Stage.' *Canadian Drama* 8.2 (1982): 129–44.

Owram, Douglas. 'The Myth of Louis Riel.' *Canadian Historical Review* 63.3 (1982): 315–36.

– 'The Riel Project: History, Myth, and Money.' *Transactions of the Royal Society of Canada* 5.1 (1986): 207–18.

Palmer, Howard, ed. *The Settlement of the West.* Calgary: Comprint, 1977.

Paquin, Elzéar. *Riel*. Montreal: C.O. Beauchemin, 1886.

Parke-Taylor, Michael. *Patrick Hayman: The Visionary and the New Frontier*. Regina: Norman Mackenzie Art Gallery, 1985.

Payment, Diane. *Batoche (1870–1910)*. Saint Boniface, MB: Éditions du blé, 1983.

Pearce, Jon. 'Moving to the Clear: Michael Ondaatje.' *Twelve Voices: Interviews with Canadian Poets*. Ottawa: Borealis, 1980. 129–42.

Pellerin, Maurice. 'Biographie de Léon-Pamphile Le May.' *Pamphile Le May, bibliothécaire de la Législature et écrivain*. By Maurice Pellerin and Gilles Gallichan. Quebec City: Bibliothèque de l'Assemblée nationale, 1986. 25–66.

Pincus-Witten, Robert. *John Nugent: Modernism in Isolation*. Regina: Norman Mackenzie Art Gallery, 1983.

Piquet, J.P.M. 'Première lettre du Frère Piquet.' Grandin et al., 23–4.

Pocock, Roger. 'The Lean Man.' 1888. *Best Mounted Police Stories*. Ed. Dick Harrison. Edmonton: University of Alberta Press, 1978. 94–107.

Podedworny, Carol. 'Riel Remembered.' *Riel Remembered: An Exhibition of Drawings on Paper by Gerald R. McMaster*. Thunder Bay: Thunder Bay Art Gallery, 1985. N.pag.

Poirier, Joseph-Émile. *Les arpents de neige*. Paris: Nouvelle librairie nationale, 1909.

– *La tempête sur le fleuve*. Paris: Jules Tallandier, 1931.

Poitras, Lisa. 'Resurrecting a Revolutionary: Interview with Best-Selling Author Maggie Siggins.' *Prairie Dog* 4.7 (1996): 3–4.

Pomeroy, E.M. *Sir Charles G.D. Roberts: A Biography*. Toronto: Ryerson, 1943.

Pope, Joseph. *Memoirs of the Right Honourable Sir John Alexander Macdonald, G.C.B., First Prime Minister of the Dominion of Canada*. Toronto: Musson, 1930.

Pratt, E.J. *Towards the Last Spike*. Toronto: Macmillan, 1952.

The Queen v Louis Riel. Ed. Desmond Morton. Toronto: University of Toronto Press, 1974.

Quesnel, Christian. *Le crépuscule des Bois-brûlés*. Ottawa: Vermillon, 1995.

Racette, Sherry Farrell. 'Metis Man or Canadian Icon: Who Owns Louis Riel?' *Rielisms*, 42–53.

Reaney, James. 'Local Grains of Sand.' Kilbourn, 26–8.

– 'Scapegoats Who Fought Back: The Donnellys.' Literary Puzzles and Mysteries Lecture Series. Peterborough (Ontario) Public Library, 14 Oct. 1999.

Rémillard, Jean-Robert. 'Pour un pendu oublié.' *Sonnets archaïques pour ceux qui verront l'indépendance, suivis de Complaintes du pays des porteurs d'eaux*. Montreal: Parti pris, 1966. 54–5.

Renan, Ernest. *Qu'est-ce qu'une nation? What Is a Nation?* 1882. Trans. Wanda Romer Taylor. Toronto: Tapir, 1996.

Rens, Jean-Guy. *L'empire invisible 1: histoire des communications au Canada, de 1846 à 1956*. Sainte-Foy: Presses de l'Université du Québec, 1993.

Reville, F. Douglas. *A Rebellion: A Story of the Red River Uprising*. Brantford, ON: Hurley, 1912.

Ribeiro, João Ubaldo. *An Invincible Memory*. Trans. J.U. Ribeiro. New York: Harper and Row, 1989.

Richard, Jean-Jules. *Louis Riel Exovide*. Montreal: La presse, 1972.

Riel, Louis. *The Collected Writings of Louis Riel / Les écrits complets de Louis Riel*. 5 vols. Gen. ed. George F.G. Stanley. Vol. 1: 29 Dec. 1861–7 Dec. 1875, ed. Raymond Huel; vol. 2: 8 Dec. 1875–4 June 1884, ed. Gilles Martel; vol. 3: 5 June 1884–16 Nov. 1885, ed. Thomas Flanagan; vol. 4: Poetry, ed. Glen Campbell; vol. 5: Reference, ed. George F.G. Stanley, Thomas Flanagan, and Claude Rocan. Edmonton: University of Alberta Press, 1985.

– *Selected Poetry of Louis Riel*. Trans. Paul Savoie. Ed. Glen Campbell. Toronto: Exile, 1993.

Riel, Sara. 'Letters of Sara [to Louis Riel].' *To Louis from Your Sister Who Loves You*. By Mary V. Jordan. Toronto: Griffin House, 1974. 106–72.

'Riel Statue to Be Moved from Legislature Buildings.' *Windspeaker*, 1–14 Aug. 1994, R1.

Rielisms. Winnipeg: Winnipeg Art Gallery, 2001.

Rivard, Adjutor. 'Préface.' Poirier, *Arpents*, v–x.

Roberts, David. 'New Bronze Statue Is the Riel Thing.' *Globe and Mail*, 13 May 1996, A2.

Roberts, Kevin. 'Riel.' Amabile and Dales, 182.

Robertson, R.W.W. *The Execution of Thomas Scott*. Toronto: Burns and MacEachern, 1968.

Rocan, Claude. 'Images of Riel in Contemporary School Textbooks.' Hathorn and Holland, 93–126.

Rock, Bob. *The Missing Bell of Batoche*. Prince Albert: Bob Rock, 1994.

Roquebrune, Robert de. *Les Canadiens d'autrefois 2: essais*. Montreal: Fides, 1966.

– 'La défense du rail.' *Contes du soir et de la nuit*. Montreal: Bernard Valiquette, 1942. 23–35.

– *D'un océan à l'autre*. Paris: Monde nouveau, 1924.

– *D'un océan à l'autre*. 2nd ed. Montreal: Fides, 1958.

Rosenberg, Charles E. *The Trial of the Assassin Guiteau: Psychiatry and Law in the Gilded Age*. Chicago: University of Chicago Press, 1968.

Rosenstock, Janet, and Dennis Adair. *Riel*. Novelization of a screenplay by Roy Moore. Markham, ON: PaperJacks, 1979.

Ross, Harold E. 'A Glimpse of 1885.' Ed. Charles Bruce Fergusson. *Saskatchewan History* 21.1 (Winter 1968): 24–9.

Rousseau, Alfred. *Les Roux*. Cadillac, SK: A. Rousseau, 1932.

Roux, Jean-Louis. *Bois-Brûlés*. Montreal: Éditions du jour, 1968.

Roy, Camille. *'Les arpents de neige.' Propos canadiens*. Quebec City: Imprimerie de l'Action sociale, 1912. 311–23.

– *Histoire de la littérature canadienne*. Quebec City: Imprimerie de l'Action sociale, 1930.

– 'Pamphile Le May.' *À l'ombre des érables*. Quebec City: Imprimerie de l'Action sociale, 1924. 9–62.

Runte, Roseann. 'Espaces politiques et poétiques: Louis Riel et Jean de La Fontaine.' *Dalhousie French Studies* 30 (1995): 17–30.

Ryan, Allan J. *The Trickster Shift: Humour and Irony in Contemporary Native Art*. Vancouver and Seattle: UBC Press and University of Washington Press, 1999.

Said, Edward W. *Culture and Imperialism*. New York. Alfred A. Knopf, 1994.

– *Orientalism*. New York: Vintage, 1979.

– *Reflections on Exile and Other Essays*. Cambridge: Harvard University Press, 2000.

Saint-Pierre, Annette. 'Préface.' Viau, 11–14.

Sanderson, George William. 'The "Memories" of George William Sanderson.' Ed. Irene M. Spry. *Canadian Ethnic Studies* 17.2 (1985): 115–34.

Savoie, Paul. *Bois brûlé*. Saint-Laurent, QC: Noroît, 1989.

– *À la façon d'un charpentier*. Saint Boniface, MB: Éditions du blé, 1984.

Schafer, R. Murray. *The Public of the Music Theatre – Louis Riel: A Case Study*. Vienna: Universal, 1972.

Schmalz, Wayne. *On Air: Radio in Saskatchewan*. Regina: Coteau, 1990.

Schmidt, Louis. 'Les mémoires de Louis Schmidt.' *Le patriote de l'Ouest* [Duck Lake, SK], 1 June 1911–17 June 1912.

– 'Mouvement des Métis à St Laurent Sask. T.N.O. en 1884.' Archives de l'Archevêché de St-Boniface, T29781–29840.

Schultz, J.W. *My Life As an Indian: The Story of a Red Woman and a White Man in the Lodges of the Blackfeet*. London: John Murray, 1907.

Scofield, Gregory A. 'Answer for My Brother.' *The Gathering: Stones for the Medicine Wheel*. Vancouver: Polestar, 1993. 82.

– *Thunder through My Veins: Memories of a Métis Childhood*. Toronto: HarperFlamingo Canada, 1999.

Scott, Frederick George. 'In Memoriam (Those Killed in the Canadian North-West, 1885).' *Poems*. London: Constable, 1910. 174–5.

Scott, Joan W. 'Fantasy Echo: History and the Construction of Identity.' *Critical Inquiry* 27.2 (2001): 284–304.

Shrive, Norman. *Charles Mair: Literary Nationalist*. Toronto: University of Toronto Press, 1965.

Siggins, Maggie. *Riel: A Life of Revolution*. 1994. Toronto: HarperPerennial, 1995.

Silver, A.I. *The French-Canadian Idea of Confederation, 1864–1900*. Toronto: University of Toronto Press, 1982.

– 'French Quebec and the Métis Question, 1869–1885.' *The West and the Nation: Essays in Honour of W.L. Morton*. Ed. Carl Berger and Ramsay Cook. Toronto: McClelland and Stewart, 1976. 91–111.

Silver, Alfred. 'The *Dancing Bear* (an Excerpt from Act II).' *Prairie Fire* 6.4 (1985): 64–9.

– *The Lord of the Plains*. 1990. New York: Ballantine, 1992.

Skirving, Adam. 'Johnnie Cope.' *The Poetry of Scotland: Gaelic, Scots and English 1380–1980*. Ed. Roderick Watson. Edinburgh: Edinburgh University Press, 1995. 411–12.

Smith, C. Henry. *The Story of the Mennonites*. 4th ed. revised and enlarged by Cornelius Krahn. Newton, KS: Mennonite Publications Office, 1957.

Smith, Donald A. 'Donald A. Smith's Report.' *Manitoba: The Birth of a Province*. Ed. W.L. Morton. Winnipeg: Manitoba Record Society Publications, 1965. 25–45.

Smith, Donald B. 'Honoré Joseph Jaxon: A Man Who Lived for Others.' *Saskatchewan History* 34.3 (1981): 81–101.

– 'Ordered to Winnipeg: Varsity Men Fought Louis Riel, but One Served as His Secretary.' *Graduate: The University of Toronto Alumni Magazine* 12.2 (1984): 5–9.

– 'Right Dream, Wrong Time.' *Globe and Mail*, 15 Dec. 2001, F6.

Smith, Doug. 'Offensive Lines.' *Canadian Dimension* 28.5 (1994): 47.

Snell, Gordon. 'Louis Riel (1844–1885).' *Oh, No! More Canadians! Hysterically Historical Rhymes*. With Caricatures by Aislin. Toronto: McArthur, 1998. 51–7.

Snyder, Gary. *The Practice of the Wild*. San Francisco: North Point, 1990.

Souster, Raymond. 'Found Poem: Louis Riel Addresses the Jury.' *Extra Innings*. Ottawa: Oberon, 1977. 78–83.

– 'Riel, 16 novembre 1885.' 1958–60. *Collected Poems of Raymond Souster 2, 1955–62*. Ottawa: Oberon, 1981. 239.

Stanley, George F.G. *The Birth of Western Canada: A History of the Riel Rebellions*. 1936. Toronto: University of Toronto Press, 1992.

– 'Foreword.' *Riel*, 1: xxxi–xxxiv.

– 'General Editor's Remarks.' *Riel*, 5: 1–22.

– 'The Last Word on Louis Riel – the Man of Several Faces.' *Eighteen Eighty-five and After: Native Society in Transition*. Ed. F. Laurie Barron and James B. Waldram. Regina: Canadian Plains Research Center, 1986. 3–22.

– *Louis Riel*. Toronto: Ryerson, 1963.

Steele, S.B. *Forty Years in Canada: Reminiscences of the Great North-West with Some Account of His Service in South Africa*. Toronto: McClelland, Goodchild and Stewart; London: Herbert Jenkins, 1915.

Stefansson, Kristinn. 'The Ninetieth Battalion.'1885. Trans. Watson Kirkonnell. *Icelandic Canadian* 54.5 (1998): 174.

Stegner, Wallace. *Wolf Willow: A History, a Story, and a Memory of the Last Plains Frontier*. 1962. New York: Penguin, 1990.

Stonechild, Blair, and Bill Waiser. *Loyal till Death: Indians and the North-West Rebellion*. Calgary: Fifth House, 1997.

Struthers, J.R. (Tim). 'Living Stories: An Interview with Rudy Wiebe.' *New Directions for Old*. Ed. J.R. Struthers. Guelph, ON: Red Kite, 1991. 17–27.

Suknaski, Andrew. 'This Side of Icon: Reflections on Riel and the Prairie Labyrinth.' *NeWest Review* 4.10 (1978): 3–4.

Swainson, Donald. 'It's the Riel Thing.' *Books in Canada* 8.5 (1979): 14–15.

– 'Rieliana and the Structure of Canadian History.' *Journal of Popular Culture* 14. 2 (1980): 286–97.

Theatre Passe Muraille, 'Mme. Tourond.' *The West Show*. 1975. *Showing West: Three Prairie Docudramas*. Ed. Diane Bessai and Don Kerr. Edmonton: NeWest, 1982. 25–38.

Thomas, Lewis H. 'A Judicial Murder – the Trial of Louis Riel.' Palmer, 37–59.

Thomson, Edward William. Letter to Archibald Lampman, 3 June 1893. *An Annotated Edition of the Correspondence between Archibald Lampman and Edward William Thomson (1890–1898)*. Ed. Helen Lynn. Ottawa: Tecumseh, 1980. 82–6.

Tiessen, Hildegard Froese, and Paul Gerard Tiessen. 'Livesay/Riel.' Hathorn and Holland, 311–25.

Tobie, Manie [Marie-Thérèse Goulet-Courchaine]. *Manie Tobie: femme du Manitoba*. Ed. René Juéry. Saint Boniface, MB: Éditions des Plaines, 1979.

Tovell, Vincent. 'Drama.' *University of Toronto Quarterly* 20.3 (1951): 272–4.

Tremblay, Rémi. 'Aux chevaliers du nœud coulant'(1887) and 'Une épopée' (1885). *Coups d'aile et Coups de bec*. Montreal: Imprimerie Gerhardt-Berthiaume, 1888. 146–8, 70–1.

Trudeau, Pierre Elliott. '[Dialogue] ... with Riel.' 1968. *PM/Dialogue*. Hull: High Hill Publishing House, n.d. 109–11.

Truss, Jan. *A Very Small Rebellion*. Edmonton: J.M. LeBel, 1977.

Turnbull, Gael. 'Riel.' *A Gathering of Poems, 1950–1980*. London: Anvil, 1983. 91.

Upisasik Theatre of Rossignol School. *Gabrielle. The Land Called Morning: Three Plays*. Ed. Caroline Heath. Saskatoon: Fifth House, 1986. 37–71.

Valade, François-Xavier. 'Report on the Sanity of Louis Riel.' Ed. Thomas
Flanagan. *Revue de l'Université d'Ottawa* 45.1 (1976): 120–7.

van Herk, Aritha. 'Progressions toward Sainthood: There's Nothing to Do but
Die.' Hathorn and Holland, 29–45.

Van Kirk, Sylvia. *'Many Tender Ties': Women in Fur-Trade Society, 1670–1870*.
Winnipeg: Watson and Dwyer, 1980.

van Toorn, Penny. *Rudy Wiebe and the Historicity of the Word*. Edmonton:
University of Alberta Press, 1995.

Vansina, Jan. *Oral Tradition As History*. Madison: University of Wisconsin Press,
1985.

Vargas Llosa, Mario. 'Novels Disguised As History: The Chronicles of the
Birth of Peru.' *A Writer's Reality*. Ed. Myron I. Lichtblau. Boston: Houghton
Mifflin, 1991. 21–38.

– *The War of the End of the World*. Trans. Helen R. Lane. New York: Avon, 1985.

Vaugeois, Denis, and Jacques Lacoursière, eds. 'La Marseillaise rielliste.'
Canada-Québec: synthèse historique. Saint-Laurent, QC: Renouveau
pédagogique, 1976. 441.

Vautier, Marie. *New World Myth: Postmodernism and Postcolonialism in Canadian
Fiction*. Kingston and Montreal: McGill-Queen's University Press, 1998.

Viau, Robert. *L'Ouest littéraire: visions d'ici et d'ailleurs*. Montreal: Méridien, 1992.

Voltaire. *Candide ou l'optimisme*. 1759. Ed. René Pomeau. Paris: Nizet, 1963.

Walsh, Frederick G. *The Trial of Louis Riel*. 1963. Fargo: North Dakota Institute
for Regional Studies, 1965.

Waters, Thomas F. 'The Red River Valley: Legacy of Glacial Lake Agassiz.' *The
Streams and Rivers of Minnesota*. Minneapolis: University of Minnesota Press,
1977. 106–31.

Wayman, Tom. 'Canadian Culture: Another Riel Poem.' *Event* 17.3 (1988): 30–1.

Weekes, Mary, As Told to Her by Norbert Welsh. *The Last Buffalo Hunter*. 1939.
Calgary: Fifth House, 1994.

Wells, Eric. 'Riel: Heritage versus History.' *Globe and Mail*, 12 March 1992, A15.

Wetherald, Agnes E. 'Conquering Heroes.' *The Week*, 23 July 1885, 538.

White, Hayden. *Tropics of Discourse: Essays in Cultural History*. Baltimore: Johns
Hopkins University Press, 1978.

White, Michèle. 'The History Cycle: The Parodic Seen / the Parodic Scene.'
Canadian Theatre Review 70 (1992): 50–3.

Whittaker, Herbert. 'Riel.' 1950. *Whittaker's Theatre: A Critic Looks at Stages in
Canada and Thereabouts 1944–1975*. Ed. Ronald Bryden and Boyd Neil.
Greenbank, ON: Whittaker Project, 1985. 19–22.

Wiebe, Rudy. 'The Death and Life of Albert Johnson: Collected Notes on a
Possible Legend.' 1978. Bessai and Jackel, 219–46.

- 'Games for Queen Victoria.' 1976. *The Angel of Tar Sands and Other Stories.* Toronto: McClelland and Stewart, 1982. 42–60.
- 'In the West, Sir John A. Is a Bastard and Riel a Saint. Ever Ask Why?' *Globe and Mail*, 25 March 1978, 6.
- 'Louis Riel: The Man They Couldn't Hang.' 1992. Wiebe, *River of Stone*, 188–215.
- *My Lovely Enemy.* Toronto: McClelland and Stewart, 1983.
- 'A Night in Fort Pitt or (if You Prefer) the Only Perfect Communists in the World.' 1989. Wiebe, *River of Stone*, 230–48.
- 'Riel: A Possible Film Treatment.' 1975. Keith, 158–62.
- *River of Stone: Fictions and Memories.* Toronto: Vintage, 1995.
- *The Scorched-Wood People.* Toronto: McClelland and Stewart, 1977.
- *The Scorched-Wood People.* Toronto: McClelland and Stewart, 1984.
- *The Temptations of Big Bear.* 1973. Toronto: McClelland and Stewart, 1976.
Wiebe, Rudy, and Yvonne Johnson. *Stolen Life: The Journey of a Cree Woman.* Toronto: Alfred A. Knopf Canada, 1998.
Williamson, Jim, dir. and writer. *From Sea to Sea.* Episode 9 of *Canada: A People's History.* CBC, 2000.
Wilson, Keith. *Hugh John Macdonald.* Winnipeg: Peguis, 1980.
Wiseman, Adele. *Testimonial Dinner.* Toronto: Prototype, 1978.
Woodcock, Connie. 'And a Happy Louis Riel Day to You.' *Peterborough* [Ontario] *Examiner*, 1 Aug. 1998, 4A.
Woodcock, George. *Gabriel Dumont: The Métis Chief and His Lost World.* Edmonton: Hurtig, 1975.
- 'Millenarian Riel.' Rev. of *Louis 'David' Riel*, 1st ed., by Thomas Flanagan. *Canadian Literature* 84 (1980): 116–18.
- 'Riel and Dumont.' Rev. of *The Scorched-Wood People*, by Rudy Wiebe. *Canadian Literature* 77 (1978): 98–100.
- *Six Dry Cakes for the Hunted: A Canadian Myth. Two Plays.* Vancouver: Talonbooks, 1977. 57–110.
Young, Egerton Ryerson. 'The Indian Problem.' *Canadian Methodist Magazine* 21 (1885): 465–9.
Young, George. *Manitoba Memories: Leaves from My Life in the Prairie Province, 1868–1884.* Toronto: William Briggs, 1897.
Zeller, Suzanne. *Inventing Canada: Early Victorian Science and the Idea of a Transcontinental Nation.* Toronto: University of Toronto Press, 1987.
Zinovich, Jordan. *Gabriel Dumont in Paris: A Novel History.* Edmonton: University of Alberta Press, 1999.
Zoran and Toufik. *Louis Riel: le père du Manitoba.* Saint Boniface: Éditions des Plaines, 1996.

Illustration Credits

Index